Praise for *Socialnomics*

"People with a passion for something can be infectious. It's obvious that Erik Qualman's passion is social media."
— Dan Heath, *New York Times* best-selling author of *Made to Stick* and *Switch*

"[P]eople are hot for social media.... Erik Qualman, who has written a book called *Socialnomics*, says it's about listening first, then selling."
— *Forbes*

"The social media revolution has raised new and important questions and is now interwoven into our lives. Whether you are an executive, a parent, or a basketball coach, Qualman's *Socialnomics* is a great guide for these issues."
— Tom Izzo, basketball coach of Michigan State University

"Erik Qualman has been doing his homework on the social media phenomenon."
— *Huffington Post*

"In *Socialnomics*, Qualman brilliantly prescribes that the key to social media success is doing rather than deliberating. This is a must read for anyone trying to leverage the social graph rather than be squashed by it."
— Steve Kaufer, CEO, TripAdvisor

"The day I met Erik, I met his mom. You learn a lot about someone from how they treat their moms. Erik is a trustworthy guy."
— Chris Brogan, *New York Times* best-selling author of *Social Media 101* and *Trust Agents*

"Qualman is to social media what Deming is to quality and Drucker to management."
— Scott Galloway, professor of marketing, New York University Stern School of Business, and chairman, L2 Think Tank

"Erik Qualman has a very bright future."
— Angelo Pizzo, award-winning writer and producer of *Hoosiers* and *Rudy*

"Social media isn't just for the next generation—it's for every generation. Whether you're an entrepreneur, a media professional, a college student, or a mom, social media will shape your future. Don't be overwhelmed by it; read Qualman's book instead."
— Jane Wooldridge, award-winning journalist, *Miami Herald*

"Social media is one of the most popular activities online today offering opportunities for both businesses and individuals to connect with a new audience. Qualman's book, *Socialnomics*, helps readers understand this emerging behavior."

— Chris Maher, president, Hitwise

"Marketing is experiencing a profound paradigm shift. In the old paradigm, marketers controlled the conversation with consumers through commissionable media— television, radio, newspapers, and magazines. In the new paradigm, marketers risk being marginalized in the electronic dialogue now taking place real-time. Erik Qualman's *Socialnomics* offers valuable insights that will help marketers in regaining control in the perplexing world of modern communications."

— Dr. Eli Cox, marketing department chair, McCombs School of Business

"Marketing and research are just the tip of the iceberg when it comes to tapping the wonderful world of *Socialnomics*. Social media is so powerful that we've seen it drive spikes in search behavior on Google. Qualman's book will provide you with a navigational map and allow you to prioritize your social media initiatives."

— Kevin Lee, CEO, DidIt

"Qualman makes a powerful case that social media has forever changed the way we live and do business. *Socialnomics* helps make sense of it all."

— Dr. Stuart Levy, professor, George Washington University

"If you need to know digital/social media in business, then you need to know Erik Qualman."

— William Hawkes, PhD, CMO, AmericasMart

"Right now an online conversation is happening about you, your brand, and the things you care about. Erik Qualman's book— *Socialnomics*— will help you and your organization join and benefit from that conversation."

— Harry J. Gold, CEO, Overdrive Interactive

"We live in a world where engagement with your consumer is critical. The one-to-many paradigm is gone. Are you prepared? If not, this book is a must read."

— Robert J. Murray, CEO, iProspect

"Qualman's intelligence on social media is a necessity for business and individuals. A 'Socialnomics Strategy' should be put in place for every person and company."

— Todd L. Young, president and CEO, ProspX, Inc.

"I am convinced Qualman can contribute to driving change toward embracing and utilizing social media with any size of company in literally any business."

—Bjorn Ulfberg, vice president of marketing, Nokia

"Qualman's lively presentation fascinated the audience, and the messages were a great start for our FTTH conference alongside the prime minister of Portugal."

—Dr. Hartwig Tauber, director general, FTTH Council Europe

socialnomics

how social media transforms the way we live and do business

second edition

Erik Qualman

WILEY

John Wiley & Sons, Inc.

Cover design: C. Wallace

Published by John Wiley & Sons, Inc., Hoboken, New Jersey.
Published simultaneously in Canada.

For general information on our other products and services or for technical support, please contact our Customer Care Department within the United States at (800) 762-2974, outside the United States at (317) 572-3993 or fax (317) 572-4002.

Wiley publishes in a variety of print and electronic formats and by print-on-demand. Some material included with standard print versions of this book may not be included in e-books or in print-on-demand. If this book refers to media such as a CD or DVD that is not included in the version you purchased, you may download this material at http://booksupport.wiley.com. For more information about Wiley products, visit www.wiley.com.

Library of Congress Cataloging-in-Publication Data:
Qualman, Erik, 1972–
  Socialnomics : How Social Media Transforms the Way We Live and Do Business / Erik Qualman. — 2nd Edition.
pages cm
  Includes index.
ISBN 978-1-118-23265-1 (pbk. : alk. paper); ISBN 978-1-118-28407-0 (ebk);
ISBN 978-1-118-28278-6 (ebk); ISBN 978-1-118-28701-9 (ebk)
Social media — Economic aspects. I. Title.
  HM742.Q83 2012
  658.8'72 — dc23

                                                              2012026725

Printed in the United States of America.

10 9 8 7 6 5 4 3 2 1

CONTENTS

FOREWORD

From Main Street to Wall Street and from schoolrooms to board-rooms, there is a revolution happening. It is being driven by a fundamental shift in how we communicate, and it is enabled by the unprecedented rise of what is commonly called "social media." Now, one may argue that we've always interacted with each other through dialogue and debate, but there's no question that the platforms and tools that are freely available to us today are taking this to the next level. It's one-to-one and one-to-many discourse in a public setting. And while we may be only at the beginning of this revolution, the effects are palpable. The historic invisible walls of the Internet are being broken down daily, locally, and globally.

Social media touches nearly every facet of our personal and business lives. In business it isn't just for the marketing and public relations departments. Rather, it is imperative for social media to be an integral part of a company's overall strategy. Whether a business is large or small, its overall success will be partly owed to its success within social media. Social media is living and breathing, and it touches every part of an organization from customer service and frontline sales to human resources and information technology. It's wherever and however your customer chooses to reach out to you. Social media is your customer today, your customer tomorrow, your employees, and others. Companies properly engaging digitally with their customers and clients have already seen the power and the payoff. At Ford Motor Company, we have seen this firsthand and it's not the result of one person, but rather the result of an entire movement.

The currency in social media isn't euros, pesos, or dollars; meaningful engagement, participation, and value creation rule the day. The World Wide Web is being categorized by billions of users across the world, and if individuals or businesses want a say in how they are categorized, they need to participate with the appropriate currency. And just as in the real world, true givers are rewarded handsomely.

For those willing to forge ahead into this new frontier, the opportunities are real and scalable. We've seen it work at Ford: the Fiesta Movement, in which we gave 100 European-specification Fiestas to digital influencers for six months, yielded amazing results. We let them do what they normally do: tweet, blog, post videos and photos, and tell everyone they know about their experience. We let their content flow through to our site in real time, unfiltered and uncensored. The results? Over 7 million views of their YouTube videos, 750,000 views of their Flickr photos, more than 125,000 hand raisers on FiestaMovement.com, 11,000 vehicle reservations, and an awareness rate of 60 percent — equal to that of vehicles that have been in the market for two to three years. All through social media.

Radical shifts in business models are also occurring elsewhere: Pepsi bypassed a Super Bowl advertisement for the first time in 20 years in order to shift those millions of dollars into social media. At Ford we've adjusted our marketing budget so that 25 percent is digital and social media. These changes aren't only for businesses. The world of politics has seen its fair share of social media influence, from the oft-used example of the Obama campaign to the rise of conservatives on Twitter with their #TCOT (top conservatives on Twitter) hashtag that has fueled the Tea Party movement.

In the United Kingdom, management of the BBC has mandated that the staff use social media tools since the BBC believes that if its employees aren't using them, they aren't doing their jobs as effectively as possible.

When the Iranian government shut off all outgoing communication channels, a revolution within the country was made known to the world via Twitter. Relief efforts poured into Haiti via texted donations and digital applications. Disasters, from flu to fires and from terrorist attacks to earthquakes, are being tracked and disseminated to mainstream news more quickly than ever before. The first photo of the US Airways plane in the Hudson River? It was uploaded to Twitter.

It's also heartening to see that many of the most popular applications and widgets are those that help people easily donate to various causes and charities. The great paradox is that this swath of society that is seemingly narcissistic and navel-gazing is also one of the most collaborative and community-minded when it comes to cause-related efforts. They want to be part of something bigger than themselves. They want to make a difference in the world, and they believe in the collective power of the crowd. To put in perspective just how powerful this can be, if Facebook was a country, it would be the third largest in the world behind only China and India. The winners in a socially driven world are numerous: good companies, good products, employees, consumers, democracy, entrepreneurial talent, and the environment—all creatures great and small. However, it doesn't come without a price; the majority of what we consider to be our personal privacy may be a thing of the past. This opens up new challenges that may be resolved over time, but Andy Warhol's well-known statement about fame may very well be flipped on its head and read something like: "In the future, we'll all have 15 minutes of privacy."

Socialnomics succeeds at helping us make sense of it all. A strength of this book is Erik Qualman's ability to take complex issues and break them into easily digestible takeaways through the use of real-world examples and analogies. He also peers into the future—seeing a world where products and services will find us via our social graph. He uses constructs that will apply in the years ahead even though the technologies are certain to change.

An item unique to this book is that as a reader you are encouraged to *not* read the book from start to finish. Instead, you're encouraged to jump around, looking for the items most relevant to you. Helpful summaries of the key points at the end of each respective chapter make this easy.

Fittingly enough, this is similar to our social media usage behaviors. As Qualman correctly points out, we no longer search for the news; rather, the news finds us. Even though you as a reader have the ability to skip sections of this book, if you're like me, you will find that most of the constructs and future models in this book are relevant and necessary to achieve success today and tomorrow. Enjoy!

Scott Monty
Global Digital Communications
Ford Motor Company

ACKNOWLEDGMENTS

Socialnomics could not have been completed without the help of many friends and family members. First and foremost, my beautiful wife Ana Maria served a dual role of sounding board and support coach. My immediate family of Dad, Mom, Jay, Helene, Matt, Mary Alison, and my loving grandparents made certain to tell me when things weren't up to standard, but were also my greatest supporters. Matt's work and insight were especially vital in beefing up our case study section. Encouragement came from my wife's family members, the Lozanos: Fernando, Margarita, José, Nicolas, and Stephanie. Special thanks go out to my John Wiley & Sons team, Shannon Vargo, Matt Holt, PJ Campell, Nick Snyder, Amy Scholz, and Elana Schulman, for having both the skill and the patience to make this happen. To talented authors Tim Ash and Brian Reich for introducing me to John Wiley & Sons. To the Muellers and Youngs for their moral support. The legal mind of Chris Norton. Julie Jawor's artistic eye. And finally, to numerous friends and family who kept giving me positive reinforcement and ideas, just when they were needed most—you know who you are, and it meant more than you know.

Social Superstar Support

Mari Smith, Dave Kerpen, Chris Brogan, Jeremiah Owyang, Mike Lewis, Brian Solis, Jamie Turner, Amber Naslund, Lon Safko, Anne Hadley, Scott Monty, Peter Shankman, Dave Carol, Guy Kawasaki, Steve Garfield, Charlene Li, Wayne Breitbarth, Tony Hsieh, Gary Vaynerchuk, Lee Oden, Jay Baer, Jason Falls, Dan Schawbel, Brian Reich, Angel Martinez, Corey Perlman, Louis Gray, Richard Binhammer, Robert Scoble, Phyllis Khare, Lee Aase, Eric Bradlow,

Sally Falkow, Don Steele, Julien Smith, Jim Carey, Michael Laze-row, Sarah Hofstetter, Mack Collier, Mike Barbeau, Jamie Turner, Alan Chan, Todd Defren, Tom Gerace, Elizabeth Pigg, Ken Rob-bins, Richard MacManus, Jon Gibs, Chris Cunningham, Paul Beck, Jesse Stay, Amy Porterfield, Mario Sundar, John Hill, Kip Bod-nar, Adam Brown, Justin Levy, Paul Colligan, Andrea Vahl, Rich Brooks, Rick Calvert, Nichole Kelly, Kelly Lester, Ana White, Matt Goddard, Chris Heuer, C.C. Chapman, Chris Penn, Shel Israel, Tamar Weinberg, Morgan Johnston, Tim Washer, Scott Henderson, David Armano, Mark Cattini, Michael Lewis, Nick O'Neil, Mike Stelzner, Sonia Simone, Adam Singer, Jessica Smith, Michael Brito, Geoff Livingston, Mike Volpe, and Wayne Sutton.

See more superstars in Chapter 9.

ABOUT THIS BOOK

This book does not need to be read from start to finish like a sultry novel, nor should it be. Rather, it provides useful insight into changes in macro trends, behaviors, and constructs as a result of social media. Just like social media itself, this book is written in sporadically digestible sound bites, and, by the magic of my wonderful editor, Shannon Vargo, it is arranged so that you, the reader, can easily select an example, particular topic, or case study that is relevant to you or your company. As such, I will occasionally repeat myself, but that's okay — studies show it takes three repetitions before something sinks in. *Hint*: If you want more tactical information, jump to the back of the book. So, while this work will not win any Grammar Girl awards, I hope you find it informative, educational, and entertaining.

Updates and augmentations to this book can be found at www.socialnomics.com. I love hearing from my readers at Twitter @equalman or equalman@gmail.com — feel free to disagree or shower me with affection. I adhere to my promise of personally responding.

INTRODUCTION

In 1992, James Carville coined the phrase "It's the economy, stupid."[1] This simple phrase was a major driver behind why Bill Clinton became our forty-second president. Much has happened since 1992, with the most powerful change being the ubiquitous adoption and assimilation of the Internet. The Internet has revolutionized almost every facet of our business and personal lives. This last statement about the Internet is hopefully not news to anyone reading this book.

What is news, however, is that today we are in the midst of yet another far-reaching revolution. This revolution is being driven by people and enabled by social media. That is why over two decades later we are taking liberties with Carville's famous quote by adjusting it to: "It's a *people-driven* economy, stupid." Although only a slight modification of words, it's a drastic adjustment in philosophy and in how people and businesses are changing and will continue to evolve in the coming years.

Socialnomics is the value created and shared via social media and its efficient influence on outcomes (economic, political, relational, etc.). Or, more simply put, it's word of mouth on digital steroids. A subset of this is that in the future we will no longer search for products and services; rather, they will find us via social media.

Socialnomics is a massive socioeconomic shift. If Facebook were a country, it would be the third largest country in the world behind only China and India. Yet, some of the core marketing and business principles of the past few centuries will still apply, while other basic practices are becoming as extinct as the companies that continue to try to force them on the unwilling public. Businesses don't have the choice on whether to do social media; the choice is on *how well* they do it.

We are already seeing the economic potential of social media in its ability to reduce inefficient marketing and middlemen. Million-dollar television advertisements are no longer the king influencer of purchase intent. People referring products and services via social media tools are the new king. It is the world's largest referral program in history. There is also less need to subscribe to costly newspapers when consumers are pushed more relevant and timely free content from their peers via social media. The news finds us. All of this can be done easily from the comfort of home or while on the go with mobile devices. These paradigm shifts, along with many others, are discussed in the forthcoming pages. More importantly, we discuss how to leverage these shifts today and in the future. The end result is that everything from purchasing a baby carriage to drafting a last will and testament is easier and cheaper for the consumer and more profitable for the seller. The following pages will give you direction on how not only to survive, but to thrive in this ever-changing world.

Socialnomics eliminates millions of people performing the same tasks over and over (multiple individual redundancy). If new parents see, via social media, that several of their closest friends have purchased the same brand and model baby seat and they all express glowing reviews, the new parents will not waste hours on research; this research and review process has already been done by people they trust. Today's winners are not the result of Madison Avenue, blueblood political parties, or monopolistic distributors. As a result of the ease and speed with which information can be distributed across social networks, the winners today are great products and services — which ultimately means that people win. Companies can elect to do business as usual at their own peril. This is a newer and brighter world for consumers and businesses; this is the world of Socialnomics.

socialnomics

Notice

This book is designed to enable readers to jump from chapter to chapter based on their individual level.

CHAPTER ONE

Word of Mouth Goes World of Mouth

A sk any Fortune 500 executive, small business owner, or sole proprietor what the most effective form of marketing is, and I guarantee the answer, without hesitation, is word of mouth. Word of mouth is not a new concept, but what happens when this is taken to another level? What happens when word of mouth goes to World of Mouth®?

As depicted in Figure 1.1, an oversimplified historical model of word of mouth works something like this: Joe User has a great experience with his Dell computer; then he tells his friend Kelly about it and why he likes it. Kelly in turn tells her friends about it and so on down the line. This is a great model. However, no model is perfect. A few shortcomings of this model are: (1) the news/information can be slow to spread; (2) the original information can be altered as it changes hands; and (3) Kelly's friends may not know much about Joe. The beauty is that social media helps word of mouth overcome these imperfections. Yet, surprisingly, as of July, 2012, 70 percent of big company CEOs have no presence on social networks.[1]

While traditional word of mouth can be slow to spread, the opposite is true for Facebook status updates. These updates are pushed via news feeds to all friends in the network. Or, to an even greater extent, a platform like Twitter gives you access to hundreds of millions of uses who have the ability to read your messaging.

Figure 1.1   Difference between Word of Mouth
and World of Mouth

This scales much better than an individual telling a few friends a
week about the new product or service he or she enjoys.

Also, social media is global in nature; one of its biggest benefits
is enabling users to stay connected with friends and family who
are geographically separated. This global connectivity extends to
positive and negative messages relating to products and services.

Also, since your opinion is in digital format, it is less likely to
be misunderstood or diluted over time. Think about the children's
game telephone. This is the game where you sit in a circle and
start with a phrase like "lightweight knickers" and it is passed
around the circle via whispers or word of mouth from child to
child until it reaches the last child and she squeals, "Bright white
Snickers!" While traditional word of mouth doesn't suffer the same
degree of degradation as a children's game, the message, over time
and distance, does lose meaning and context. However, when that
message is passed digitally, as is the case with social media, it is
less likely to lose its original intent. That digital string is passed

intact. Along with the benefit of the message remaining intact, the viewer/reader can also see who was the originator of the initial thought. Beyond this, one can often see helpful information about the originator like age, education, hobbies, location, and so forth.

Is Social Media Just a Fad?

Why is there even a need for social media? In less than three years it became the most popular activity on the web,[2] supplanting pornography for the first time in Internet history. Even search engines weren't powerful enough to do that.

Remember years ago when the last three to four seconds of many television commercials prompted viewers to use various America Online (AOL) keywords? You don't see or hear that anymore, do you? What do you see? People are sending this traffic to social networks. A good example of this is CBS, which sends a majority of its March Madness basketball traffic not to its own website, but to www.facebook.com/brackets.

Why has social media's popularity been so meteoric? Its rapid ascent is due in large part to its ability to help people avoid *information indigestion*. At first glance, this would seem counterintuitive because, inherently, social media actually produces *more* content and information (e.g., status updates, tweets, social bookmarks, video sharing, and social media's photo commenting). Because of this increase in information, you would think that it would cause more confusion, not less. But, when we dive deeper, we can see why this is not the case.

In his groundbreaking book *The Long Tail*, Chris Anderson succinctly describes the ability of the Internet within free markets to easily and effectively service small interest groups:

> *The great thing about broadcast is that it can bring one show to millions of people with unmatchable efficiency. But it can't do the opposite — bring a million shows to one person each. Yet that is exactly what the Internet does so well. The economics of the broadcast era required hit shows — big buckets — to catch huge audiences. Serving the same stream to millions of people at the same time is hugely expensive and wasteful for a distribution network optimized for point-to-point communications. Increasingly, the mass market is turning into a mass of niches.*[3]

As we have seen, this is powerful stuff. This is terrific for individualism, but it greatly fragments the market. Life was much simpler when we knew that all our world news would come from *Time* and *Life* magazines. Fragmentation can be stress-inducing for people.

As human beings, we have the dichotomous psychological need to be individuals yet feel connected to and accepted by a much larger social set. Accordingly, people are willing to keep *open running diaries* as a way to stay connected and accepted. In his Hierarchy of Needs study, Abraham Maslow indicates that after the basic needs of survival and security, humanity's greatest need is to feel accepted. Being social animals by nature, we were highly receptive when social media came along.

However, as humans we experience an ongoing struggle between protecting our privacy and being accepted by others. As a result, there is often give and take when it comes to privacy and acceptance, and much depends on the individual and such factors as age, race, ethnicity, religion, and location. Often this struggle is resolved by balancing the acceptance we receive with the privacy we sacrifice:

> *If you can make something more relevant to me by having less privacy, well, that is a small price to pay.*
>
> — Bill Tancer, General Manager,
> Global Research, Hitwise

Everyone has a different privacy requirement, but whatever that level may be, most of us still have a yearning to understand what other people are doing.

It was much easier to know what the majority was doing when all you had to do was tune in to Casey Kasem's *American Top 40* to find out the latest and greatest in music, or flip through *Vogue* magazine to quickly grasp fashion trends.

Who Cares What You Are Doing?

Why do I care if my friend is having the most amazing peanut-butter-and-jelly sandwich? Or that someone is at her child's dance recital? These types of questions are often posed by someone who doesn't understand social media, rather than by someone who hasn't embraced social media; there is a difference. These questions are usually posed by people who are frustrated, because they don't understand what social media is about.

Heavy social media users actually don't care about every little thing happening in their friends' lives all the time. Yes, there are the exceptional few who view every post, photo, tweet, or comment. Individual users make personal choices about how they establish their settings (privacy being one big item here) and, more importantly, viewing behavior.

This is similar to a BlackBerry, Android, or iPhone where users can customize their settings so that the unit vibrates every time a message comes in or they can disable that setting and download messages at their leisure, thereby avoiding what's called *crackberry* syndrome (addictive immediate response to every incoming message).

The key with social media is that it allows you to easily stay abreast of people you want to stay connected with via casual observation. Someone might argue, "Well, I already don't have enough time in my day; how can I possibly follow anybody else or keep those following me informed? I can't waste my time like that!" This is a fundamental misunderstanding. One of the key maxims of this book is that *investing time on social media actually makes you more productive.* Let's look at an example with a fictitious character dubbed Sally Supermarket.

We find Sally Supermarket at her favorite place and namesake. It's Fourth of July weekend, so all of the checkout lanes are congested. It's going to be a 10-minute wait until she reaches the cashier. During these 10 minutes, she can:

A. Ruminate about how upset she is that she has to wait in line for 10 minutes, for which she definitely doesn't have time.
B. Flip through a magazine she has no interest in.
C. Be rude and place a call on her cell phone, most likely annoying the others in line around her and potentially the person receiving the call as well, because it's noisy in the supermarket and she might have to hang up the call at any time.
D. Check on updates from her friends and family via social media.

Sally chooses option D, and here's what occurs:

- *Sally's status:* "Bummed that the supermarket is out of mayonnaise — I was planning to make my cold chicken curry salad for the annual picnic tomorrow."
- *Friend 1's status:* "Excited to be boarding a plane to D.C. for the weekend!"
- *Friend 2's status:* "Who knew my kids would love mandarin oranges in a can?"

- *Friend 3's status:* "I'm pregnant!"
- *Sally's daughter's status:* "Excited! Got an A on my psychology exam — off to get a Frappuccino to celebrate!"
- *Friend 4's comment:* "Sally, plain yogurt is a great substitute for mayo — use a third more curry than normal to kill the bitterness. I recommend Dannon. It's healthy, too!"
- *Friend 3's status:* "Going in for first ultrasound. We've decided not to find out if the baby is a boy or a girl ahead of time."
- *Friend 5's post:* "Great video on bike decorating for the Fourth of July is found here: www.tinyurl.com/4th/."

After reading the status updates from her friends on her phone, Sally still has about four minutes before she'll be at the front of the checkout lane, so she runs to get some plain yogurt (per Friend 4's recommendation). While checking out, she sees a $10 gift card for Starbucks hanging above the magazines. She purchases this gift card with the intent of mailing it to her daughter as a congratulatory surprise for doing well on her exam and to let her know she's thinking about her.

Sally will see Friend 3 tomorrow at the picnic and be able to congratulate her on her pregnancy. Staying up to date on Friend 3 means that Sally won't spend time speculating whether Friend 3 is just putting on extra weight. Sally can also avoid asking if the couple knows whether the baby will be a boy or a girl, because based on Friend 3's last updated social media message she already knows that they are waiting. Sally knows from firsthand pregnancy experience how tiring answering the "Do you know if it's a boy or a girl?" question can become — if only she'd had social media back then!

On the way home, Sally's husband calls her.

Sally says, "Hey, honey, I'm on my way home from the supermarket — how are you?"

"Struggling — Jack and I are trying to decorate his bike, but it's not looking so hot, and the crepe paper keeps tearing in the spokes."

"Not sure if this will help, but Friend 5 just bookmarked a video about bike decorating — maybe you could check it out for some ideas."

This Sally Supermarket example is a little played up for the purpose of illustration, but it certainly isn't far-fetched. This

10-minute snapshot is just one simple example of why social media is a time *saver* rather than a time *waster*.

JetBlue Helps Reduce the Travel Blues via Twitter

Like many others, my wife and I experienced firsthand the ability of social media to help save time and stress. We were in Austin, Texas, for the SXSW Conference, where I was a keynote speaker, when my wife's departing JetBlue flight on Sunday was canceled due to bad weather in Boston. In fact, all flights to the Northeast on all airlines were delayed due to the extreme weather conditions. My wife tried calling JetBlue and a few other airlines that operated out of Austin, but most of the hold times were in excess of two hours. In our dismay, we turned to JetBlue's Twitter account and posted the following:

> *Wife's flight canceled to Boston, what are our choices?*

JetBlue normally has exceptional customer service on Twitter. However, due to the high volume on this day, they couldn't get to all the thousands of tweets pouring in, including ours. We witnessed several others who tweeted almost the same question that we posted. While JetBlue couldn't get to the tweet, some fellow Twitters could. In the next few minutes we received several tweets from different users, but most were similar to this one:

> *Got thru to JB. First JB flight isn't until Thursday. If you need to get back BOS use Continental out of Houston. DFW sold out too.*

This allowed us to hang up on the phone call and start taking action to try to book a flight on Continental Airlines out of Houston. It also saved us the hassle of figuring out our potential options out of Dallas–Fort Worth (DFW), since several people had told us (via Twitter) that DFW was not an option. For JetBlue, it also helped reduce its call volume as we weren't the only ones with the question about how to get back to Boston. Several other people were able to hang up their phones. As a reminder, it wasn't JetBlue that answered the question; it was other JetBlue customers. However, JetBlue enabled this to occur by having a robust Twitter presence so that people knew to turn there for viable information; whether that information came directly from JetBlue or JetBlue customers is immaterial.

Foreign Friends Are Not Forgotten

This depiction by German-based social media user Christoph Marcour is a quick example of how social media can easily keep us globally connected:

> One thing I enjoy about social media is staying in touch with my friends in America. Before, I would occasionally travel to the United States for work, primarily to New York and Houston. I was generally very busy leading up to these trips and often didn't have time to e-mail or call my friends—all of whom lived in Indianapolis. My friends from Indy also traveled for work quite a bit. So, ironically, we'd often be in the same city at the same time and not know until months later.
>
> However, today we are more likely to meet up if I'm traveling to the United States. It's primarily the result of the fact that even if I'm not directly reaching out to them, if I put in my status "Packing for New York" or "Bummed that my flight to Houston is delayed," they see that, just as I see similar items that they are updating.
>
> Geolocation tools like Facebook Places and Foursquare also come in handy for people attempting to stay in touch with others' whereabouts. These tools are especially helpful when attending massive conferences or conventions.[4]

Search Engines and Social Media

The Internet's greatest strength—rapid and cheap sharing of information—is also its greatest weakness. Search engines have and will continue to help users quickly access the one morsel of information they need out of the trillions of bytes of data. The inherent fault of search engines is that users need to know what they are looking for in the first place. For example, if users type in "great Father's Day gift" they do receive some helpful nuggets, but the results are often an overwhelming sea of confusion. And, if what you need is not on the first results page, it might as well not be anywhere, because only roughly 5 percent of users go to the second page. In 2010 the Chitka Network reported that going from the 11th spot to 10th sees a 143 percent jump in traffic, proving that a very small percentage of users click through to the second page while searching online.

With the excess of information on the web, people require a tool to make sense of it all. Social media is that mechanism.

Search engines are getting better and better at understanding our individual search needs. Search engines have advanced technologically to recognize that when my 13-year-old cousin searches for "Paris Hilton," she is looking for the pseudo-celebrity, but that when my mother searches for "Paris Hilton," she wants a hotel room in the City of Lights.

While these are nice improvements, if the searcher types in generic terms like "chocolate" or "shoes," the results will be relatively the same as everyone else's results. So, even though search results are getting better, you still can't type in "best rib-eye steak in New York" and quickly get what you are looking for. The advancement in semantic search will largely depend on who wins the search engine wars. If a virtual monopoly exists (e.g., Google), the advancement in search technology could potentially be slow. Someone could argue that the core offering and search engine results have not advanced much in the past five years. This isn't surprising given Google's relative dominance of the space over this time period. Can one blame Google for not changing things too radically? Why would Google try to *fix* something that is making record profits for its shareholders? This isn't a book about search, but we touch on it because social media and search are so closely tied to each other.

Google, Baidu (China), Bing, and other search engines are recognizing this shift, and they are trying to make their offerings more social. At the writing of this book, we don't know whether Google+ will become a serious competitor to Facebook. What we do know is that part of Google's strategy to launch Google+ is to compete head-to-head with Facebook so that Facebook has less time to focus on a robust social search capability. We also know that some Google+ features like Huddles (group video chats) and circles (an easier way to categorize your softball buddies separately from your co-workers) have forced Facebook to increase its innovation to match these capabilities. Social network competition means the consumer wins. Understanding this, Bing announced that they were becoming a social search engine — helping to supply information from our friends and peers based on our search queries. Old and new players alike are racing to win the battle of social search. The competition will be fierce because much of social search will be directly tied to social commerce. Social commerce will be counted in billions of dollars. Beyond social search, the titans of digital are starting to intrude on each other's turf. Google, Facebook, Amazon, Apple, and LinkedIn are fighting for the same people in dollars when it comes to music, e-readers, social, mobile, search, recruiting, tablets, advertising, contacts, and beyond.

We No Longer Search for the
News — It Finds Us

We no longer search for the news; rather, the news finds us. This is
evident when looking at key newspaper statistics. According to data
from the Newspaper Association of America, advertising revenue
for newspapers declined 18.1 percent, national advertising sales fell
18.4 percent, classifieds sank 30.9 percent, and online advertising
sales dropped 3 percent.[5]

During the 2008 U.S. presidential election, Tina Fey, a cast
member on Saturday Night Live (SNL), was a dead ringer for Republican vice presidential nominee Sarah Palin. There were several
skits done by Fey mimicking the vice presidential hopeful, and
some argue that they played a large role in the election itself. The
most popular of these episodes was the premier. What was interesting about this five-minute video was: (1) the popularity of it and
(2) where people watched the video clips.

NBC estimated that over 50 million people viewed the "Palin"
skits. According to research conducted by Solutions Research
Group, more than half of those who saw this SNL video viewed
the clips over the Internet.[6] Many viewed the video on the popular social video network YouTube, while the majority of others
had it pushed to them and played right within their social media
network.

As a result, SNL's television viewership increased more than
50 percent over the previous year (2007), allowing NBC to profit
from both ends of the spectrum (online exposure and TV ratings).
This resulted in SNL developing SNL shorts specifically tailored
to be passed around socially. The power of Socialnomics isn't just
online; it can also drive activity in the opposite direction — to the
offline world. This makes sense because the roots of social media
and the social graph (an individual's multiple online connections to
friends, peers, and family) come from an offline world (book clubs,
men's clubs, garden clubs, athletic clubs). Technology has enabled
us to go to a whole new level with our networks or clubs when they
become digitized.

As an aside, it's important to note that these Sarah Palin skits
are another good example of social media being a time saver
rather than a time waster. Historically, a viewer would have to
sit through 90 minutes of SNL content, a majority of which may
not be germane to that particular viewer. Instead, with the help
of social media tools, the relevant five minutes (in this case Palin
skits) of that particular SNL episode are pushed the viewer's way

by like-minded friends, which in turn saves 85 minutes that can be repurposed accordingly.

Old marketers used to conjure up 30-second commercials that were so entertaining they would be discussed around the watercooler. However, what happens when the watercooler now exists for the sole purpose of dispensing water? Watercooler conversations are now happening online in real time.

Newspapers and Magazines Diminish in Power

If we are no longer walking down to the end of our driveway in anticipation of reading what is going on in the world, and if we are no longer even going onto our favorite Internet news sites to find the news, what does this mean for the various news outlets and the businesses that support them?

We have shifted from a world in which the information and news were held by a few and distributed to millions to a world where the information is held by millions and distributed to a few (niche markets). This has huge ramifications for traditional media outlets. The Internet caused major newspapers and magazines to rethink their business models. While these traditional mediums were still trying to grasp how to handle the upshot of blogs and user-generated content, social media suddenly came along, causing yet another significant upheaval in the status quo.

Traditional newspapers and magazines need to recognize that people are having their news pushed to them from friends and automated free subscriptions. This means newspapers and magazines need to change what their content delivers—otherwise their decline will continue. Newspapers should no longer be just reporting the news; instead, they should be commenting on the news and what it means. Even if they do this, their chance of survival may still be slim and only a few, if any, will survive.

In fact, it was interesting to see legendary advertising and marketing columnist Bob Garfield start his 2010 presentation at the SXSW Interactive Conference by announcing, "I and traditional marketing and advertising are [slow reveal to a presentation slide] Fu%#ed!"

Despite these doomsday scenarios for traditional marketing, social media is more of an "and" thing than an "or" thing.

A quick ironic example is that as more and more companies cut down on direct mail (expensive to print, slow, environmentally damaging, more difficult to track than digital, etc.), the few companies that continue direct mail pieces may actually see an uptick in results, because there is less clutter in the mailbox.

This book is actually a microcosm of the newspaper/magazine phenomenon. By the time this goes to print, many of the news items and examples in this book will be outdated; in fact, some websites listed in this book will no longer be market leaders or even exist at all. There may be only a handful of paper newspapers left, as well. Hence, the importance of the material in this book, as well as in newspapers and magazines, is to provide helpful commentary on what the news means and be able to identify constructs that have occurred before and will potentially occur again. Please note that new examples and updates to this book can be found at www.socialnomics.com. The irony is that it prompts the question: With e-readers, iPads, tablets, and the like, why can't I as an author simply continually update the digital version of the book you are currently reading? I see this coming soon and am surprised it hasn't happened already.

This digital shift will continue to present an uphill battle for traditional publishers because they still need to maintain the best and brightest columnists and experts. But how do they retain these experts when their platform is no longer as strong as it once was? In the past, newspapers had almost full control because they managed the distribution. Today, the experts (i.e., writers, journalists, reporters, bloggers) have increased leverage because the price to entry for them to gain mass distribution is close to zero. While it still means something to have the *Wall Street Journal* on your resume, it doesn't mean nearly as much as it once did. In fact, in the technology world it probably means more to have a *Mashable* byline than to be the technology writer for *Newsweek*.

Playboy and the *Sports Illustrated* Swimsuit Issue Are Stripped Down

A salient example of this is the once-famed *Sports Illustrated* Swimsuit Issue. People in the 1980s and 1990s used to talk in anticipation for weeks prior to the Swimsuit Issue landing in mailboxes across the country. The most popular person in school or the office that week was whoever received the magazine and brought it in. *Sports Illustrated* was able to charge up to three times its usual rates to advertisers.

For a supermodel, landing on the cover of this issue was life changing. That was then; this is now. The luster of this issue quickly faded with the seemingly limitless photographs and videos on the Internet. When was the last time you heard the *Sports Illustrated* Swimsuit Issue mentioned in a conversation? It went from part of pop culture to irrelevance. Even Hugh Hefner's venerable *Playboy* reduced its guaranteed magazine subscriber base by 13 percent in 2009, from 3 million to 2.6 million. Christie Hefner, daughter of the founder, stepped down as CEO at the start of the year.[7]

Craigslist, LinkedIn, Monster, CareerBuilder, TheLadders, and many others have eviscerated the one-time newspaper monopoly in recruitment advertising since the technology bubble burst, resulting in a loss of $4.9 billion, or 56.3 percent, of classified revenues between 2000 and 2007.[8] In turn, LinkedIn will most likely make HotJobs, Monster, and CareerBuilder obsolete. This is how fast business cycles move these days. Today, 80 percent of all companies use social media tools to recruit, and of these, 95 percent use LinkedIn, according to the 2009 Jobvite Social Recruitment Survey. The online recruiting market is so lucrative that Facebook announced plans in 2012 to offer a competing service to LinkedIn.

The first step that some major periodicals took was to place their content online; this was a logical step. Of course, they still needed to make money, and the model that they understood was subscription based. This worked well for a few years for major publications like the *New York Times* and the *Wall Street Journal*; but if you have a good understanding of Socialnomics, you can see how over the long haul this is a somewhat flawed strategy. To effectively leverage the social graph, every company has to understand that it needs to make its information easily transferable.

Idaho Bloggers Are Better Than New York Reporters

It's important to free your content from being trapped in a walled garden, because people have quickly grown accustomed to the news finding them, and there is no turning back. That is a key construct of the book: The world as it was no longer is. Good, bad, or indifferent, it is a fact that will not change.

People expect and demand easy access to their news; any hurdle, no matter how small, can kill potential distribution. If distribution is limited, then the eventual effectiveness and ultimate viability will be doomed. So let's quickly showcase an A to B comparison of how this works in Socialnomics. For those who believe bloggers can't report as well as a traditional newspaper reporter, this section is for you. Also, note that in 2012 a blogger (from the *Huffington Post*), for the first time in history, was awarded a Pulitzer.

News Site A

Site A is one of the world's largest and best-known newspapers. Historically, it has generated revenue from print advertising, as well as paid subscriptions. In the past decade, it has put even more information on its website, along with additional video content, multimedia, and so on. It has seen tremendous growth in its online revenue, but that's not enough to offset the loss incurred by its traditional offline revenue model. The newspaper still has a substantial staff of expensive writers, large office buildings that need to be maintained, along with trucks and various types of overhead to distribute the paper. As a result of these high costs, the paper requires a paid subscription and login for online content in the hope of generating enough revenue to offset these costs.

Blog Site B

Jane the blogger works out of her house in Boise, Idaho. She has plenty of time to write because she works only three days a week in the state courthouse. She uses a popular free blogging tool (e.g., WordPress, TypePad, Tumblr, Blogger) and pays $20 per year to have the vanity URL www.idaho-senators.com. Since she likes to stay current with events outside of Idaho, she pays for a subscription to News Site A. Her husband is a big Boise State football fan and gets a free subscription to the *Idaho Statesman*, and Jane enjoys reading the political section. Her only other cost is the time she spends reading these news sources. One could argue that in this instance this is no cost at all because she finds intrinsic value in (aka enjoys) discussing the political topics on her blog about Idaho's U.S. senators.

To keep abreast of the latest news on her two senators, she uses free social media tools and alerts to push the news her way when either of the two senators' names is mentioned. She also carves out time to review and edit the various wikis (e.g., Wikipedia) across the web on each respective senator. Her interest started when a high school friend, Julie Patterson, was elected to the Senate. Patterson still holds her Senate seat in Idaho.

Situation

The other Idaho senator (i.e., not Patterson) is involved in a drunk driving accident early one Saturday morning where he is at fault. There was one passenger in the car — the senator's babysitter — and she was killed in the accident. The driver of the other car was a Supreme Court judge who was in Idaho on vacation. The Supreme Court judge is in critical condition at a local Boise hospital. As you might imagine, this is going to be big world news coming out of Boise, Idaho.

Jane the blogger finds out about the accident from one of her friends from the courthouse prior to it appearing on local or national news. Surprisingly, no citizen was there with a digital phone to send a picture off via Twitter or Facebook. Jane is already familiar with the Idaho senator, so no background is required; in fact, she knows that he has a history of overindulging with booze and has had a previous DUI incident that went through her courthouse a few years before he became a senator.

Meanwhile, News Site A's field reporter for that area is on vacation; consequently, the assignment goes to a reporter based in the paper's Manhattan headquarters. This reporter is not at all familiar with the Idaho senator, so she immediately goes to her favorite search engine and types in the senator's name. Guess what site comes up in the top five rankings on the search engine? You guessed it: www.idaho-senators.com. The reporter reads background information on the senator and then hops on a flight to Boise. On the flight, she begins writing the story.

Jane the blogger and the reporter both post stories about the event. Because of her background and experience on the subject matter, Jane the Blogger posts her story an hour or two before News Site A. Not only that, but to presell her more in-depth story, she originally breaks the news she received from the courthouse via a microblogging tool like Twitter. She immediately becomes the recognized expert on this story. Microblog posts were the first to break such noteworthy news events as the 2009 U.S. Airways emergency landing in New York's Hudson River and the 2008 California forest fires, and will continue to grow in importance in the reporting and consumption of breaking news.

The purpose of this Jane the blogger example isn't to showcase who produces better stories — bloggers or traditional reporters; there are plenty of great articles about that. This example demonstrates the availability of free, great content on the web and the fact that some of the most qualified people to write a story are bloggers who actually do it for free—because they enjoy it! Most of these people aren't doing it for advertising revenue or subscription revenue; they are doing it because they want to be heard. It's not just for news stories, either. As we cover later in this book, this has ramifications for commercial transactions. A study conducted by Jupiter Research in 2009 found that 50 percent of Internet users consulted a blog prior to making a purchase. A Nielsen study indicated that an astounding 81 percent consulted reviews prior to their holiday purchases. Ninety percent of us trust peer recommendations,[9] while only 14 percent of us trust advertisements.[10]

Pundits try to broad-brushstroke bloggers and microbloggers (e.g., Twitter, Facebook) as "all bad and uninformed" or "regurgitating the same news and facts" when in fact there are varying levels of quality in the blogosphere. There are certainly bloggers who act as leeches, can't source a story, and don't fact-check properly, but there are many who provide valuable original content and information.

Later in this book, we discuss how social media helps pinpoint the good sources of information and distinguish them from the bad ones. Understandably, traditional journalists who bad-mouth bloggers have a biased opinion; after all, these new outlets are stealing their journalistic jobs.

Not All Bloggers Are Bad

Getting back to World of Mouth, let's continue with this example to show why the public turns to nontraditional outlets. During this scenario, for argument's sake, let's assume that the stories of News Site A and Blog Site B are exactly the same in terms of quality. There are three reasons why Jane the blogger's story has a higher chance for success than News Site A's story:

1. She is the most qualified expert on this particular niche subject.
2. She posted first.
3. She has Socialnomics on her side.

The first two reasons are self-explanatory and have been touched on in other publications, so let's look at the Socialnomics aspect by continuing our story example with Trevor in San Francisco, California. Trevor is an avid follower of politics, and has used some social media tools to alert him once a day about stories that are related to senators. He receives these two stories (Jane the blogger's and News Site A's) in his daily newsfeed via really simple syndication (RSS) technology. Trevor has no idea how the technology works; he just knows that his favorite stories show up on his MyYahoo!, iGoogle, and Facebook home pages. Let's see what happens to each story. If these tools inform him, the stories would be pushed his way by his friends and peers via social media tools like Twitter.

News Site A's Story

Trevor looks at the link for News Site A and likes the catchy title and brief summary of what the story contains. He notices "subscription required" listed next to the link, but he has seen this before and sometimes he is able to get enough of the story before hitting the pay wall. Keep in mind that many readers would have stopped here as soon as they saw "subscription required" — they would not have bothered to click on the hyperlink to the story. However, Trevor is hopeful, clicks through, and the page promptly displays a login screen for subscribers only. News Site A has put a hurdle in Trevor's path. As a result of this hurdle, this is the end of Trevor's experience with News Site A for this particular story and most likely for future stories.

Quick recap of Trevor's experience:

1. He clicks on the headline within his feed for News Site A.
2. He notices "subscription required" for News Site A.
3. He clicks anyway but encounters a login screen for subscribers only.
4. The end.

Jane the Blogger's Story

Trevor still wants to read about the drunk-driving senator so he clicks on the next related headline in his feed, which is Jane the blogger's post. He also sees a link to this same story in his Twitter account. Here's what happens:

1. He clicks on the headline within his feed.
2. He reads and enjoys the story.
3. He posts to his 245 friends on Facebook and 45 followers on Twitter.
4. Forty of his friends/followers read the story.
5. Twenty of his friends/followers who read the story also repost it.

6. Ten of his friends/followers rate and tag it on social media bookmark sites (e.g., Delicious, Digg, Reddit).
7. A few other websites and blogs link to this story.
8. Steps 4 through 7 continue in recurring multiples like Russian nesting dolls.

Search engines read these social bookmarks and hyperlinks and rank the article high in their organic rankings for news around the keywords "senator drunk driving." It's important to note that a key aspect of social media is the ability to tag items. In this example, anyone reading the story could add a tag such as "Idaho senator" or "drunk senator," similar in concept to a tag you would use when organizing a manila file folder in a steel filing cabinet. This is done for quick reference later, but it is also extremely helpful in cataloging the Internet for other potential readers. This is instrumental in social media; via tagging, users help other users make sense of all the information available on the web. (People tell search engines what various pages and articles contain by the tags they apply.) Other forms of tags may include #idahosenators for tools like Twitter. This is called a hashtag (#), and hashtags are helpful in categorizing conversations: #ford, #bpoilspill, #jokes, #doughnuts, and so on.

So, as we mentioned in the opening pages of this book, even though social media helps produce more content, it actually causes less confusion and helps make sense of the morass of information on the web for everyone across the globe. Search engines rightfully look for and aggregate these tags as well as the names of the links to help in ranking items.

Jane the blogger receives tons of direct traffic from the various direct links to her story. She receives even more traffic from the search engines because so many voted for her by social bookmarking it, reposting it, retweeting about it, or linking to it. She has thousands of eyes looking at her story that a marketer would be happy to pay decent money for. Her gain is News Site A's loss.

As reported by Facebook, the average person on Facebook has roughly 130 friends—there is a lot of viral potential when one person posts a story or video.

Barriers to entry, like required subscriptions, can cause an unfavorable ripple to cascade into an inevitable crescendo of failure. This example isn't to show that subscription-based news models are a bad thing, although we anticipate that by the time you read this book there will be limited subscription-based content models on the web (most will probably go to more of an app model on tablets or a bundled subscription price where you have access to both offline and online subscriptions), but rather it is to indicate that most companies need to fundamentally rethink their business models.

The mind-set of "We've always made money this way for the past 100 years, and we are going to stubbornly keep doing it this way" is flawed. Just as flawed is thinking, "Let's 'digitize' our current offerings but use the same business model" (in this example, putting newspaper content online but charging the same subscription price). This model isn't going to work in a time where competitive free digital offerings have similar content, as evidenced by the Tribune Company filing for bankruptcy at the end of 2008. Tribune is the second largest newspaper conglomerate in the United States and has such well-known properties as the *Los Angeles Times* and the *Chicago Tribune*.

We see this type of flawed thinking time after time, and it keeps repeating itself because companies are having a difficult time understanding how to leverage these dynamic digital shifts. Instead, many forge ahead and try unsuccessfully to impose outdated business models on a newly informed customer.

In 2009, the Associated Press (AP) asked Google not to feature its content in the search results. Other companies and publishers pay search experts to help them be high in the rankings because they want more traffic, yet the AP did the exact opposite. The AP was telling Google not to list its articles at all. It was putting up a distribution hurdle, which, as we previously mentioned, is a bad idea.

The AP's decision is similar to cutting off your nose to spite your face.

More progressive thinking is what the *New York Times* has done. It has tested several different types of subscription models for e-readers and tablets, even going so far as to have an intimate relationship with Apple at one point. It is too soon to tell if it has found a model that will work, but it has a better chance than the models that are attempting to cram a square peg into a round hole. The *New York Times* did a smart thing by looking at the success of Apple iTunes' charging 99 cents per song and by trying to work with Apple. There is no need to re-create the wheel if you can just as easily learn from the mistakes and successes of the past. History repeats itself because nobody listens the first time.

There are no physical fees (printing press, website maintenance, delivery trucks, paper, ink, shipping, and so on) for the

New York Times, but most importantly, it meets the users' desire to have news pushed to them in real time to their preferred mobile device. We don't know if this new model will work, but we do know that the old model does not.

Crowd-Sourced Information

Tim Russert was the well-known anchor of the popular television show *Meet the Press* for 17 years. When he unexpectedly passed away in 2008, his Wikipedia page was updated even before Fox News announced it. Entertainment blog TMZ and Wikipedia also scooped the untimely death of Michael Jackson. The online newspaper-subscription model works well if you are the only one holding the information. However, it breaks down if free information is available faster. Social media enables this "free and faster" information to exist. Online newspapers would argue that their information is more credible, and that Wikipedia isn't a reliable source.

While this argument may hold true for smaller niche topics, it's not likely to hold true for the more popular topics. Ironically, major media outlets are designed to cover the big news stories, not the minor niche ones. This makes sense because these niche stories were historically reserved for the local media outlets.

Our major media outlets are now competing against Wikipedia and other social collaborative sites, and these outlets continue to increase in power and relevance. As far back as December 2005, studies were conducted showing the accuracy and viability of Wikipedia. One such study was conducted in the journal *Nature* and posted by CNET.

For its study, *Nature* chose articles from both the *Encyclopædia Britannica* and Wikipedia in a wide range of topics and sent them to what it called "relevant" field experts for peer review. The experts then compared the competing articles side by side — one from each site on a given topic — but were not told which article came from which site. *Nature* collected 42 usable reviews from its field of experts. In the end, the journal found just eight serious errors, such as general misunderstandings of vital concepts, in the articles. Of those, four came from each site.[11]

Back in 2005, when Wikipedia wasn't fully vetted, this study was showing that it was as accurate as the *Encyclopædia Britannica*. One could debate (and many have) the validity of this study, but one thing that is very telling is that *Britannica* itself launched its own version of a wiki (however, it does censor and does have final approval) in 2009. Wikipedia should be more accurate for major topics — if you have 1,000 experts contributing, versus three to five experts, the social graph will win every time. Conversely for niche products, however, where you have two or three contributors versus two or three encyclopedia experts, the experts, in most instances, will provide more reliable information.

Wikipedia is successful as a result of scale and self-policing. As a result of the success of Jimmy Wales's Wikipedia experiment, others have started to leverage the social graph. For the first edition of this book, one hotly debated topic was between Wikipedia and the *Encyclopædia Britannica*. Many where appalled that I indicated that in many instances the Wikipedia model was a better one. Well, in 2012, *Britannica* decided to do away with its traditional printed encyclopedias and move to a model that closely resembles Wikipedia's. I would be so bold as to suggest a partnership with Wikipedia — if you can't beat them, might as well join them.

One prime example of free and faster information is the Zillow site (www.zillow.com). Zillow allows users and Realtors to investigate the estimated values of various real estate properties. It aggregates various public data (most recent sales price, up-to-date selling prices of the surrounding houses in the neighborhood, asking prices, quality of schools, etc.) into an algorithm to obtain the estimated property value. To augment this third-party data, Zillow allows its user base to update various aspects. For example, a user can update the number of rooms or bathrooms in a particular home. If you are the homeowner and you added a bathroom in the basement, who is a more qualified expert than you (the homeowner) to update the listing?

Google Maps offers a similar wiki functionality by allowing users to move or otherwise modify items on the maps so that they are more accurate, such as updating a store that may have gone out of business in the past few weeks. This model works well. Google establishes a baseline product offering (map of the area) and then allows the public to help fine-tune and grow it.

This is a slightly different but just as effective model as Wikipedia's. The difference is that Wikipedia doesn't produce a baseline; rather, everything is developed from scratch. In January 2008, Facebook introduced the Translations application, effectively turning the translation process over to its users. And why not? The users are the people who understand Facebook and their languages best. Even Facebook was blown away by the success. The site was translated into Spanish in two weeks; French followed soon after and was translated in just 24 hours. At the start of 2012, Facebook is available in more than 70 languages, all translated by Facebook users using the Translations application.

Wikipedia proves the value of collaboration on a global basis. The output of many minds results in clarity of purpose and innovation. The lesson to be learned is that if collaboration among strangers across the Internet can result in something as useful as Wikipedia, think about how collaboration among colleagues can transform business. Many businesses are even starting to use social media collaboration tools like Yammer in the workplace. The theory behind tools like Yammer—a social networking tool for use inside companies—is that employees often communicate via e-mail, which is antiquated. Social media tools offer the possibility of better collaboration in the workforce. Please note that at the writing of this book there weren't very many proven success stories using social tools to collaborate in the workforce. Often the adoption at the beginning is high, but then the stickiness wears off as employees' time is being allocated to other areas.

It's important to keep in mind that not all uses of social media are golden, so this may be an instance where social media doesn't prove successful. There is a lot of collaboration potential here for employees to share their collective knowledge. However, only time will tell how many companies and organizations successfully pull this off. While social media will play an important role in most of our lives, it's certainly not a panacea for everything.

A Touch of Bacon Salt on Your Social Media

The success of Bacon Salt is a great example of how the social graph can even result in a product going from a crazy idea to production. Bacon Salt was an idea that was born out of the minds of two Seattle buddies, Justin Esch and Dave Lefkow, who over a few beers jokingly posed this question: "Wouldn't it be great if there was a powder that made everything taste like bacon?"

The genesis of their success was when Lefkow started a My-Space profile (remember MySpace?) dedicated to Bacon Salt. They then used data openly available on MySpace to seek out people who had mentioned bacon in their profiles—they found over 35,000 such people. They began reaching out to these people to gauge their interest in Bacon Salt, and not only did they find interest, but they started receiving orders when they didn't even have a product yet!

World of Mouth took over from there. As Lefkow describes it, "It was one person telling another person, telling another person.

It was amazing and scary at the same time. We weren't prepared for the onslaught." The viral aspect of this experience branched into non-social media channels, and they even received a free endorsement from the Gotham Girls Roller Derby team. It's one thing to get buzz about your product, but it's another thing to sell it—and sell it they did. The spice that made everything taste like bacon incredibly sold 600,000 bottles in 18 months. "We didn't even have a product at the beginning; instead, we bought cheap spice bottles, printed out Bacon Salt logos and Scotch taped them onto the bottles."[12]

The Bacon Salt product and brand were built entirely using social media. Similar to JetBlue, Starbucks, Dell, Zappos, and Comcast, the founders of Bacon Salt started following what people were saying about their product and responding to them. They did other activities, but, as Lefkow and Esch readily admitted, they wanted to keep some of their social media insights to themselves: "We don't want them [big companies] to get on our gravy train."

Micro Revenue Streams Huge for Social Media

The Bacon Salt case study is a good example of a potential revenue stream for the social networks. For a small business owner, it is still very daunting and cumbersome to figure out how to set up a website for that business. As evidenced by Lefkow and Esch, you can get a fan page, profile page, group page, and so on up and running on your favorite social network in literally minutes. The best part is that as of this writing, the social networks don't allow for much customization.

How can noncustomization be a good thing? For small business owners, this places everyone on a level playing field, which means it comes down to the product you're selling versus the glitz and flash of your website.

The functional solution that social networks will provide in the future will be the ability to have an automatic shopping cart and transaction model easily established. The social network will take a small percentage of all transactions. This is similar to what the Obama presidential campaign excelled at—small payments that add up to millions of dollars. Ninety-two percent of Obama's donations were less than $100.[13] Essentially, this is almost a micro payment model for small businesses. Small businesses can be up and running in a few hours on a social media storefront, and the fractions of pennies that the social media platform captures from transactions would hardly be missed by that small business, but would be a huge revenue generator for the social media platform when collected from thousands of businesses. Companies like the T-shirt supplier Threadless are successfully completing e-commerce transactions on social networks.

Dancing Matt — Something to Chew On

Later in this book, in more than one example, we show how companies try, some in earnest (TripAdvisor — "Where I've Been") and some halfheartedly (Hasbro — Scrabble) to leverage existing successes. These efforts often fall short, and, as a result, companies often develop their own similar marketing programs — sometimes to grand success and other times to failure.

One company that was able to leverage an overnight sensation was chewing gum brand Stride (Cadbury). The story begins with Matthew Harding, a video game developer from Westport, Connecticut, who had stints at Cutting Edge Entertainment and Activision. Many of these games were primarily shooter games. Saying he "didn't want to spend two years of my life writing games about killing everyone," Matt quit his job and began traveling, which led to the production of his first "dancing" video.

All of us are known among our friends for something peculiar or quirky. Matt was known for a particular dance. So, while traveling in Vietnam, his travel buddy suggested he do his dance, and they filmed it. The video was uploaded to his website for friends and family to enjoy, and they loved it! The dance can probably best be described as a five-year-old on a Halloween sugar rush.

Matt decided to perform his unique dance whenever he was visiting an exotic location on his journey. After the trip, he was able to string together 15 dance scenes in exotic locations. All the scenes had him center frame, with the background music "Sweet Lullaby."

This second "dancing" video was passed around by e-mail and eventually became viral, with Matt's server getting 20,000 or more hits a day as it was discovered country by country. The beauty of the video is that there are no language barriers; it's simply Matt dancing in various locations.

It was a natural fit for Matt to upload it to YouTube. Stride saw a huge opportunity and approached him, offering to help sponsor his travels. Matt was delighted because he had been traveling on a shoestring budget — originally using a tour offered by a college travel company, STA Travel. With the help of Stride, Matt was able to produce a third video.

This video was the result of traveling to 42 different countries over 14 months and included shots from 70 different cities and locations.

One of the founders of YouTube, Jawed Karim, stated that Matt's video was his favorite. Karim said that he particularly liked the "Dancing Matt" video because it "illustrates what YouTube is all about — namely that anyone who has a good idea can take that idea and make it happen." When told that Matt had been hired by Stride to go dance around the world, Karim said, "Sounds good to me."[14]

This sounds good to Stride as well. As of May 2012, over 60 million people had viewed Matt's two most popular videos on YouTube. Keep in mind that this doesn't include all the ancillary videos like "How the Hell Did Matt Get People to Dance with Him?" and "Where the Hell Is Matt's Girlfriend?" That video also produced a few million views.

If you type in "Matt" in Google, he shows up as the top result. He was voted a Top 40 Internet Celebrity by VH1, and he made guest appearances on *Good Morning America*, *The Ellen DeGeneres Show*, *Jimmy Kimmel Live*, and *Countdown with Keith Olbermann*, just to name a few. For the nominal fee of sponsoring Matt's travel costs, Stride was paid back in millions of dollars' worth of brand equity. The best part is that the video is still being viewed by the millions, which is completely different from a *one and done* television commercial. In fact, this video is often showcased on one of the giant flat screens in New York's Times Square.

A main reason the campaign was successful was that Stride kept the integrity of the original concept — it was always about people; it wouldn't be prudent to all of a sudden make it about gum. Stride helped Matt improve on his original formula by suggesting that he try to surround himself with locals also joining in the dance, whereas previously the somewhat reserved computer programmer would have, at most, one or two people in the video with him. This produced some genius results — one of the most inspiring being Matt surrounded in Poria, Papua New Guinea, by a tribe of Huli wigmen dressed in their indigenous garb. The beauty of this sponsorship is that Matt and his girlfriend Melissa continued to do all of the legwork.

Prior to the third video, Matt sent out communications to the various cities he'd be visiting so that he would have people to dance with. He received over 25,000 responses, and he needed to get release forms signed prior to the filming. This was quite a bit of work that could easily have gotten bogged down in the legal department of a large corporation. In this instance, Matt and his girlfriend were continuing to produce the videos from point A to point Z.

Stride also could have made Matt wear a Stride T-shirt and pass around free samples of gum, but the company was smart enough to leave well enough alone. Instead, Stride had a tactful message at the end of the video (i.e., post roll) and also had a discreet logo in the upper right-hand corner of some of the videos. Stride showed how successful a brand can be by simply associating itself with social media that is already virally successful, which gives other brands something to chew on.

Flying the Not-So-Friendly Skies

A good example of the viralness of social media can be seen in this American Airlines example. Over the course of four days, American Airlines had to cancel 3,000 flights as a result of a large percentage of its jets not meeting the maintenance requirements mandated by the Federal Aviation Administration. This was not the result of bad weather or security threats; it was pure negligence on the part of American Airlines. A spokesman for American Airlines expressed its strategy in handling the situation:

> We fly over 100 million passengers a year, and they are all important to us. A large percentage of them fly with us exclusively, so the most important goal was to stay in contact and let them know what was going on. And we used every communications channel we have available to us.
>
> This included some new plays, including monitoring blogs, as soon as the crisis started. That was an important part of our strategy. And we felt, in general, that the information was generally correct and balanced enough to where we didn't have to get involved in the conversation. Some of the remarks were tough to take and on some blogs people were actually defending us.[15]

I underline two important pieces in this statement. The first is that "we used every communications channel we have available to us," yet there is no specific mention of social media. The second is "we didn't have to get involved in the conversation." As an individual or company, you should feel compelled to become part of the conversation; people want to hear from you. A strategy based on only entering a conversation if it gets ugly is generally flawed logic in the sense that the damage will be done before one can react. This is similar to trying to time the stock market; it's very difficult.

Website complaints to www.aa.com increased 25 percent over the same period as the year before and 9 percent over the previous week.[16] American asked consumers with complaints about the cancellations and inconveniences to e-mail them. This caused a 13 percent increase in e-mail complaints. What jumped out was a 74 percent increase in downstream traffic to social networks.[17] This is compelling in the sense that users were most likely going to social media to vent and widely disseminate their own personal issues with the crisis. This large increase couldn't be caused only by teens, because teens index low on travel volume. Also, as noted, in the previous quote there was no mention by the American Airlines spokesman of specifically monitoring social media outlets — only blogs. This type of rabid activity on social media can affect an airline's brand equity, yet as stated by the spokesman, American Airlines wasn't using the popular social media tools, listening to what was being said, and attempting to address it. The airline chose to ignore these important conversations. Later in this book, we will show how JetBlue has correctly taken the appropriate measures to make sure it is listening and responding within social media to disgruntled consumers.

Chapter One Key Points

1. Despite niche fragmentation caused by the Internet, people still desire an understanding of what the majority is doing. Social media is that mechanism.
2. Spending time on social media makes you more productive. Social media is the mechanism that allows users to avoid information indigestion. Recall the Sally Supermarket example in which she uses social media to turn 10 minutes of historically wasted time into 10 productive and enjoyable minutes.
3. Business models need to shift. Simply digitizing old business models doesn't work; businesses need to fully transform to properly address the impact and demands of social media.

(continued)

(continued)

4. Traditional magazines and newspapers are struggling for online survival because some of the most qualified people to write a story are freelance bloggers who write for the sheer joy of it! They aren't writing in hopes of subscription revenue; they are posting free content (opinions, videos, facts, etc.) because they want to be heard. It's tough for traditional journalists and publications to compete with *free*.

5. We no longer look for the news; the news finds us.

6. A key aspect of social media is the ability for millions to tag items just like you would label a manila folder. This helps catalog the information on the web and makes it easier for all users.

7. Not all great viral marketing ideas need to originate in the marketing department. It is prudent to team up with already successful grassroots programs (e.g., chewing gum company Stride and "Dancing Matt").

8. World of Mouth is an advancement of word of mouth as: (1) it disseminates the information quickly and globally, (2) its digital aspect allows the original integrity of the message to remain intact, and (3) it is traceable to an original source.

9. People want to know what their friends and peers think about products and services. Social search drives social commerce.

10. Businesses don't have a choice on whether to do social media; their choice is how well they do it.

11. Socialnomics = word of mouth on digital steroids.

CHAPTER TWO

Social Media = Preventive Behavior

We covered in Chapter One why there is such a thirst and demand for social media and that it is now a driving force in most strategic business decisions. But what does social media demand from us? While hundreds of millions of people have discovered the benefits of social media, some people and companies have also experienced the potential pitfalls of such mass transparency.

More than a few students have been kicked out of universities for collaborating on Twitter, hi5, Facebook, MySpace, and the like on assigned individual school projects. It's old news that potential employers haven't hired some people because of inappropriate content or associations on their LinkedIn or Facebook pages. Or how about the teachers who have been asked to step down for overtly sexual content within their social networks? There's also the famous Jeff Jarvis blog post about Dell's inadequate customer service.

So what does this all mean? Are social networks powerful enough to cause an adjustment in personal and corporate behavior on a macro level? You bet your camera phone they are. This is why we are seeing governments starting to step in to help try to regulate social media. Hopefully, the social media suppliers can self-regulate as much as possible.

The 20-something now thinks twice about getting so drunk that she blacks out and can't remember how she wound up in the hammock of a stranger's backyard. Cameras document everything, and technologies like Facebook's Mobile Upload and tagging can disseminate a naked keg stand to your network faster than you can count to five.

Sure, many still have the desire to put their deepest and darkest thoughts and behaviors into a black box, but they are less likely to be able to keep their actions secret.

Staying in Touch with Your Teenagers

When you get home from a hard day at work and ask your kids what happened in school, many respond with the same answer that you did when you were a teenager—"Nothing." They aren't intentionally being difficult (at least most of the time); they are just teenagers being teenagers. They do not understand that the fact that their classmates Holly and Suzy were pulling each other's hair in gym class is incredibly intriguing, or that the substitute teacher went an entire class period not knowing she had toilet paper on her shoe would provide much needed levity to a parent returning from a stressful or monotonous day at the office.

In many instances, social media can help bring families a little closer by enabling parents to unobtrusively follow their kids' lives. Oftentimes in today's busy world, parents and teenagers share time only around the dinner table, and then everyone goes about his or her own life. Many families don't even share the luxury of sitting down together at dinner.

To some extent, social media can bring families together—it connects parents to their kids as never before. "I think one of the real beauties of social media is the passivity of it. Unlike e-mail that requires a response, a mother or grandmother can passively observe the whereabouts and activities of her children or grandchildren," indicates Steve Kaufer, CEO of TripAdvisor.

While ignorance can sometimes be bliss, social media provides insight for parents into the day-to-day activities of their children. But you shake your head and say there is no way that kids would allow their parents to spy like that. You would be right, but it's not universally true. Although some junior high students don't mind being seen with their parents at the movies, others would rather be dead than be spotted with their parents in public. Also keep in mind that some parents will not bless their children's social media usage unless they are a part of their child's network. Sixty-nine percent of parents indicate they are friends with their kids on Facebook, according to insurance company Liberty Mutual's Social Media and Personal Responsibility Benchmark Survey. The same study revealed that the vast majority (73 percent) of parents believe it's acceptable for their children to have Facebook or MySpace accounts. However, those same parents claim they will monitor their children's social media profiles until they are 18 years old.

Obviously, if their parents are in the social network, then teenagers will be taking on preventive behaviors. Keep in mind that teenagers will also take on preventive behaviors not only for their parents, but also for some of their classmates. For example, if a rowdy, partying guy is trying to impress a particularly reserved girl, his behavior in the social network might be a little more refined after she becomes a part of his network and is privy to his activities and behavior.

There is also so-called Facebook dating. This is where teenagers change their profile to reflect who they supposedly are dating. However, in the real world the two aren't really dating, and have never held hands or even kissed. Simply put, if a girl likes a boy she can simply change her profile to reflect she is dating the dreamy guy in her geometry class.

Preventive Behavior for Business

The great thing about technologies like Twitter (microblogging) for businesses is that this is a tool that enables a company to search for a brand name like Hershey or Prada and see what millions of people are talking about. Good companies do this, but savvy companies take it one step further and act on it.

Comcast, which has had notoriously terrible customer service, did a progressive and great thing from the beginning when it came to microblogging. Comcast assigned a person to monitor conversations for any mention of the term "Comcast" and, more importantly, also gave that company representative the authority to respond and act. This first came to the public's attention when famous blogger Michael Arrington of TechCrunch had his service down for over 36 hours and was getting no help from customer service over the phone. He ranted on Twitter about how much he despised Comcast's service, and pals like Jeff Jarvis ("Dell Hell") started reposting the story. To Arrington's surprise, he was contacted within 20 minutes by a Comcast representative who was following rants on Twitter, and his issue was resolved by the next

day. Another example of Comcast's progressiveness was posted by
C. C. Chapman on the blog "Managing the Gray":

> *I just had an amazing experience in customer service from Comcast. . . .*
> *With all the flack they have gotten over the years, I've actually been*
> *very fortunate to have a mostly good experience with them and the*
> *last 24 hours really proves that when a brand pays attention to the*
> *conversation happening out on the web about them and actively works*
> *to engage in that, good things can happen.*
>
> *. . . [L]ast night I made a snide remark about the lackluster quality*
> *of my HD picture on Comcast during the Celtics game. Comcast saw*
> *that and tweeted me back minutes later. This morning I got a call*
> *from their service center. This afternoon someone came out. Now*
> *my HDTV rocks! THAT, my friends, is customer service and how it*
> *should work all the time.*
>
> *Brands need to wake up to the fact that "new media" isn't going*
> *away and in fact, I'd argue that it isn't new anymore, but is here and*
> *at the forefront so you either wake up and pay attention or you lose*
> *business to the company that is paying attention.*[1]

JetBlue also engaged in trying to keep a pulse on its customers.
When a company starts to follow you on Twitter, it may seem a
little too Big Brother, but if the company is transparent, then the
consumer's concerns about too much information sharing go away.
For example, this is a typical response from JetBlue:

> *Sorry if we weirded you out by following you on Twitter. @JetBlue*
> *isn't a bot, it's merely me and my team keeping our ears to the ground*
> *and listening to our customers talk in open forums so we can improve*
> *our service. It's not marketing, it's trying to engage on a level other*
> *than mass broadcast, something I personally believe more companies*
> *should try to do.*
>
> *Because corporate involvement in social media is a new and*
> *evolving discipline, I also take a specific interest in conversations*
> *revolving around our role here. I'd have messaged you directly if you*
> *allowed direct messages, so please also forgive me for following the*
> *link on your Twitter page here to send you this note.*
>
> *You and Lisa are no longer being "followed" as you indicate.*
> *Again, my apologies.*
> *Morgan Johnston*
> *Corporate Communications*
> *JetBlue Airways*[2]

Notice what Morgan Johnston says: "It's not marketing, it's
trying to engage on a level other than mass broadcast."

In another use of Twitter, authors are constantly doing vanity searches on Twitter to determine if people are talking about them or about their books. One author says,

I was doing a vanity search on my name within Twitter when I saw a post out of Billings, Montana, that had happened in the last two minutes and the exchange went something like this.

Author: *My husband just handed me a book by Tim Ash called* Landing Page Optimization. *Is this any good?*
Tim Ash: *Yes, it's a great book.*
Author: *Aren't you the author?*
Tim Ash: *Yes, I am.*
Author: *Well, if I don't like this book will you refund my money?*
Tim Ash: *Yes, I'm so confident that you will like the book that I will refund your money if you don't.*

As you read this, you may say wait, this isn't necessarily new; good companies have been responding to comments on message boards for several years now, especially after popular blogger Jeff Jarvis flamed (no pun intended) Dell in his "Dell Hell" post in 2005.[3]

The concept of responding to customer unhappiness is certainly not new and especially not new on the web. The difference with social media is the speed and ease with which this occurs as well as the sphere of influence.

A post on a message board can take a company quite some time to find (i.e., time measured in days), if they find it at all. This can also be a labor-intensive and costly process for companies to follow. The key problem is that it is also often very labor intensive for the user to post a complaint. To post on a message board, you generally are required to set up an account for that particular message board. Message boards are sometimes difficult to navigate to a particular topic area, and so on.

In the past, millions of frustrated customers didn't bother to comment. According to a study by the Strategic Planning Institute, historically 96 percent of dissatisfied customers don't bother to complain. An astounding 63 percent of these silent dissatisfied customers will not buy from that company again.[4] Hence, companies didn't know they had hundreds of frustrated customers. Now, it is so much easier to provide feedback from anywhere (in particular from your mobile device) that more and more customers are doing it. With programs like Facebook Connect and Friend Connect (Google), one can use an easy-to-remember login (Facebook or Google) no matter what site you happen to be on, whether it's CNET at www.cnet.com or CBSSports.com. Or, if you don't feel like posting a comment with one click of a button, you can simply Facebook "like" a particular website, brand, or company. The American Express Global Customer Service Barometer report showed that a person who contacted the company via social media customer service channels was three times more likely to tell a friend about the experience.[5] These same social customers say they'd spend 21 percent more with companies who deliver great service, compared to 13 percent on average.

With social media tools, you can post a comment or video in seconds directly from your laptop or most likely your mobile device. This is critical because it allows frustrated customers to instantly post their exact feelings at the point of frustration. They haven't had time to ruminate, so it is unbridled. Similarly, the posts are easy for companies like American Express and Burberry to see. It's not laborious at all to find problems; in fact, they can assign one person to help handle most situations, which means they have more time to focus on the solution rather than spending time finding the problem.

This gets to another point on how savvy companies philosophically approach critical posts on the web. Ineffective companies that aren't in touch with their customers view negative posts as nuisances. These companies approach negative feedback by attempting to figure out how to technically scrub or manipulate it by means of posting bogus "good" user comments or applying pressure to the site(s) via anti–trademark infringement laws to remove the post.

Effective companies and people relish critical online feedback. They use this information to make themselves more competitive by improving their products and services in the eyes of the consumer. These companies don't waste their time attempting to manipulate online systems; rather, they spend their time (like in the JetBlue Twitter example) trying to resolve the issue with the disgruntled customer and learning from it. Good companies view it as an opportunity to prove to that customer they are willing to go the extra mile for the customer. From the previously mentioned Strategic Planning Institute study, of the 4 percent of unhappy customers who do complain, 7 out of 10 will do business with the company again if their concerns are handled properly, and 19 out of 20 will do so if their grievances are dealt with swiftly. Rapid response is even more critical when it comes to tools like Twitter, where 10 minutes is considered a lifetime.

A good everyday analogy of constructive feedback is a friend who lets you know when you have an unsightly poppy seed stuck in your teeth prior to a big blind date. This friend is much more valuable to you than the politically polite and silent friend. Perhaps the biggest difference between these examples and traditional message boards doesn't have anything to do with the tactical aspect or the technology. It has to do with the sphere of influence of the person posting.

If the fictitious Peter Poster places something on a message board, he doesn't know whom he is reaching, and the reader most likely doesn't know who Peter is. With social media, Peter posts a status update on Facebook, LinkedIn, Twitter, and so forth. This status update is sent to people within his network who all know him personally. By knowing Peter, they can readily identify with the position Peter is coming from.

If Peter complains about a Boston cream doughnut from a particular bakery, his followers may discredit it and say, "That Peter is always so fickle when it comes to eating. It's rare if he likes any food item that his mother doesn't make." Conversely, if Peter complains about the poor customer response from a phone provider, a follower may say, "When it comes to eating, Peter is fickle, but he is very patient and forgiving otherwise, so if he says his phone company has poor customer service, I'm going to make certain that I steer clear of that phone company."

> *Someone who has stayed only at five-star hotels will rate a five-star hotel differently than a honeymooner staying at a five-star hotel for the first time.*
>
> — Bill Tancer, General Manager,
> Global Research, Hitwise

One step would be to find someone you don't know on general review sites who appears to have similar tastes; however, the next logical and more rewarding approach is locating a person in your social network whom you know and who you are confident (via personal knowledge) has the same preferences you do.

To underscore the importance of social media, let's perform a quick calculation based on the average number of followers that someone on Twitter has. The old rule of thumb was that a person who had a bad experience would tell 6 to 10 people about it. The average person on Twitter follows 100 people. If you take that and assume that 10 percent of the people following someone will pass it along, then you get to the number 10 ($100 \times 0.10 = 10$). Ten people will be influenced directly. If those 10 also have 100 followers each and only 5 percent pick it up, then another 50 individuals will be influenced indirectly, and so it goes on down the line. That's quite an impact. The American Express Global Customer Service Barometer report found that the average customer with a good experience would tell 42 people through social media channels, and one with a bad experience would tell 53 people.[6]

Chapter Two Key Points

1. Businesses and people are willing to have open diaries within social media as a way to stay connected, because their ultimate desire is to feel a part of something larger than themselves. With this openness comes responsibility for both businesses and individuals.
2. What happens in Vegas stays on YouTube.
3. Individuals and companies are starting to lead their lives as if their mother or board of directors is watching their every move — because they probably are.
4. Social media enables customers to instantly post what they like and don't like about anything from products to government.
5. Negative comments and posts are easier for companies to find with social media. Hence, those companies have more time to focus on the solution rather than spending time finding the problem.
6. Effective companies and people embrace critical feedback. Digital comments that identify areas for improvement are invaluable.
7. Ineffective companies spend time attempting to obfuscate or manipulate negative comments within social media. Good companies spend time addressing and resolving customer complaints.
8. If done properly, one can use social media to get hired versus fired.

CHAPTER THREE

Social Media = Braggadocian Behavior

The second, more exciting behavioral change is braggadocian behavior. As people continue to microblog and update their status via social media, it often becomes a competition of who's doing the coolest thing. What once took place only periodically around the watercooler is now happening in real time.

Would you rather post "I'm watching reruns of *Saved by the Bell*" or post "Just snowboarded down a double-black diamond run at Aspen and highly recommend it for those who love Colorado snow!" Over time, each of these posts contributes to *your* individual brand or social tattoo.

As a society, this is a good thing. It allows people to take stock of their collective lives and what they're doing throughout the day, rather than letting years go by and looking back on their wasted youth, saying, "What did I do with my life?"

People are actually living their own lives rather than watching others. As a company, it's imperative that you produce products and services so that people want not only to be associated with your brand, but also to take ownership of it.

Social media is in.

Out: Reality TV.

In: Reality social media.

Just Do It, Did It

Nike understood how to take advantage of users' appetites for competition as well as users looking to brands for helpful tools (creators of content). That is why Nike created an avatar named "Miles" that people can place on their desktops and smartphones. Miles helps users by tracking the miles they run or their jogging patterns compared to others inside and outside of their network. Miles encourages you to run and keeps you aware of local weather, running events, and promotions. This tool can easily be used wherever you are (iPhone, social network, iPad, desktop, etc.).

Companies need to focus on providing content and tools to consumers, which is the opposite of traditional marketing. Instead of providing consumers with a one-way communication stream, companies today need to focus on supplying something of value. People are grateful that Nike is able to provide them with a tool to track how many miles they run and to tell them which songs from their music playlists seem to stimulate them to run their best, as well as allowing users to see what songs stimulate other runners.

This social media technique also helps align Nike, Amazon, and Apple with additional revenue. More songs will be downloaded and more shoes will wear out and need to be replaced. Every time a person's running profile is updated, it broadcasts this to their social graph, helping increase Nike brand awareness. In fact, joggers are encouraged to challenge others to virtual races in which their respective performances are tracked via the tracking technology placed in the shoes.

Stationary bicycle manufacturers have picked up on the social aspect of exercising and the ability to enable connections via social media technology. Some of these bikes have built-in monitors with connectivity to the Internet that allows Joe in his gym in New York to compete against Suzy in her spa in Santa Fe. Looking at the digital screen, you see real-time avatars of other people cycling across the world, and you can virtually pass or be passed by these cyclists.

This also allows for the introduction of celebrity athletes; yes, you could be virtually competing against Lance Armstrong. This is a huge opportunity for advertisers, who can sponsor the Lance avatar or could even sponsor Joe from New York if he became the most proficient within the virtual racing world. Many of the world's top gamers are currently sponsored — they are treated similarly to successful athletes. Some even make a living from professional gaming.

Social Media Is the New Inbox

The killer tool of the first part of the Internet boom was e-mail, and then along came e-commerce, e-care, search, music, video, and now social media. E-mail has held on through the years as, arguably, the king of the Internet, used by the old and the young. However, the new inbox is shifting toward social media.

"I have a 16-year-old cousin, and she listed her favorite websites and applications and failed to mention e-mail, so I asked her about it," said Mike Peters, 41, of Detroit, Michigan. "I was shocked by the incredulous look on her face and even more shocked at her response that she didn't use e-mail that much since it was too formal; she would rather use instant messaging (IM) tools on her phone or post comments based on people's activities in social networks." It turns out that Generations Y and Z find e-mail antiquated and passé, so they simply ignore it.

While this is shocking to some generations, it fits within the scheme of Socialnomics. E-mail isn't going away entirely; it just may not be the first means of digital communication in a Socialnomics world. Messaging is much easier to manage within mobile social media versus e-mail because it acts like a real conversation among friends.

"As a salesperson, I see social networks like LinkedIn and Facebook as invaluable tools," said Allison Bahm of Response Mine Interactive Agency. "It doesn't necessarily shorten the sales cycle, but what it does is keep the information flow more open and it also allows for a much deeper relationship than e-mail. I've started relationships and signed contracts exclusively within social networks. It is revolutionary for sales; it's much easier than telephone calls and e-mails."

Whereas e-mail functions in a nonfluid manner:

"How are you doing?"
"Fine."

Open conversations within social media have an easier flow to them and replicate a normal conversation. Also, the conversational content is broken down into bite-size chunks and is associated into more easily recognized compartments rather than just a long and daunting slew of 45 e-mails that you need to wade through systematically.

Kids today prefer one-to-many communication; e-mail to them is antiquated.

— Bill Tancer, General Manager,
Global Research, Hitwise

People are updating their status—"I'm depressed" or "I got a new job"—and it is much easier to read this and stay connected than to send a series of e-mails asking how someone is doing or what that person is up to. In a sign of the times ahead and for the first time since e-mail was invented, Boston College and other universities will no longer be giving out e-mail addresses to incoming freshmen. Many colleges and even kindergarten classes are distributing iPads as the de facto learning tool. Education is being revolutionized as a result of advances in technology.

"At Apple, we generally hire early adopters. That being said, I was still blown away when we recently hired a 22-year-old and he had literally never sent an e-mail," said a director of Apple. "Via his iPhone he had always communicated with his friends either by Instant Messenger, text, phone call, or comments within Facebook. I believe he is not alone and this is a trend we will continue to see with the next generation."

"Are You on Facebook?" Is the New "Can I Get Your Phone Number?"

The main underlying factor for this new inbox may be the seismic shift in the way people exchange information. Let's take a quick look at the evolution of dating over the past 10 years. First, people used to give out their home phone numbers. Then, people began to give out their e-mail addresses instead.

At first it seemed odd to ask someone for a date over e-mail, but then it became quite natural. Then we progressed to mobile phone numbers because some people didn't have landlines anymore. Besides, it was easier to text message one another—it was less intrusive and awkward: "What are you doing tonight?"

Today with social media, when people meet, it's common for one of them to ask the other person, "Are you on Facebook?," "Are you on Vkontakte (Russian social network service)?," or "Can I follow you on Weibo (Twitter in China)?" Just as people use the word Google as a verb—"Google it"—they now use phrases like "Facebook me" or "Send me a tweet." People are no longer exchanging e-mails; they are exchanging each other's social media information. In many instances, people wouldn't give out their e-mail addresses for fear of spam (broken marketing model). Today, if they desire an e-mail communication stream, social networks have inboxes of their own that replicate and replace e-mail.

Executives are still holding hard and fast to the concept of the traditional inbox. In a survey of 180 chief marketing officers of $1 billion corporations that was conducted by GfK Roper Public Affairs and Media, the researchers found that while 70 percent were decreasing their marketing budgets, the area in which they were least likely to make cuts was e-mail.[1] You can't necessarily blame them for this type of thinking. This has been one of their best-performing channels for years, and they've spent money building and managing their databases.

Now and in the future, marketers need to adjust their way of thinking, because it's no longer about building out the existing database. Instead, you could be in communication with fans and consumers on someone else's database (Facebook, YouTube, Foursquare, Twitter, etc.). Yet, many companies fail to grasp this new concept. They build elaborate YouTube or Flickr pages, placing callouts and click actions that send the user outside the social site, often to their company website or a lead capture page. These companies still believe they need to get users into their prospecting databases in order to market to them. They are doing a disservice to their loyal fan base and in turn a disservice to themselves.

It's analogous to meeting a pretty girl in a bar and asking if she would like a drink. When she responds "Yes," rather than ordering a drink from the bartender, you grab her, rush her into your car, and drive her back to your place; after all, you have beer in your fridge. This is not a sound courtship strategy, nor should companies employ comparable social media strategies in courting potential customers. It is best to be patient rather than to rush into things, because without consumer confidence, just like in dating, you have nothing.

Deep Dive into Dating 101

Let's digress back to our dating scenario on social media. Social networks are fantastic for meeting new people and dating. If a girl meets a guy out on the town and they exchange names and connect within a social media network, it's a virtual gold mine of personal data.

The more friends you have in common within a shared social network, the more secure you feel knowing the other person isn't some form of lunatic. Photos are helpful, especially if the night before was a bit wild and a little fuzzy. If you are listed in a network for "*Star Trek* Fanatics" or "Dracula Oprah," that will be even more telling about who you really are. What you do, who you work for, and where you live and have lived all provide additional insight into your personality.

If all checks out fine, that first date is more like a fourth date; you don't have to ask questions like "Where did you go to college?" or "What are your hobbies?" You will still probably ask these questions to show a polite interest or to avoid coming across as a stalker, but it is a completely different dynamic than the world in which baby boomers, or even Generation Xers, grew up. Social networks make it easier to stay in touch with someone new before you are at the "Let's grab a drink" stage. It's easier than face-to-face because you avoid awkward silences, you don't have to worry about who is going to pay the bill, and you don't experience potentially embarrassing situations (poppy seed between the teeth, anyone?).

Mobile geolocation tools and apps like Foursquare, Yelp, and Gowalla alert you when people of interest are in your area. Going one step further, some tools recommend locations based on your mood. Instead of listing the top 10 restaurants in the SoHo area of New York, they list the top 10 romantic restaurants or the top 20 hip, laid-back restaurants; so, if it was your first date, it wouldn't be awkward being at a place with white-glove service and dining by candlelight.

The benefits of these types of relationship-building tools certainly hold true from business to consumer, as well. Businesses capture more information via social media about their consumers than ever before. Good businesses realize that the relationships they have with their consumers still need to be cultivated (e.g., the grabbing the girl from the bar analogy). Good businesses realize that it's not all about the instant win of getting someone into a database. Rather, it is cultivating that relationship via social media. If it's done correctly, you will have a relationship that lasts a lifetime.

Assess Your Life Every Minute

The examples presented in this section stress a crucial maxim of this book. Social media allows individuals to take real-time inventories of their lives and helps answer the age-old question "What am I doing with my life?"

Bill Tily, 87, says:

I actually made a habit of physically printing out my social media updates from the previous month and going through them one-by-one and highlighting updates that weren't necessarily contributing to a "full" life. Over time, I reduced the amount of "waste" and actually became so cognizant of it during the actual act of updating my status that I'd recognize in that specific moment in time what I would deem an "unfruitful activity" and cease engaging in it immediately. My life is much more fulfilling because of this! I wish these social media tools had been around a long time ago![2]

Heather, a mother of three, has her own story about how social media is helping her lead a more productive life:

I had a close friend who was married without children. One day she confided in me that she didn't know if she was ready for children. She thought she was but then she mentioned something that floored me; the conversation went something like this:

"Heather, I'm just not sure that I'm up for it. I mean you are probably the most with-it person that I know and it seems like your kids are all that you can handle."

To which I responded, "Yes, having kids is life-changing and presents its new challenges, but it's not as bad as people let on; for every one thing my kids do bad, they do nine things that light up my life."

"Really? That's good news to hear and helps alleviate some of my concerns, but to be blunt, it's also a little surprising given the social media status updates I receive from you."

I was obviously surprised to hear this revelation from one of my closest friends, and I didn't think it had much validity. So, later that day, I wanted to prove it was unwarranted. I pulled up the last several weeks of updates, which didn't take me too long since I did only one or two updates per day. There it was staring back at me in black and white; my friend was exactly right! While my kids were the greatest joy in my life, you would never know it from reading my updates. My kids provided 90 percent of all the new wonders and happiness in my life, yet I was conveying the exact opposite in my status updates. For every one positive status update about my kids ("Lilly gives the best hugs" or "I posted Will's beautiful finger painting on the fridge"), I'd post nine negative ones ("Have a massive headache from the kids' nonstop screaming" or "Not sure I can handle a full day at the zoo with the kids again").

The reality of the situation shocked me, and I was afraid that there was a possibility that I was also projecting this negative attitude onto the kids. The answer to this came sooner than expected. For the next few weeks, I made a concerted effort not to post anything remotely negative on the social media platforms I used, or at least [to] have it reflect my reality, nine positive posts for every single negative post. Then one day, about two weeks into practicing this experience, it really hit home when my four-year-old tugged at my shirt and looked up at me with her big blue eyes and said, "Mommy, you seem a lot more happy, and I really like it."[3]

Updating your status or tweeting about what you are doing is an immediate reminder of exactly that! And, if you pause, like Bill, and look back over a day, week, or month of what you posted, it is extremely enlightening because it shows you how you are spending what precious time you have.

Millennials — All about Giving Back

In 2008, Millennials (Generation Y) showed up in record numbers to vote. In comparison, jaded Generation Xers never stepped out to vote when they were in their early twenties, despite all the *Rock the Vote* promotions being blasted on MTV at the time.[4]

In 2008, the most popular Facebook application wasn't a fancy game, music, or TV show. It was an application called Causes, with almost 20 million active monthly users.[5] The application was quite simple in its description: Causes lets you start and join the causes you care about. Donations to Causes can benefit over a million registered nonprofit organizations. Not surprisingly, this was a far cry from the Me Generation of the 1980s. Recall that one of the popular songs of that era was Madonna's "Material Girl."

Generation Y is a by-product of the 1980s, and after witnessing the horror that can be caused by narcissistic behavior, they want to do everything in their power to correct it. They don't want their kids to grow up as latchkey kids. The social community aspect simply doesn't stop at discussing the hottest young pop star. No, Generation Y has a strong sense for making the world a better place.

While the majority of this book stresses the many positive aspects of social media, we'd be misleading if we didn't highlight the potentially negative aspects as well. One trend we are starting to see is Generations Y and Z's difficulty with face-to-face interactions.

The Next Generation Can't Speak

The desire and ability to meet new people has rapidly eroded so much that humans fear public speaking more than death. This led comedian Jerry Seinfeld to quip, "According to surveys on what we fear . . . you are telling me that at a funeral, most people would rather be the guy in the coffin than have to stand up and give the eulogy?"[6]

Difficult and awkward subjects are much easier to deal with when hiding behind instant messaging or social media tools than when confronting them face-to-face.

And even written skills have eroded from living in a 140-character world.

A study by the nonprofit group that administers the SAT and other placement tests (the National Commission on Writing at the College Board) found:

- About 50 percent of teens surveyed say they sometimes fail to use proper capitalization and punctuation in assignments.
- Some 38 percent have carried over IM shortcuts such as LOL or U.
- Approximately 25 percent of teens have used :) and other emoticons.
- Some 64 percent have used at least one of the informational elements in school.[7]

So yes, there are downsides to not having as much face-to-face interaction, and that's a challenge these two generations and future generations face because technology is an intrinsic part of their lives; but the positive aspects are plentiful.

These generations have an understanding of their place in the global community and are more collaborative. They don't mind challenging the status quo — which is much different than simply not respecting it. They expect a better work-life balance, are better at prioritization, and are adroit at multitasking. On the flip side, these generations need more guidance in management skills, project planning, and business communication.

They are also less likely to understand boundaries, whether that is answering e-mail from a friend during business hours or taking e-mail from a manager at 11 P.M. To them, things are just more fluid; it's not a 9-to-5 world, it's a 24/7 world, and it's up to the individual to properly balance the hours in the day. Generation Xers and Yers think it's laughable that a company would block Facebook or YouTube during work hours (as of this writing 54 percent of companies block social media sites to their employees) — you are either getting the job done or you are not getting the job done. Aside from that, these blockers aren't very effective since most can access what they need via their mobile phones. Workers realize that if they play during the workweek they will have to work on

Saturday to complete the necessary tasks. But that is a conscious decision they make.

Consumers Own Your Brand

The Young Adults Revealed global survey conducted by Synovate in partnership with Microsoft was designed to find out how much young adults interact and engage online with brands on a daily basis. The research included 12,603 people 18 to 24 years old from 26 countries. The survey found that 28 percent say they talked about a brand on a discussion forum, 23 percent added brand-related content to their IM service, and 19 percent added branded content to their home page or favorite social sites.[8]

The research concluded that young adults are more than willing to add brand content to their instant messaging services, web home pages, and social networking sites. The researchers found that respondents spent an average of 2.5 hours online daily in nonworking-related activity. Synovate's global manager of syndicated research, Julian Rolfe, stated:

> *The research shows that young people are not only comfortable with the idea of branded content and branded entertainment, but also reveals they are openly willing and eager to engage online with brands.*
>
> *They clearly feel their opinions about brands are important, they want to associate themselves with brands they see as "cool" and this is why we see them uploading clips to their social networking sites and IM services.*[9]

Synovate found that 1 in 10 said they passed along viral ads and marketing clips.[10] For brand marketers, this should be welcome news. Your consumers want to have a relationship with you and even help out where they can. All it takes is honesty, transparency, listening, and reacting. Because not every company can do these well, the ones that do will win decisively.

Kids Ages 2 to 17 Don't See Advertisements

A Nielsen study found that kids ages 2 to 11 endure the least amount of advertising on the Internet. The group experiencing the second lowest ad exposure is the next age group in succession (12 to 17). The amount of advertising someone is exposed to is somewhat correlated with age; the 65 and older demographic sees the most ads.[11]

This speaks to the infancy of social media, because this is where a lot of teens spend the majority of their time. It also speaks to the fact that social media companies realize that they shouldn't force fit an old advertising model into a completely new and different space (i.e., insert a square peg into a round hole). The limited ad exposure of kids under 12 years of age is due in part to protection laws coupled with the fact that many of the more popular kids' sites (e.g., Webkinz) carry few, if any, advertisements.

The upside to this as a marketer is that if you are able to integrate your content (note we say content rather than advertising), then it will have a better chance to stand out since there is less clutter.

Turning Lemons into Lemonade with Fizzle

A salient example of companies less steered by their legal departments is the Diet Coke and Mentos experiment. This started with two scientists experimenting in a laboratory one day and discovering that if you dropped five Mentos (chewable gumlike candy with a hard outer shell) into Diet Coke, a fairly volatile chemical reaction would ensue. They perfected these geysers, having determined that five Mentos on a fishing line dropped into a two-liter bottle of Diet Coke with the cap on and a tiny hole at the top would result in the most dramatic effect.

Since it was so visual and dynamic, YouTube was the perfect platform to make it globally famous. Before the existence of a social media site like YouTube (first video was shown on April 23, 2005), only a select few in the science community would have known about it. In the past, the Coca-Cola Company could possibly have handled this quietly behind closed doors; however, in today's world with its heightened social media exposure, Coke was forced to deal with the situation. Let's look at how Coke handled it.

In the past, Coke would have been alarmed by this discovery, and rightfully so. There was potential for the public to jump to the incorrect conclusion that Coke must be highly toxic and it would be undesirable to have this type of reaction going on in the stomach. *If shaking up a bottle of Diet Coke and Mentos can create a 20-foot geyser, imagine the havoc it would cause in my stomach!* The end result would have most likely been a long court battle by the Coca-Cola Company to discredit and shut down these activities.

The transparency and rapid distribution of information enabled by social media (blogs, Twitter, YouTube, etc.) don't allow for events and news to be handled discreetly anymore. Equally important for Coke to consider was the reaction by the competition (e.g., Pepsi).

During their testing, the scientists, Fritz Grobe (the short one) and Stephen Voltz (the tall one), had discovered that the best results came from using Diet Coke. Sprite, Diet Pepsi, Coke Classic, and Dr Pepper produced a reaction with Mentos, but not the same dramatic effect.

Hence, a window was open for Pepsi to do something if Coke didn't (the mind-set that if you don't do something, someone else will). Pepsi could have shown that its products didn't have the same explosive reaction and compared them side-by-side with Coke using a proactive question of "Which would you rather have in your kids' stomachs?"

Weighing these factors, as well as other World of Mouth ramifications, Coke decided to embrace the exposure of this experiment and actually hired Grobe and Voltz as spokesmen. They, in turn, went on to do a much more elaborate video on YouTube that won Coke many marketing awards and has resulted to date in over 11 million views on YouTube. The transparency and exposure of social media are having the positive effect of companies starting to embrace items that they historically would have either ignored (in hopes they'd go away) or shunned for fear of legal liability or consumer backlash.

If a company or individual has something to brag about now or in the future, we will see that the company or individual is going to let the world know through every social media tool available. The great thing is that if people or companies don't have anything to brag about, then they will presumably alter their behavior (e.g., watching TV) to something more interesting (e.g., writing a screenplay), which in turn, one could certainly argue, has them contributing more and more to improving society as a whole.

Chapter Three Key Points

1. Social media allows individuals to take real-time inventories of their lives and helps answer the age-old question, "What am I doing with my life?" This benefits society because it encourages more people to engage in productive or charitable activities that they can brag about.

(*continued*)

(continued)

2. Reality TV has been replaced by reality social media — it's all about *my* friends and *my* reality.
3. Social media is the new inbox: Younger generations find e-mail antiquated and passé.
4. The interpersonal communication skills of Generations Y and Z have been retarded by reliance on social media tools that aren't face-to-face or verbal.
5. Many in Generations Y and Z have a desire to contribute to the greater world around them and leverage social media for social and charitable causes.
6. Consumers want to take ownership of your brand and brag about your product; let them!

CHAPTER FOUR

What We Can Learn from Politics

John F. Kennedy was helped into the White House by the increasing popularity of a new medium, television. The same can be said about Barack Obama. He also was greatly helped by a new medium, but rather than television, it was social media. While the 2008 election was groundbreaking in that it forced traditional broadcasters such as ABC, NBC, and CBS to adjust how they covered election news — otherwise people would find content elsewhere (YouTube, Wikipedia, blogs, podcasts, etc.) — the constructs are a good blueprint for how we can leverage change, whether it's within politics or in any other endeavor. The blueprint for success will constantly evolve, but it's important for us to recognize recurring old constructs that we can utilize to apply to the latest shifts in society and technology. As you read this chapter, think about how you can leverage change, like the Obama campaign did, to drive your own personal success.

"We should be careful of these zero-sum games where the new media drives out the old," said Andrew Heyward, a former president of CBS News who consults for the Monitor Group. "I think what we see is growing sophistication about making the channels work together effectively."[1]

Perhaps due to his widespread appeal to younger audiences, but more likely due to limited funding at the outset of his campaign in the Democratic Party primary, Obama embraced social media from the beginning—knowing that he had a chance to dominate this medium over his Democratic opponents. Attempting to dominate traditional media (newspapers, television, radio) would have been a tactical error against his well-known opponent, Hillary Clinton, and, more important, the Clinton political organization. In many respects, the Obama campaign workers weren't geniuses for embracing social media; it was the only card that they had against a stacked deck.

As a result of the hard-fought battle with Hillary, Obama was well positioned from a social media perspective when he won the Democratic nomination and entered the presidential race.

His social media followers and supporters weren't going away; rather they were growing and contributing in record numbers—with $5 and $10 donations quickly adding up to a multimillion-dollar arsenal. Obama raised a record amount of money, and 92 percent of his donations were in sums of less than $100. This disrupted the old model of getting giant donations from a handful of donors or so-called whales. What old models are holding you or your business back that you can use technology to disrupt?

By the time Obama was elected, he had over 3.1 million fans on his Facebook fan page. This number didn't include the various other fan pages and groups like "Students for Obama," "Pride for Obama," "Michelle Obama," "Florida for Obama," "Michigan for Obama," "Pennsylvania for Obama," "Women for Obama," and so on. If you added only the rest of the top 20 groups, Obama would have an additional 2 million supporters. This is in stark contrast to John McCain, who had 614,000 supporters for his fan page the day of the election and whose next largest fan page was for his wife Cindy with only 1,700 fans. That's 5.1 million (Obama) to less than 1 million (McCain).[2] On MySpace, Obama had 833,161 friends to McCain's 217,811, and this type of disparity also held true on Twitter, where Obama attracted 113,000 followers to McCain's 4,650.

You and YouTube

Looking to YouTube, the disparity was even greater as the election neared. The BarackObama.com YouTube channel had over 20 million views, whereas the JohnMcCain.com channel had just over 2 million views.[3] A year and a half prior to the election, a young woman had released the "I've Got a Crush . . . on Obama" video. Amber Lee Ettinger, later nicknamed "Obama Girl," would appear on many national television shows and be included in *Playboy* magazine.

This was prior to Obama becoming a household name; in fact, it was items like this that helped Obama rise from being an unknown candidate. This video was viewed 11.5 million times in the months leading up to the election.[4] In McCain's defense, his voting base skewed older, and they didn't use these types of social media tools at the time, which meant a huge advantage for Obama. Obama used social media to his advantage in both the Democratic primary and the national race to become the president of the United States.

This leveraging of peer-to-peer communication helped mitigate the violent swings that can be caused by traditional media and is one significant reason why Obama was able to overcome some controversial issues (e.g., Reverend Jeremiah Wright, William Ayers) during his campaign for the Oval Office.

"No one knows the impact of quasi-permanency on the Web yet, but it surely has changed the political world," said Allan Louden, a professor who teaches a course on digital politics at Wake Forest University. "The role of gatekeepers and archivists have been dispersed to everyone with Internet access."[5]

Open Those Closed Doors

Obama's team was also creative by providing their own original footage of events that the networks covet — behind-the-scenes moments. They were able to splice these together with decent, yet not too high-end, production quality. Even if they had the money, candidates wouldn't necessarily want top-level editing because that destroys the authenticity of the organic ambiance they are attempting to create and, more importantly, can increase the lag time to get the content in the hands of influencers and tastemakers. Viewers want timely information they can relate to; spending time and money on high-end production can often create distance between candidate and viewer. Viewers are interested in how a person acts when the lights of Hollywood aren't on — how do the candidates interact with their families and those closest to them on a day-to-day basis? That's why we see millions following Lady Gaga, Ellen DeGeneres, and Shaq on Twitter.

Social media user Lance Muller of Decatur, Georgia, said, "I have been an Obama Facebook friend since his speech at the 2004 Democratic Convention. In social media, he actually virtually 'pokes' me and sends memos and stuff. I don't know if it is really him, but it makes you feel more in touch with the process. His team is smart in utilizing social networks to reach people like me so that I feel connected personally."[6]

The Obama camp also was smart in appealing to their voting base by introducing a chief technology officer (CTO) position to the president's cabinet, which would be dependent on an Obama victory. Aneesh Chopra became the first CTO of the United States on August 7, 2009. The main role of the CTO is to "ensure that our government and all its agencies have the right infrastructure, policies, and services for the twenty-first century."[7]

As we will discuss throughout this book, advertisers need to become providers of content. Obama's campaign did just that when they placed ads pushing an early voting message in Electronic Arts (EA) video games, most prominently in a racing game called Burnout Paradise. These games are socially interactive, with players being able to compete with each other around the globe. Obama's objective for this particular campaign targeted players in 10 battle-ground states. The key to this form of advertising is that it benefits the player of the game. The game appears more real-time with seamless and wireless updates to allow for such real-time product placement — in this case, the product placement was Obama with the specific message of early voting.

When you look at total views for Obama via YouTube, they accounted for 110 million views. This was estimated at 14.5 million hours of viewing on YouTube, according to Democratic political consultant Joe Trippi. He estimated that amount of time would have cost $47 million to purchase in commercial venues.[8]

"If not for the Internet, Barack Obama would not be president or even the Democratic nominee," claimed Arianna Huffington of the liberal Huffington Post website.[9] Overall blog mentions of "Obama" and "McCain" varied greatly during the election (and we can't delineate positive versus negative posts); close to 500 million blog postings mentioned Obama since the beginning of the conventions. During the same time period, only about 150 million blog posts mentioned McCain.[10]

Obama's almost micropayment style approach to raising funds allowed him to outspend McCain nearly three to one, which was a testament to the capabilities of social media. By engaging constituents directly, he was able to raise a staggering $660 million in campaign contributions.[11]

Close to 65 percent of the American population voted in the 2008 election, the highest turnout since the election of 1908.[12] These results are telling: a Democrat had not won Virginia and Indiana since then, either. Obama captured both.

Support came from everywhere for Obama during his historic and meteoric political run. Some help came from unexpected places. The famous Budweiser "Whassup?" commercials, which debuted in 1999, immediately helped sell millions of Bud Lights. The ad became a part of U.S. pop culture following its exposure during the 2000 Super Bowl. Could this same "Whassup?" idea be resurrected to help Obama's cause for change? You bet.

The parody used the same characters from the original spots and opened in the exact same fashion, but instead of a guy comfortably relaxing on a couch, he was sitting on a foldout chair in a boxed-up apartment as a subtle hint at the housing crisis that was sweeping the country in 2008.

From there, the spoof segued into a series of "Whassup?" conversations in conference call fashion. The characters ranged from one friend stationed in Iraq and another fighting a hurricane to someone looking for help to pay for pain medication because of a broken arm. The star of the original commercials, "Dookie," steals the show again as he contemplates hanging himself after seeing his entire stock portfolio plummet essentially to zero. Dookie, being overweight, pulls the entire ceiling fan down in a failed attempt; hence, the ad keeps its original light tone while at the same time connecting with the audience and sending a strong message. At the end of the video, one of the characters asks again, "Whassup?" And the main character replies, "Change. Change, that's whassup," from his boxed-up apartment as he watches TV images of Senator Obama and his wife.

"It's a great juxtaposition of the original ads," said author and political campaign expert Brian Reich. "It shows how the lives of these characters have dramatically changed in the past eight years — going from carefree and relaxed beer buddies to being confronted by a shift in global dynamics, an economic collapse, and all in all an unbelievable amount of personal challenge and difficulty. Being able to identify with the characters is what makes this video so strong, and they never once say or state Obama's name; rather it's a subtle glimpse of Barack and Michelle Obama on the television that the main character is watching at the end of the spot with a huge smile on his face. The short video ending with the word 'Change,' just like in the 1999 commercials that were followed by the word 'True,' was both powerful and brilliant."[13]

Brian Reich was a key member of the Howard Dean interactive team largely recognized as the originators of many of the political Internet tactics that Obama successfully leveraged.

Charles Stone III, who was the idea man behind the original Budweiser ads, created this satire. The ad was posted on October 24, 2008, on YouTube a little over a week prior to the election, and received over 4.8 million views along with 14,891 user comments. Also, 21,746 viewers took the time to rate the video, and it received the difficult-to-achieve five-star rating.[14]

Stone was paid roughly $37,000 by Anheuser-Busch and Omnicom Group's DDB Chicago for the rights to license the concept for five years. Stone had originally created a "Whassup?" film that had caught Omnicom's attention. The fact that neither Anheuser-Busch nor its agency owned the rights to the concept is unusual in the advertising business, but in this instance, it allowed Stone to make his popular and effective parody. Stone appears in both the original and satire ads with his friends — who also happen to be African American. Stone felt that he could use the same concept to "make a difference" for a politician he believes in.[15]

In this instance, the brand is Obama. The Obama camp could have asked Stone to remove the video out of concern that the hanging scene and the soldier in Iraq might have crossed the line. A traditional brand would have probably stopped the video or diluted its viral power. Obama's advisers did not do this; instead, they allowed someone (Stone) outside of the Obama camp to take ownership of the brand and promote it. As a result, he exposed his message to 4.8 million people right before the election without spending one penny or lifting one finger. That is the power of social media for brands; yet many aren't willing to take the risks.

However, it's important to not underestimate the potential bumps in the road when your supporters are a little too aggressive with your brand. This was the case with another video that was in support of Obama. This one was aptly named "Politics as Usual" and was produced by famous hip-hop artist Ludacris. One of the lines was "Obama would paint the White House black." This was tame in comparison to dismissing Hillary Clinton as a potential vice presidential running mate — "that bitch is irrelevant." Attacking the Republicans, Ludacris stated that John McCain should be able to sit in the "big chair" only if he is paralyzed. Prior to the election, this rap video received over a million views on YouTube.[16]

It was a tough spot for Obama to be in because he still wanted the support of the influential hip-hop community, but he also needed to avoid the controversy that these lyrics stirred. In the end he took corrective action, quickly and publicly denouncing it, calling the music video "outrageously offensive."

"While Ludacris is a talented individual, he should be ashamed of these lyrics," Obama campaign spokesman Bill Burton said in an e-mail statement.

"Of course, Obama and his people have to condemn the rap, because it does say some vulgar things. If you're running for president, you're supposed to be an upstanding individual," said John McWhorter, author of *All About the Beat: Why Hip-Hop Can't Save Black America.*[17] Many companies and politicians make the mistake of stopping there, but Obama went the extra mile to have a private meeting with the rap star. Rapper Ludacris said Barack Obama disapproved of the song he wrote because it insulted his rivals.

"The song was my artistic expression and was meant to get people who weren't involved in the political process involved. Being as though it was the first mix tape to reach the United States government, it was a bit overwhelming," said Ludacris. He indicated that when he met with Obama, they didn't just discuss the song. "What myself and the president spoke about is confidential, but I took it upon myself to not speak about the song."[18] By acting quickly and decisively, Obama was able to turn a negative into a positive, for he kept the support of Ludacris's fan base while distancing himself from the controversial content.

Can Google Predict the Next President, Product Trend, or Flu Outbreak?

In the early part of this century, Yahoo! started to leverage the search data that was flowing into its data centers. At the time, Yahoo! was the world's preeminent search engine. It was noticing that it could predict some pop-culture trends, often six weeks in advance. It actually leveraged this data for one of its biggest advertising clients at the time, Pepsi-Cola. Yahoo! identified through its buzz index that searches for an up-and-coming pop star by the name of Britney Spears were indexing high and rising rapidly. As a perk to its important client, Yahoo! disclosed this information, and Pepsi seized the opportunity. With little investment, Pepsi was able to sign Spears to a relatively cheap endorsement contract a few months before she became one of the music industry's biggest and brightest stars.

Fast-forward to the present. Because of the transparency that social media demands, search engines don't hold this data hostage anymore. Much of the search data is open for public consumption.

Though the data is in aggregate (meaning privacy policies are upheld since you can't identify an individual) and the data isn't absolute (meaning there are indexes rather than the actual number of searches — otherwise financial analysts could extrapolate data to predict quarterly financial performance for the search engines), it is very helpful for many reasons.

Is the Flu a Virus or Just Simply Viral?

It appears that people make a habit of entering phrases like "flu symptoms" or "flu remedies" into search engines prior to actually seeing a doctor. When you multiply this across millions of searches around the globe, you have something like a neighborhood watch for fast-spreading flu outbreaks.

Google flu trends is a service provided by the company's philanthropic arm (Google.org), released to do just exactly that. Historically, the Centers for Disease Control and Prevention (CDC) based in Atlanta, Georgia, was the only source for tracking spikes in viruses like the flu. Comparing the CDC data to Google's data showed that Google's insight was roughly two weeks ahead of the CDC's. The CDC data is inherently slow as a result of its dependence on data being supplied and analyzed from thousands of sources (e.g., doctors, labs, health insurance).

Search and social data is powerful stuff that can help stifle the spread of disease and ultimately save lives. A simple definition of big data is all the information and items that we, as individuals, produce. A simple post on Facebook or tweet contributes to big data. The amount of data we produce is mind-boggling. Did you know that Google has crawled less than 1 percent of all the data out on the web?

This big data is unstructured and the key is trying to put structure around it so we can make predictions. Google is able to combine flu search data with its robust mapping tools to quickly showcase where the disease is spreading across the world. The potential doesn't stop at influenza, but can be used for all forms of disease and outbreaks. The CDC data and other data can also be combined with search data to make it even more accurate. "Most forecasting is basically trend extrapolation," said Hal Varian, Google's chief economist. "This works remarkably well, but tends to miss turning points, times when the data changes direction. Our hope is that Google data might help with this problem."[19] The key is that the data has existed for years and in some instances was being used (e.g., Pepsi and Britney Spears), but Socialnomics has been a main driver behind it being shared for such beneficial causes.

In 2009, Prabhakar Raghavan, the head of Yahoo! Labs, said search data could be valuable for forecasters and scientists, but privacy concerns had generally stopped Yahoo! Labs from sharing it with outside academics. "I think we are just scratching the surface of what's possible with collective intelligence," said Thomas W. Malone, a professor at the Sloan School of Management at MIT.[20] For business and politics it is very intriguing: Do more people search "cheap travel" or "travel"? "Coke" or "Pepsi"? "Obama" or "McCain"?

This last one was particularly intriguing. Could search and social data help predict the next president of the United States?

Digital Data: The New Exit Poll?

We compared U.S. search trends in April 2008 for the terms "Clinton," "McCain," and "Obama." Total searches for Obama far exceeded those of Clinton — for every Clinton search, there were 1.60 Obama searches. Yet for every Clinton search, there were only 0.48 McCain searches.[21]

This makes sense, given the Democrats' heated primary. What's interesting is that Obama had so many more searches than Clinton. Keep in mind that the Clinton result is artificially inflated by the fact that it contains searches having nothing to do with Hillary (e.g., people looking for Bill, Clinton Township, etc.). "Obama" is a unique term, so it has less statistical noise. Also, the data doesn't factor in searches done for "Barack." So, Obama's 1.60:1 ratio was most likely even higher than the numbers indicated. It's important to note here that if you are launching a new product or brand, the more unique the name, the easier it is to crawl and collect data digitally. For example, Puma (shoes, jungle cat, purse, older female, etc.) has a much more difficult time crawling for data than Adidas has.

Google Insights data also pointed out that in April 2008 searches for Obama in the state of Indiana greatly exceeded those of Clinton. It would've been easy to predict that Obama was closing the gap on Hillary in that state. After all, if the voters had already decided to vote for Hillary, there wouldn't be a need to search for information on Obama. Obama was supposed to lose handily in Indiana; but just as the data predicted, he closed the gap, narrowly lost the state, but was well on his way to achieving the nomination afterward.

Using this same construct, in the 2012 Republican primary race, Facebook and political blog Politico.com teamed up to share data. Politico took comments on Facebook around the primaries and was able to accurately predict the state-by-state election results, based on the data that individuals were posting on Facebook. This is an example of taking unstructured data (Facebook posts) and putting structure around it (aggregated to identify patterns and make predictions).

Capturing Geographic Interest and Intent

Data from Google Insights also gave a strong indication that Obama would defeat John McCain in the presidential election. Thirty days prior to the election, Obama searches outperformed McCain almost 3:1 even though McCain had gained 11 percent in search volume over the same time period. Predictably, U.S. allies (Canada, United Kingdom, etc.) seemed the most interested in the election, judging by their search behavior. Global searches indexed even higher for Obama over McCain by a 4:1 ratio, indicating that the world was anticipating an Obama victory or interested in learning more about Obama.

In the United States, not surprisingly, most searches for Obama and McCain came from those living in Washington, D.C., and in the college towns Austin, Texas, and Raleigh, North Carolina, which indexed within the top 10, primarily due to the younger voters being so involved in this election.[22]

McCain and Obama each tried to build up their respective brands in the eyes of voters. They used search data to answer questions such as whether it would be better to print "Obama" or "Barack" on promotional posters. There were 3.5 more searches done on "Obama" than on "Barack,"[23] which was pretty helpful information.

Just like in the political race, search data can also be used in the world of business to help guide companies in making strategic decisions. Should Coke use the term "soda pop" or "soda" to describe the products on its website? What regions in the world search for "Coke" more than "Pepsi"? Which cities seem to show the most interest, based on data, and could be ideal places to launch a new product? More and more companies are adding the role of a chief of analytics as they comprehend that those who better understand the Big Data around them will better understand the marketplace. This is a definitive competitive advantage.

Even more than search, social media tools like Twitter are becoming extremely instrumental in predicting trends, from flu outbreaks to the spread of natural disasters like forest fires. In one celebrated case in March 2010, actress Demi Moore's Twitter account played a vital role in stopping a teen from committing suicide. When one young man posted his intent to commit suicide, Moore asked if he was serious; the reply was yes. Another actress, Nia Vardalos (*My Big Fat Greek Wedding*) saw the post as well and called the Florida police and the suicide prevention hotline. Vardalos stayed on the phone with the police until she knew the young man was okay and was being taken to the hospital. Hundreds of others also tweeted their support.

Fireside Chats and Presidential Texts

In a text message sent to supporters on the eve of the election, Obama reaffirmed that they would be part of the presidency: "We have a lot of work to do to get our country back on track, and I'll be in touch soon about what comes next."

Obama was diligent in not abandoning social media once he took over as president. He realized that the people who had elected him to office wanted to stay connected, and he also knew this would be key to success while in office. Just as users are willing to take ownership of brands when given the chance, if they believe it is their government and not just Obama's, then there really is a true chance for change; change comes from within, not externally.

Social media allows for this two-way conversation. The U.S. president, for the first time, can cultivate grassroots communities directly, where people discover, create, and share information online. Obama has pledged to involve Americans in his decision making, by giving them five days to comment online on any nonemergency legislation before he signs it. Whether he delivers on this promise remains to be seen.

To help with this conversation, Obama has resurrected the principles of FDR's fireside radio chats; only this time, the chats will be on YouTube or another online video format, which allows for commentary, posts, rebuttals, and ongoing dialogue. His cabinet members are committed to having their own chats as well. The goal is to make the political process more transparent and give an identity to the White House. This is exactly the same strategy that good brands employ: transparency and having people connect and identify with the brand because the brand helps define them. Good companies put customers' needs first and foremost.

Whether you're a Republican, Democrat, Independent, or member of the Bull Moose Party, you can't deny the power of real-world community relations combined with the reach and engagement of online social communities and networks to change politics as usual. It's important to note that this isn't about using the latest shiny new toy out there. The key resides in the ability to identify and internalize issues that help precipitate change. Action, not merely words, earns support.

As addressed in the preventive and braggadocian behavior chapters of this book, it is important for the president to be transparent by showing the behind-the-scenes inner workings of the White House without sacrificing national security. It is irrelevant whether you like the transparent demands of social media; the fact is that society has drastically changed as a result of social media—this isn't just a nice perk for the president to use; it is something the public now demands. For the first time ever, the press, specifically NBC, was granted access to the Situation Room in the White House to describe what the moment was like in the room during the running of the operation to capture and eventually kill Osama Bin Laden.

This is an opportunity for government, whether it is led by Republicans or Democrats, to meet demands by using new and influential channels to address voters' needs and win people over, one citizen at a time.

The office of the president, whether it's in the United States, France, Colombia, or beyond, will never be able to satisfy everyone, but if social media is utilized correctly, it will supply the ideas, insights, support, concerns, and satisfaction of the public. It allows for a government to be more in tune with the citizens and to truly run the country as a democracy by stripping away the politics and getting to the core of what matters.

The Gartner Group hypothesized that social media would complement and even replace some functions of the government. To some people, this may seem laughable, but isn't that what a democratic government is supposed to be about—a government of the people, by the people, and for the people? This will become even more prevalent with Obama's successors, whether they are Republican, Democrat, or Independent. As the 2008 presidential campaign's reliance on social media to persuade voters indicates, this will become an integral part of every candidate's campaign in the years to come, particularly considering that the 2008 election's online campaigns will be scrutinized more than any before. "There's going to be a lot of analysis of the campaign online this time around," Borrell's VP of research, Kip Cassino, told *ClickZ News* in November 2008. "This is absolutely a groundbreaking election for digital marketing and the candidates, and it's not just the money involved. It's the techniques that were developed and the knowledge that was gained."[24]

Is the White House More BlackBerry or Mayberry?

Of course, everything wasn't all roses for Obama and his pioneering ways. Days after the election, a decision had to be made on whether Obama could keep his BlackBerry, something that he, like many others, had become dependent on in his daily life. In fact, in one White House meeting, everyone was asked to put their BlackBerry in the middle of the table to ensure each person was paying attention. This was something new for Washington, but not for businesses where the device's addictive ways has earned an apt nickname — *crackberry*.

The reason for the discussion about whether Obama would need to relinquish his BlackBerry did not center on overuse. Rather, it revolved around the fact that his text messaging, tweets, status updates, and e-mails would be a part of the public record. When George Bush entered the White House, he had to give up his America Online (AOL) account (G94B@aol.com) for this exact reason. So, Obama's friendly joshing and sidekick conversations with his friends about the latest Bears playoff game would be on the public record. However, relating back to our discussion on preventive and braggadocian behavior, has Obama been around social media long enough to have established the correct behavior and fail-safes associated with it?

Perhaps so, which then allows for the use of such devices as a BlackBerry to transform information into an asset. Rick Sanchez of CNN used Twitter to grow his user base. He raised his CNN program to third in the ratings, behind only Fox News's *O'Reilly Factor* and MSNBC's *Keith Olbermann's Countdown*. Because of Sanchez's success, viewers' microblog posts became a part of almost every CNN broadcast, and they continued to expand engagement with the viewer via social media. At the 2012 SXSW conference it was even rumored that CNN would be purchasing social media blog Mashable for $200 million.

Does a president's transparency become an enormous asset? Can he go from 1 million followers on Twitter to 100 million? As president, his public record may be quite different from that of Joe the Plumber's, but the reasons for utilizing it are the same — to openly communicate with many. People are using these mechanisms as a public record. There are no secrets; we are living in a world of glass houses. That is why Obama is the first president to keep his BlackBerry or have the first presidential laptop computer. We know the positive impact of these tools, and one of the most powerful people in the world should still have the option to use them.

To Sarah Palin's credit, she seemed to be practicing correct preventive behavior. When her Yahoo! e-mail was hacked, there was not much dirt to be found, despite these being private conversations; it was *not* a social media forum. San Francisco Mayor Gavin Newsom agreed that for national politics, the Obama campaign used social media to an unprecedented level. "Now I'm more concerned with what it means when we can use this unfiltered conversation with people. How will it help construct public policy?" he asked.[25]

While Obama benefited enormously from the power of social media, there are still social media detractors. A Facebook group was formed prior to Obama even taking office with several hundred members called "Impeach Barack Obama." Social media has the good, the bad, and the ugly for everyone to see. When it comes to politics, isn't that the true beauty of social media? Its power speaks for itself; before social media, Obama would not have won his own party's nomination, let alone become the 44th president of the United States.

The 2010 oil spill crisis in the Gulf of Mexico also showcased how social media can provide political pressure as well as raise money for a good cause. Some creative minds took out the Twitter account BPGlobalPR and posted such snarky tweets as: "If you find any oil in the Gulf of Mexico please return it because it's ours" and "We don't forbid our workers from wearing respirators because it looks bad in photos, we just want to see their smiling faces." This parody account had over 120,000 followers only weeks after it launched. Greenpeace utilized the social sharing site Flickr to run a BP Parody Logo campaign. One of the better ones submitted, by Russ A, had an image of the Twitter Fail Wail being lifted out of the Gulf ensconced in oil with the tagline "BP Fail." You could order these logos on T-shirts, and the campaign helped raise thousands of dollars to aid the Gulf. Most importantly, these social outlets applied political pressure on BP and Obama's cabinet to increase efforts to resolve the issue.

In 2012 Congress attempted to pass the Stop Online Piracy Act (SOPA). While the intent of the bill sounded good in theory (stop people from stealing and misusing others' creative works), the execution wasn't feasible or reasonable. In one example, if you were filming your child playing baseball but there was music playing in the background, then YouTube would have to pull this video since you, the parent, didn't have rights to this music. At one point exasperated members of Congress stated, "We need to get the nerds in here to help us figure this out."

The online community rallied, with sites like Wikipedia and Google shutting down for a set day to showcase that the Internet wouldn't function properly if this bill were to pass. These various sites listed the contact information for each state's senators and representatives in Congress. The sites also collected signatures needed to stop the bill from passing. This is the promise of social media and democracy. While it was only one day and one bill, this form of involvement will hopefully be more prevalent in the future. It only makes sense on major initiatives for the public to digitally weigh in and voice their concerns. Heck, I even placed a phone call to Senators Kerry and Brown of Massachusetts to voice my displeasure with the bill — all because Wikipedia listed their phone numbers.

More important than a privacy bill was the role that Twitter, Google, and Facebook played in the overthrow of an Egyptian dictator. Some citizens of Egypt were so thankful that they started naming their children Facebook.

Free Pancakes, Anyone?

Starbucks, Ben & Jerry's, and others gave freebies on Election Day — did it work? Remember the free pancake breakfast you used to get as a kid down at the fire station? Of course it wasn't free; your parents would pay a donation to help out the firefighters, but it seemed like it was free, didn't it? Your parents likely donated more than they would have paid at the local Denny's for a Grand Slam breakfast, yet they, too, felt it was free — probably better than free.

This is the sense of community that human beings long for, and it is something that is strengthened with social media. In fact, it is part of the reason for social media's meteoric ascendancy in our lives. Face-to-face interaction still can't be beat on certain levels, but social media does help you feel as though you are part of a community. Social media can help a national or global item feel intimate.

In years past, there have been many campaigns that attempted to increase voter turnout (e.g., MTV's "Rock the Vote"), but few have seemed to work. In 2008, voter turnout was predicted to be strong for many reasons, but as a friendly reminder and incentive, several companies gave away freebies on Election Day. Generally, most marketers steer clear of anything political, but in this case the brand marketers wanted to be a part of a community, and the community in this instance, thanks to social media, was the American community.

Some of the more high-profile giveaways included a chicken sandwich from Chick-fil-A, a tall cup of coffee from Starbucks, a free scoop of ice cream from Ben & Jerry's, and a star-shaped doughnut with patriotic sprinkles (i.e., red, white, and blue) from Krispy Kreme. Along with many other factors, these freebies helped drive the highest voter turnout since 1908.[26]

For users to get their freebies, they were asked to show their "I Voted" stickers, but in most cases they could simply say they voted. (After all, isn't community all about trust?) One entity that doesn't believe in trust is the government; it almost rained on this feel-good parade by highlighting a federal law that stipulates you can't give incentives to encourage people to vote. Fortunately, several companies didn't let this hurdle stop them and were able to work within it.

That is another example of the changes we are seeing with the advent of Socialnomics — it's a new way of thinking. In the past, large multinationals would have been shrinking violets and would have let their well-paid legal counsel pontificate on doomsday scenarios and suck the life out of the marketing and public relations departments until they gave up on the idea.

Today we are seeing less of this, partly due to the intense competition forcing companies to adopt the mantra: *If we don't do this, someone else will.* Part of competition is coming from foreign entities that don't have the same legal requirements as U.S.-based entities. Most of all, though, we are seeing companies and people within them with the conviction to drive what they believe is best for the company even if it clashes with the opinion of legal counsel. If companies have confidence in what they are doing, then they will overcome the hurdles that formerly may have stopped them.

Contributing to this, in part, is the flexibility and real-time nature of social media. In the past, if Ben & Jerry's was going to promote a free giveaway via the expensive development of television, radio, and print advertising, it would have had to think twice about the concerns of the law shutting down its good intentions, because that would be quite costly. However, given that the primary push for the Ben & Jerry's promotion was sending an alert to the followers on its Facebook fan page, there were few up-front costs, and the action of taking down the promotion would have been roughly only 20 to 30 minutes of work.

The variable cost of how many people actually show up for the freebies remains a factor, but it is the fixed costs of print and production of advertising that cause marketers to think twice about a promotion if there is a chance that it would be shut down for legal reasons. Social media helps mitigate these concerns because the up-front costs are so minimal that if a legal issue shuts down the program at the last minute, so be it. Also, social media allows things to be shut down in a few minutes, and for word to travel just as quickly. In this instance, if Ben & Jerry's had needed to shut down the giveaway, it would have simply informed its 285,000 Facebook fans and let them spread the word virally.

As we will constantly reiterate within social media, it's not how cool Ben & Jerry's is that matters. Rather, the concern is whether the ice cream company can give its loyal fans something to pass on that makes *them* (loyal fans) look cool. "I didn't know about the B&J free ice cream giveaway until my friend Stephen in Texas pushed it my way on Facebook," said Kim Estes, of Nashville, Tennessee. "It was good to know he was thinking about me, and I felt like I owed him a scoop of ice cream."[27] During the promotion, Ben & Jerry's added over 100,000 fans to its Facebook fan page.

Starbucks promoted its coffee giveaway almost exclusively via social media mechanisms. The company ran only one ad on *Saturday Night Live*, which was primarily viral during the time because of the success of the Tina Fey–Sarah Palin spoofs (more than 50 percent of the views were within social media). They also ran 30 TV spots on Hulu and displayed placements on Facebook. The spots took advantage of the well-known Starbucks brown recycled-paper coffee sleeve to animate and script a quick message helping to convey two salient points — we care about the environment and we care about the country. The message was: "What if we cared so much every day about these things?" In a rare instance, it covered off-branding (what Starbucks stands for) and also gave a call to action (come to our store). It is estimated that Starbucks spent less than $400,000 for this promotion, which Oprah Winfrey quickly paid back by giving it some major coverage on her show, as did every other media outlet (including this book). On YouTube alone, the promotion received 386,000 views.

One measure that tracks this type of viral buzz (the number of people who are talking or writing about your brand) indicated that Starbucks's buzz increased 26 percent as a result of this effort.[28] Starbucks would not disclose how much coffee was given away, but in some stores it was plenty: one Chicago franchise handed out 300 steaming cups of java and goodwill.[29] Facebook users also started downloading the application "Which Drink Is Meant for You?," resulting in almost 100,000 active monthly users and driving the Starbucks fan page to nearly 200,000 fans.[30] In order for companies to truly benefit from social media, they have to become part of the community. Is your company serving up fresh pancakes or serving up stale messaging?

Social Media Creates and Solves the Problem of Long Voting Lines

To help assuage concerns about long lines due to record voter turnout, a Twitter Vote Report was established. Voters who were at the polls could use the microblogging tool to help supply real-time data on polling conditions. These messages and alerts were aggregated and applied to a Google Mapping tool so people could see any voting issues in their area in the hope of avoiding crowds and hassles. It was very simple to send in reports using your mobile device:

#wait:90 = Wait time is 90 minutes.
#machine:30 = Wait time is 30 minutes due to machine issues.

Users who didn't use Twitter could also send text messages to #voterreport or to 66, or could call an automated hotline. Hashtags (#) are very convenient when using microblogging tools or text messaging, as they allow items to be easily tagged and categorized—which has been a dramatic part of the social media revolution. Convenient items like this contributed to the 2008 election having the highest voter turnout in 100 years.[31] Higher voter turnout is, therefore, one positive influence that social media has had on society. Moving forward, mobile geolocation tools like Foursquare, Gowalla, and Google Latitude will make it even easier to share this type of information.

Online Voting — The Future Is Now

If the political use of social media accelerates in the future, what new and exciting tactics can we expect? One thing that is surely inevitable is the introduction of online voting. Having the capability to easily cast votes via online mechanisms makes too much sense for it not to become a reality. For those who have always screamed that online voting is less secure than offline voting, you possibly do not understand the current offline process to obtain an absentee ballot. Let me explain.

For the 2008 presidential election, for the state of Florida, which one could argue should have the tightest system after the difficulties the state experienced in the 2000 election, the offline security was less than tight. For example, prospective voters were required to know merely their (1) birth date and (2) address number (not the entire address, just the mailbox number!). If you had these two relatively easy-to-access pieces of information, the state of Florida was happy to send you an absentee ballot at any address that you specified.

If you were a legitimate absentee voter and dutifully filled out your form, you proceeded to drop it in the mail. The outside of the envelope boldly proclaimed ABSENTEE BALLOT, and it also bore your authorized signature. Anywhere along the way this ballot could have been conveniently lost or stolen by numerous people. That doesn't sound nearly as secure as an online process that has point-to-point encryption, with only those two points having the proper access key.

This is analogous to when the Internet was first introduced as a place of commerce, aptly named e-commerce. It's hard to believe now, but at the time people were afraid to give out their credit card numbers online because of the false belief that it was unsafe to do so. Yet these same people had no problem giving their credit card numbers to some random clerk along with their signature at the local convenience store. For now, let's assume that great minds are able to solve the major security holes in online voting (they will). Imagine the tremendous increase in voter participation when this occurs. In a SodaHead study, 79 percent of the respondents said they wouldn't wait an hour to vote during the 2008 presidential election.[32]

People can argue that not everyone has a computer or mobile device that can access the web. While this is true, there are more people who have the ability to access the web than have voting machines in their homes. Those who don't have access to the web can go to their local library or voting station just as they have done in the past. The cost savings associated with no longer dealing with paper, staffing, parking, administration, voting machines, police protection, and so on would be significant. The increase in productivity would also be mind-boggling.

Assuming the U.S. population is approximately 310 million, and according to the latest U.S. Census Bureau data, 68 percent are of voting age, this equates to 210 million possible voters.[33] If the average hourly wage (factoring in white-collar wages) is close to $16, and keeping in mind that the physical act of voting takes a rough estimate (very rough) of two hours (including drive time), the summation is startling. This is $6.7 billion in lost productivity (210 million × $16 per hour × 2 hours)! All that could be saved by a few simple clicks online.

The harder decisions aren't necessarily based on whether we introduce online voting, but rather on how it will function when it is introduced. There are several social behavioral pieces to keep in mind. Is early voting online a capability? It makes sense. In an online voting model, are the early results disclosed to the public so that everyone can see how the race is projecting? If someone has already cast his or her vote, is that person allowed to go back and change it anytime before the election? In other words, how social would the government allow online voting to become? It would make sense to make it very social. For example, early voters could click on a radio button or have a form field for the main reason they selected or didn't select a certain candidate. Imagine — candidates could then address the concerns of the voting public during the election process itself. Sounds very democratic to me.

Even the Army Is Sharing Information

In an effort to relate with its desired target audience of 17- to 24-year-olds, the U.S. Army launched a tool called "Straight from Iraq." It was designed to allow potential recruits to get a better sense of what war is like from the people who know best. This is a long way from the days in Vietnam where television coverage was carefully screened. "Straight from Iraq" was historic because it was the first time candidates could ask direct questions of soldiers in combat.

"The goal is to provide those considering the Army — along with parents and others who influence their decisions — with verifiable information about what being a soldier is really like, what combat is really like," said Lt. Gen. Benjamin C. Freakley, commanding general of the Army Accessions Command in Fort Monroe, Virginia, overseeing recruitment at the time.[34]

"The campaign was successful in conveying the benefits of 'Army strong'—the physical, emotional, and mental benefits," said Ed Walters, chief marketing officer for the Army at the Pentagon.

"We wanted to more clearly articulate that," he added, "through efforts like sharing with civilians the video clips of real soldiers' stories."[35]

As we point out throughout the book, these types of open, social media conversations are much more effective than a unilateral communication to your audience. The best part, too, is that they are much more cost effective. In this example, while the Army couldn't disclose exact figures, it easily exceeded its recruiting goals for 2006 to 2008.[36]

For cost-effectiveness comparison, the Army has spent roughly $170 million per year on such high-profile items as NASCAR sponsorships and rodeos. I'm sure it's fun for the Army's director of marketing to watch his NASCAR automobile go around the track every Sunday, but how effective is this, and how accurately can you track such a thing? The average sponsorship cost for a NASCAR car is in the $15 million to $20 million range. In comparison, the social media campaign costs between $200,000 and $300,000.

Chapter Four Key Points

1. Open, multilateral conversations are much more effective than unilateral communications to your audience, for politics and for business. Social media enables these open conversations. Utilizing free social media tools and placements is more timely and cost effective than traditional advertising.
2. By engaging voters, social media has had a positive impact on voter turnout (the highest since 1908 and the highest youth participation).
3. The adoption of online voting in the future could save an estimated $6.7 billion in lost productivity (U.S. presidential election).
4. We are just scratching the surface of what's possible with collective intelligence of big data in terms of being able

(continued)

(continued)

to predict and control influenza outbreaks, predicting the United Kingdom's next prime minister, and so forth.

5. Fortune 500 companies should learn from Obama's 2008 social media campaign, allowing the public to take ownership of his brand and growing it to success.

6. Just like businesses, politicians and governments need to keep up with advancements in social media; otherwise, they will be left behind. Successfully leveraging social media in politics pays big dividends.

7. Social media can help provide important political pressure and also raise money, as evidenced by the Gulf of Mexico oil spill, democratization of Egypt, and earthquake rescue efforts in Haiti.

8. Business should watch how politicians advance their use of social media as it may foster new ideas.

CHAPTER FIVE

I Care More about What My Neighbor Thinks Than What Google Thinks

S ocial commerce is upon us. What is social commerce exactly? It is a term that encompasses the transactional, search, and marketing components of social media. Social commerce harnesses the simple idea that people value the opinions of other people. What this truly means is that in the future we will no longer seek products and services; rather, they will find us. Nielsen reports that 90 percent of people trust their peers' opinions.[1] This is neither a new concept nor new to the web (e.g., Epinions, Complaints.com, Angie's List).

What is new is that social media makes it so much easier to disseminate information. As the success of social media proves, people enjoy spreading information. This explains the popularity of Twitter, Foursquare, Open Table, Yelp, TripAdvisor, and so forth. These tools and products enable users to inform their friends what they are doing every minute of the day ("I'm having an ice cream cone," "Check out this great article," "I'm listening to a keynote speaker," etc.). Twitter is interesting from the standpoint that its popularity began with older generations and then Generations Y and Z started to embrace Twitter. This is the exact opposite trend of Facebook, which was originally popular with the younger generations and then Generation X and the baby boomers started to engage.

Social media is creating something that I think eventually is going to be very healthy for our economy, and that is institutional brand integrity.

— *John Gerzema,*
Chief Insights Officer,
Young & Rubicam[2]

The most popular feature of Facebook and LinkedIn is status updates. Status updates enable users to continuously brag, boast, inform, and vent to everyone in their network. This simple tool allows users to easily stay connected with their network. As a result, there are 60 million status updates per day![3] Let's take a look at a couple of examples of social commerce in action.

Buying the Right Child Car Seat

Steve and his wife are expecting their first child. With this addition, they are in the market for a lightweight, but safe, child seat for their car. Steve doesn't know the first thing about child car seats and is dreading the hours of researching and searching on the Internet to find the appropriate one. Steve, like many fathers, is also fearful that he might, despite all of his diligent research, make a mistake. Making sure you provide the appropriate safety for your child can be stressful and at times overwhelming. The good news is that the majority of these purchase challenges, concerns, and sources of unwanted stress will become things of the past with social media. Here's why.

If you enter "buying a child car seat" on a search engine, you are likely to receive a series of irrelevant search results and a bevy of sponsored ads. Not all of the search results are unrelated, though. Some will prove fruitful, but it may take some time-intensive trial and error before you wean the helpful results from the not-so-helpful results. Yet, as social commerce becomes more and more mainstream, when Steve performs a social search by entering the query "buying a child car seat" he will discover the following:

- Of Steve's 181 friends, 23 have purchased a child car seat in the past two years.
- Fourteen of them purchased the same make and model online.

- The average price for the most popular model was $124.99 (10 of the 14 purchased online).
- Three are looking to sell their used car seats because their children have outgrown them.
- Seven different online videos showcasing this seat have been bookmarked — tagged by people in Steve's network.
- Four different reviews and articles have been bookmarked — tagged by his network.
- Eleven of the 14 have posted positive reviews on the seat, two of which are video reviews.

Steve respects the opinions of the 14 people who purchased the same seat, so he clicks on one of the reviews to find out more, and gets the following information:

We have three kids and have used this same baby seat model for all of them. My sister used Cheekie Brand's baby seat and it was clunky, awkward, and heavy. When she saw mine, she immediately went out and got one for her baby. I highly recommend these seats!

— Gab Fernandez

Steve can now confidently purchase the seat without the usual research, stress, and time required if he were starting his search from scratch. Once Steve starts to use the seat, he takes on a different role within the same social media conversation; he is actively using the product and can provide his own insight into features and benefits that the seat provides. Steve may notice that it's too easy for his child to undo one of the seat straps. Compelled, he may point this out to his network via a quick video example that may be relevant to his social network of friends. This then presents an opportunity for product improvement, which the manufacturer can act upon.

If the manufacturer's marketing team is listening and watching, then they will be able to quickly share this with the design and production team and hopefully get a quick resolution and improvement for future buyers. This is not only a benefit for the manufacturer, but a benefit to society as well, because future children will be much safer based on the quick advancements.

Correspondingly, just like his friends before him, if Steve finds features he really enjoys about the car seat, he will feel compelled to write about them, since his friends facing a similar purchase decision will benefit from his experience. When I was at EarthLink, one of our key findings when working on referral incentives was that the main reason people recommended EarthLink was not for the referral incentive, but that they liked being viewed as the subject matter expert within their social graph. The same holds true in social media.

> *The popular belief that people take the time to post something only when they want to vent or discuss a bad experience is simply not true, at least in our experience. The majority of the over 20 million reviews and opinions we have received on TripAdvisor are positive ones. People are simply compelled to give back to a community that has given to them.*
>
> *— Steve Kaufer,*
> *CEO of TripAdvisor*

When it comes to social search, many pundits speculate that one major reason that Google started Google+ (its social network) was a defensive strategy against Facebook. The popular thought was that if Facebook engineers had to make adjustments to their general platform due to threats posed by Google+, those engineers wouldn't have time to focus on developing a social search tool (which we discussed earlier). As of this writing it seems to have proven successful, as Facebook's search capability is woeful at best. Social search is a huge opportunity, and whichever company figures it out may eventually win the social networking wars. More importantly, companies need to shore up their products and services so that when social search is commonplace their brand is positioned to win a World of Mouth world.

Minivan or Hybrid?

Steve and his wife eventually go on to have their second and third children, and their two sedans won't cut it anymore; they are in the market for a bigger vehicle. Having vowed to himself and his friends that he'd never own a minivan, he's considering an SUV or a crossover vehicle.

Steve is dreading the hours of searching on the Internet to find a vehicle that suits the family's needs. He's even dreading having to leave work early to visit the car dealerships to test-drive selected vehicles and then the ensuing haggling process. Despite hours of research, Steve is also fearful that he and his wife may make a big purchase mistake when the moment comes. Again, most of these concerns are mitigated when we move to a social commerce model: Steve performs a search on his favorite social network—he types in "buying a car." Rather than receiving a series of irrelevant ads for car trader sites, he discovers the following:

- Of Steve's friends, 23 have purchased a car in the past year.
- Sixteen of these new car owners are married with two or more children.
- Fourteen purchased an SUV or a crossover vehicle.
- Nine purchased the same vehicle.

Steve respects the opinions of the nine people who purchased the same vehicle, so he clicks to find out more, and gets the following information:

I test-drove Crossover X and Crossover Y. Crossover Y was the much better feel, and it was easier to get into the backseat. Coupled with the fact that it gets three more mph to the gallon, it was a no-brainer.

To further illustrate the importance of viralness today, a study conducted by online market research firm Marketing Evolution on marketing campaigns from Adidas and video-game publisher Electronic Arts found that 70 percent of the return on investment was the result of one consumer passing information to another virally. Social commerce is a referral program on steroids.

Blowing Out the Candles

Karen (age 48) just received a birthday check from her mum for 470 euros. She feels like treating herself by buying something, but doesn't have anything particular in mind. Karen quickly taps into her social network to see what other people she respects (friends/peers) are buying and whether they like or dislike their choices.

Within five minutes, she decides to purchase an Apple iPad because her friend Molly bought one and loves it. The fact that Molly has an iPad and likes it assuages Karen's fear of technology because Molly is even more of a technical neophyte than Karen is. Knowing this about Molly drove 95 percent of Karen's decision process within minutes. This intimate knowledge of people within your social network is key, and is the main reason why reviews via social media have gone to the next level compared to other online reviews in the past.

The big social networks (Facebook, LinkedIn, Twitter, QQ, etc.) will eventually dominate this portion of social commerce.

Sites like ThisNext, Kaboodle, WeShop, and WishPot helped push the adoption of this market opportunity by enabling buyers to quickly share their purchases and reviews with friends. These sites were designed for people to go to for ideas about what products and services they should be purchasing and using.

Bon Voyage, Online Travel Agents?

Suzy (age 34) has set aside a budget of £1,400 to take a trip this year with her husband. The only thing she knows at this point: destination, South America. In the past, she would have performed a search on Google, which would have taken her to some helpful online travel agent sites (e.g., Travelzoo, TripAdvisor, Go Ahead Tours, Lonely Planet, Orbitz, Priceline, Travelocity). She probably would've narrowed down the choices after hours of research. She would then begin the arduous task of finding the best deal for the flight, hotel, and so on.

As a result of social media, this process becomes much easier for Suzy. She simply goes to her social network of choice and searches for "South American vacations." The results pop up: five of her friends have traveled to South America in the past year. Conveniently listed are their itineraries, hotels, and resorts, as well as prices and recommendations.

Suzy sees that two of her friends took a trip to Chile through Go Ahead Tours and rated it highly. It's within her budget, and the same package is available. She quickly snatches it up before it's sold out. She saved hours of painstaking research and the fees of a travel agent.

If she has only 10 minutes before going to pick up the kids at day care, is her time better spent scrolling through 400 reviews by people she doesn't know on a travel review site (some of which will be spam from the competing hotels), or looking at the recommendations from her friends? The time is much better spent with her friends' experiences and recommendations. Social commerce has given her peace of mind and the anticipation of an enjoyable adventure. That is why TripAdvisor incorporated Facebook Connect into its site. Now you can see hotel reviews from your friends via TripAdvisor's connection with Facebook.

Listed alongside the qualitative reviews are certain data points for each friend: price, travel supplier, places recommended, day excursions, and so on.

We could continue with other examples, like trying to figure out what the trendiest online video game is for Christmas. This has several challenges; the first is trying to figure out what the *it* game is. The second is to determine if that game is age-appropriate for your child (e.g., sex, violence). Third, if it is the *it* game, the task of obtaining the game will be a challenge. Fortunately, social media lessens many of these worries, as some of your early-adopter friends can show the way by providing insights into their purchase history and experiences. If a friend you trust bought the game for her child, that would be more insightful than trying to decipher the confusing game ratings for graphic and sexual content to determine if the product is age-appropriate for your own child.

Social media has a much easier time tracking when the purchase is made online. It enables users to know where goods or services were purchased — which in turn may be a good indication that the item is in stock. This is done using cookie-based tracking that follows users (if they opt in) as they traverse and transact on the web. A *cookie* is a tiny piece of code that is placed in your web browser.

What does this mean for brand marketing? Well, it means that companies and marketers had better start spending more time listening to their customers and less time spending countless hours creating the next award-winning (but not customer-getting) 30-second television commercial. Consumers are taking ownership of brands, and their referral power is priceless.

Just as important as listening to the customer is acting on the information received. This entails all parts of the organization working more in harmony than ever before — the speed of social media demands it. These certainly aren't new constructs, but in this new age, your brand will experience a quick death if these constructs aren't adhered to. The days of traditional brand marketing aren't necessarily dead; they're just taking on new forms.

In the years ahead, social media will help eliminate multiple individual redundancies (MIRs). This is beneficial to the user, and it's mission critical for businesses to understand that this impacts almost everything they do from marketing to operations to manufacturing. As people increasingly look to social media for advice and recommendations, marketers need to make certain they are part of the consideration set. In order to accomplish this, companies need to create great products and services rather than rely on advertising campaigns to bail them out. When a transaction occurs, marketers need to encourage or give incentives for users to complete product and service reviews — good, bad, or indifferent. Companies that are able to encourage this information sharing from their consumers, both online and offline, help water the seeds of viral success. Money to water these seeds will come from traditional advertising budgets (television, outdoor, radio) and will go directly into the consumers' pockets. This is another reason why consumers will take more ownership of the brands they associate with, and it makes the traditional referral model look like a dollhouse alongside the Taj Mahal.

Ken Robbins, founder of Digital Agency Response Mine Inter-active, sums up the challenges and opportunities that individuals and companies face with social media:

> *Social media has evolved from a mere post it–answer it model (bulletin boards and blogs) to instantaneous publish-subscribe models (i.e., Twitter and Facebook updates). Combined with the portable surfing of today's phones, this pub-sub model has both fantastic and dire implications for businesses. It's fantastic from the standpoint that one can not only stand in front of a refrigerator in a store and check out reviews of that model; the consumer can Twitter his network to get advice on all models, this brand, and this store instantaneously. If the product and store have good reputations, buying hesitancy is removed and the purchase takes place. The dire side of this is that if the price, the model, or the store has a poor reputation, the transaction will definitely not take place. We are moving to a world with total retail and product performance transparency for the consumer. The market will be much less tolerant of poor service and poor products and high margins with this social communications infrastructure.*[4]

Many may take issue with the two points or assumptions being made. One could make a good argument that people aren't going to want to share their purchase decisions. This is true; some will not. Others will share only certain purchase decisions and price points, while still others will share everything and anything. However, from an online buying perspective, the technology for this to occur is there, and as we have seen from the transparency of other social media usage, it's only a matter of time until purchases will be pushed to everyone who is willing. Not everyone will share, just like not everyone comments on TripAdvisor or edits on Wikipedia. However, as we've seen over the past few years, particularly with younger generations, people have an unbelievable willingness to share. That is why Facebook has a billion users.

The other piece that people will be concerned about is whether buyers will be motivated to write a review. It's possible that a true tangible incentive may not be necessary, but what is certain is that more effort and marketing dollars will be used to implore customers to write a review of a product. This incentive model isn't anything new; when a hotel or airline asks you to fill out a suggestion card, it is usually with the hook of potentially winning a sweepstakes or a free meal.

The hope is that incentives aren't necessary for reviews, but even if they are, that doesn't mean that the person will write a good review. This type of transparent review may not be for everyone, as some people like to remain anonymous, but that brings up another key point: All reviews don't necessarily need to be public to everyone — some people may feel comfortable posting reviews only to their own network. All of this is a lot to digest for Generation X and beyond, but it's a way of life for the generations born after 1980, as they have grown up in a transparent world.

We can see a dramatic shift in that 92 percent of consumers now cite word of mouth as the best source for product and brand information, up from 67 percent in 1977.[5] That is one reason why in this book we say we've moved from word-of-mouth to World-of-Mouth marketing.

Looking to Friends for Medical Advice

Other major societal benefits from social media will be made in the health care arena. Survey results from online advertising agency iCrossing in 2008 showed that 34 percent of Americans turn to social media for health research. While that is substantial, we are certain the percentage is even higher today. Twenty percent of the online health searchers went to Wikipedia for information. Other social networks were also used, and the average age of people using social media for health-related questions was 37, whereas the average overall age for patients searching for health information was 44.[6] It is not surprising that the former are younger, but it does again show that social media users aren't all teenagers; social media use will be mainstream sooner than people expect. When health consumers turn to social media, they are in a decision-mode process. Needs range from finding out costs for certain operations or medical devices to the reputation of a certain provider or doctor.

When engaged in face-to-face or phone conversation, it can be awkward or even rude to discuss medical conditions. Social media eliminates this awkwardness. A simple post like "Has anyone ever had their tonsils removed? I've had a sharp pain in my throat for the last day. Let me know" or not even asking the question but simply stating "Burned my finger with boiling hot water—top of the tea kettle fell off" will often elicit such responses as:

> *Sorry to hear that—the key is to run it under cold water for 10 minutes—don't use ice! After that, use Neosporin to disinfect and make sure to keep it covered and clean. I did this once, and it will heal in about a week, but it hurts like heck!*
>
> *— Sandy*

> *Don't use ice on it, only cold water. No need to go to the hospital even though I'm sure it looks red and awful.*
>
> *— Logan*

After their physicians, nurses, or pharmacists, people look within their network to those they trust for good advice on medical treatments and medications. In the iCrossing study, more than 60 percent list "Consumer Opinion Leader" as "extremely important" or "very important." Some even list the advice from their friends above that of their physician.[7]

In the same study, 75 percent indicated that they use social media in health to "connect with other consumers to exchange information or obtain support"; 55 percent noted that the most important reason to use social media over other online sites is to get cost information for a procedure or medical equipment.[8] Consumer-generated health content is increasing in both supply and demand. Society is benefiting from this shift. Perhaps the largest benefit of this will be seen outside the United States where in some small towns the local physician is revered as a demigod. This is fine if that physician is capable and altruistic at heart, but that is not always the case. Social media allows for an inexpensive and relevant second, third, and four hundredth medical opinion, especially in underdeveloped regions of the world.

Jared and Subway's Almost Missed Opportunity

One of the most successful marketing campaigns in history nearly didn't get off the ground. Jared and his Subway weight-loss story did not come from the top down; rather, it came from the bottom up. Jared actually started the now famous diet of his own accord, long before receiving royalty payments from Subway. Jared's unique diet story made its way from a college campus newspaper to a savvy executive at an advertising firm. Jared was attending the University of Indiana at the time, and the advertising executive sent an intern to Bloomington, Indiana, to track Jared down on the university's serene campus.

Once Jared was found, the advertising executive and his agency pitched the idea to Subway. The marketing executives at Subway headquarters rejected the idea, but the ad agency and this particular executive were so convinced of the idea that they sold it to local Subway franchisees, and the agency paid to run the spots out of its own pocket! Only after proven success did the marketing executives at Subway's headquarters relent. This turned out to have a happy ending, but how many such ideas have never seen the light of day? If this agency executive hadn't been willing to stick his neck out and pay for the original campaign, it would have been another idea that went into the garbage can.

In the Subway campaign, recall that Jared was an avid user of a company's product and service — in this case, low-fat submarine sandwiches. This is another reminder that executives and companies who want to excel need to be comfortable in knowing that not everything related to the brand will be owned by them; their customers will take ownership. This is a good thing, because straightforward and true stories resonate well with consumers, and this particular story has helped Subway overtake McDonald's as having the most restaurants in the United States. Similarly, the world's largest advertiser, Procter & Gamble, laid off 1,600 of its marketing and advertising personnel since more and more of the brand ownership was being handled by the actual end consumer/customer.

The beauty of social media is that fewer of these great stories will remain hidden, and, as a result, companies will benefit. One of the top 10 viral videos in 2008 was "Christian the Lion."[9] This is a clip of two Australian men who raised a lion cub in the city of London. One year after the young lion was returned to the wild, the men went to Africa to reunite with a giant hug. (Remember, this is a lion!) This story was from 1969 and, despite Broadway Books publishing a book about it in 1971, prior to 2008 it was relatively unknown. Then along comes the social medium of YouTube, and the story spreads globally in little time at all by using the film footage from 1969. Imagine, this incredible story was known by only a few until the advent of social media — what a shame! Ironically, it has come full circle, and a second book has been published on this story: *A Lion Called Christian: The True Story of the Remarkable Bond between Two Friends and a Lion* by Anthony Bourke, John Rendall, and George Adamson (Broadway Books, 2009), and it became a best seller! This is also an example of how social media can drive offline revenue in new forms as well.

The Choices We Make

Businesses, both large and small, have to realize that they no longer own relationships. Yet, when it comes to social media, many companies haven't shaken their old tried-and-true marketing models. Other companies quickly figured it out. Next, we discuss three companies that all had the same goal when they set out, but wound up experiencing different levels of success based on their strategies. While these examples are old, the constructs are sound today. After reading this case study, reflect on which approach you would have taken. Ask yourself what question you are wrestling with today or perhaps arguing with your boss or colleague over. How can you use this case study to help you make the right decision today with your current dilemma?

In 2007, Facebook introduced the ability for developers to make applications (tools/widgets that allow users to do everything from tracking a favorite sports team's scores to playing a game of tic-tac-toe against a friend in another city) to enhance the Facebook experience. When the application platform was originally introduced, three separate travel companies correctly surmised that people would want to input and track all the places in the world they had visited. Each company set out with a different strategy, resulting in various levels of success. The three companies were:

1. Acme Travels (a large, traditional, publicly traded tour operator).
2. Where I've Been (a new company).
3. TripAdvisor (a popular online travel agent).

One of the top executives at Acme Travels had a relationship with someone at Facebook and was aware that Facebook was planning to open its application program interface (API) allowing any company to develop useful widgets within Facebook. For example, Delta Airlines could develop an application in which users could view upcoming flights on Facebook, or Crayola could have you fill out some simple questions and tell you what color crayon your personality reflects.

Acme Travels thought it would be helpful for the users to be able to easily track where they had traveled. The idea sprang from an employee who had invented an Excel spreadsheet that allowed you to check off boxes next to countries traveled. This spreadsheet was based on other people using maps tacked to a wall with a pushpin for every place traveled.

The idea for the application was a good one because within the first few days, hundreds of thousands of Facebook users downloaded the application. Understanding also the braggadocian behavior of social media, Acme Travels set up the application so that people could send an alert to their friends whenever they traveled to a new city. So, if Kim went to Auckland, it would alert everyone in her network, "Kim indicated she has traveled to Auckland within Acme's travel application."

Acme Travels was ecstatic at the success of its application; it estimated that the internal cost to build the application was $15,000, and it was receiving 50,000 downloads per day, which meant it was capturing 50,000 names to put into its prospect database.[10] To go into this particular aspect a bit further, the download process for Facebook applications doesn't require users to forfeit their e-mail addresses — yet Acme Travels made the decision to place an extra page in the middle of the download process indicating it was mandatory for a user to supply name, mailing address, and e-mail address in order to use the application.

About a week into the process, Acme received word from 20-something Craig Ulliott. Craig's belief was that the additional page during the application download process was cumbersome and would discourage many users who didn't want to disclose personal information to get the application, ultimately hurting the overall success of the application. Acme Travels pondered the suggestion from Ulliott and conceded that there probably were people who were being turned off, but then again, Acme was getting 50,000 names on some good days, so things were going very nicely. Besides, the Acme executives thought, this was the entire reason they were doing social media marketing: it was a carrot to get names for the database. Why should they fix something that wasn't broken?

Things continued successfully for Acme Travels for a few weeks. Meanwhile, Craig Ulliott wasn't your typical user; rather, he was a very established programmer. He liked the idea of the mousetrap that Acme Travels was offering, but he thought he could build a better one. So, he continued with his own vision, a very similar application called "Where I've Been." This application was graphically more appealing and also contained some sexier pieces of flash programming that made it easier to click on a particular part of a map to indicate you'd traveled to a certain place. However, the key difference was that Craig didn't insert the additional page during the download process that required users to enter their personal information. He simply used Facebook's standard two-step process. Here's what happened next.

Where I've Been quickly became one of the must-have applications and also the top-downloaded travel application. It was so successful that Craig was able to help form a seven-person company under the same name. With 800,000 active monthly users, Craig was attracting the attention of the big online travel agents like TripAdvisor, Priceline, and Travelzoo.

TripAdvisor was savvy enough to realize that an application like this would be an unbelievable marketing tool for their business. TripAdvisor began behind-the-scenes negotiations with Where I've Been. By this time, Craig had joined forces with an experienced and dynamic Internet travel guru named Brian Harniman to head up his strategy. The asking price for Where I've Been was a little steeper than TripAdvisor had originally expected. TripAdvisor had hoped that it would be dealing with some wet-behind-the-ears kid and get the application for a bargain price.

TripAdvisor came within a whisker of buying the application for $3 million—so close, in fact, that a story was released. Then it did something very smart—it begged, borrowed, and made better. TripAdvisor pulled back, took a deep assessment, and calmly said, "We think we can do this better." Instead of investing $3 million, TripAdvisor decided to build its own application for a fraction of the cost. Now, it's important to point out that TripAdvisor used two very good tactics. The first one was a prudent attempt to leverage an already proven and successful product application in Where I've Been.

On discovering the expensive asking price, TripAdvisor reassessed the situation and correctly decided there was enough opportunity for more than one company to succeed. With Facebook counting user growth in millions, TripAdvisor was hopeful that this type of travel application had not "jumped the shark." Jumping the shark is an Internet term for something that is past its prime or no longer *in*. According to Wikipedia, the specific definition is as follows:

> Jumping the shark *is a colloquialism used by TV critics and fans to denote that point in a TV show or movie series history where the*

plot veers off into absurd story lines or out-of-the-ordinary characteri-
zations. In the process of undergoing these changes, the TV or movie
series loses its original appeal. Shows that have "jumped the shark" are
typically deemed to have passed their peak. According to the theory,
once a show has "jumped the shark" fans can designate the point of the
show's perceived decline in overall quality with the "jump the shark"
moment.[11]

The term was taken from one of the later *Happy Days* episodes
where Fonzie, leather jacket and all, attempts to jump a shark on
water skis. Suffice it to say, it was *not* one of broadcast television's
finer moments. The tech community eagerly snapped up this
television term, and today it is more recognized in the Internet
community as the moment that something goes past its prime. For
instance, most MP3 players had a "jump the shark" moment when
the iPod was first released.

Anyway, TripAdvisor moved forward with building a bigger,
better version of Where I've Been. Within a month the company
released Cities I've Visited. It was smart to name the application
something very tangible and to stick with cities. TripAdvisor leveraged Google Maps so travelers could place pins on the digital map
just like many people do in their home or office on paper maps.
Using Google Maps was smart in four ways:

1. People were familiar with Google Maps.
2. Using Google Maps was free.
3. No development was needed.
4. It worked.

That old adage that you can have only two out of three — cheap,
quick, or quality — doesn't hold true within social media, because
you can often leverage preexisting human capital or preexisting
products and solutions. In this instance, TripAdvisor was doing
both — it was leveraging the idea (human capital) that Where I've
Been and Acme Travels had produced before it, and it was leveraging Google Maps (preexisting product). So, its cost investment
was approximately $20,000. What it received in return is somewhat
staggering. In April 2009, TripAdvisor's application had 1,779,246
monthly active users, while Where I've Been had 885,577 monthly
active users.[12] In June 2010 TripAdvisor's application had grown to
5,187,366 monthly active users, while Where I've Been was up to
1,031,902 monthly active users. Both were very successful. That's
over 5 million people who actively interact with TripAdvisor's

brand every month, and Craig was able to help start a company due to the success of his application. That is truly the power of social media.

> A key thing to note is that for every successful Cities I've Visited or Traveler IQ application we had just as many, if not more, not achieve wild success. The importance in a social media age is to be nimble and not afraid to make mistakes. The more things you can test or try, the more chances you have for success. I have a sign outside my door that simply says Speed Wins. We have adopted this as our motto and it serves us well. If our development team says something will take four months, we challenge ourselves to do it in four days, and more often than not we succeed. It may not be perfect for that initial beta launch, but that is okay, because with the help of our users we will make small, rapid changes to constantly improve. If you aren't constantly evolving along with your customers, you will be doomed to fail.
>
> — *Steve Kaufer,*
> *CEO, TripAdvisor*

Marketing to Zombies

We introduced the term *active monthly users*. This term was coined by Facebook in 2007 and is an important one. Historically, most tracking just dealt with pure volume. How many hits did you get on your website? Then it was determined that hits weren't really relevant since hits were tracking the number of times certain elements on a page were served up. If your website home page had several images and form fields and one person visited this site, the unique visit could equal 13 hits; this type of count is not too helpful. So, tracking progressed to visits; this wasn't very good, either, because it could be the same person coming back several times. The next logical step was to measure unique visitors.

Social media has changed the paradigm of tracking again. Originally, Facebook rated top applications by how many times they were downloaded, but downloads aren't necessarily relevant; what truly matters is how active the users are. If a user downloads the application and never returns, that's not very valuable to the creator of the application. If a million people download something but never use it, then in a sense it is worthless to both the user and to the creator. Or, if 500,000 people like your brand on Facebook but never return to the page, comment, share, or post anything, they may not be particularly valuable. This is why Facebook tracks most items by active users, which changes everything.

Having 12 million e-mail addresses in your database doesn't mean much if only 1,000 open and click on your e-mails. It's much more important to have 10,000 e-mails with 9,000 people opening and clicking. With social media, marketers are able to measure user activity and capture helpful information such as age, sex, education, hobbies, interests, and so on. This assists marketers in one-to-one conversations between companies and consumers.

Going one step further is just how powerful the social graph is. Take, for example, the 9,000 active people mentioned earlier. E-mail is generally a one-to-one conversation. If you have an e-mail that contains something particularly entertaining, then you could be lucky and those 9,000 people forward it on, and so forth. This is powerful, but not quite as effective as social media. The main reason is that the viralness of e-mail is really related to that one particular e-mail, whereas in social media people are constantly pushing content to their network. In e-mail it's an anomaly, whereas in social media it is inherent.

To showcase this point, in April 2009 EF Educational Tours had roughly 800 Twitter followers — people who actively wanted to know the latest news from EF Educational Tours. If you looked at the number of followers these 800 people had, though, then the social graph influence was 8.5 million people (based on results from a query on http://twinfluence.com/).

Leveraging Success

The TripAdvisor story doesn't end with the brand value derived from the application; that was only the beginning. The beauty is that 1.8 million users are feeding TripAdvisor information. These augment their 30 million user base — talk about a large focus group! The days of advertising executives sitting behind two-way mirrors munching on stale chips and M&Ms will become a distant memory. More important than healthier marketers is the opportunity this vast amount of data presents. For example, companies can provide this data to reporters as part of their public relations efforts (e.g., "Top five cities that people want to travel to in the coming year" or "35- to 45-year-olds more likely to travel to Australia, teenagers to Europe").

Reporters and bloggers are always looking for this type of hard data that is of interest to consumers. What they learn in real time can also help shape their products and services. The level of demographic information passed within social media is unprecedented. If TripAdvisor sees in October that 80 percent of males 60 to 65 are putting Machu Picchu as a place they desire to visit when historically only 20 percent have been selecting that destination, then it would make intuitive sense to change the TripAdvisor home page to have a callout for a Machu Picchu Seniors special. This is where marketers' jobs are changing drastically. This data is being collected from the website, as well as all the social media touch points.

Marketers need to be joined at the hip with their production team to ensure they are getting this real-time information. They also need to recognize that they are no longer sending a one-way message but are serving more as a conduit. "Those who will succeed need to act more like publishers, entertainment companies, or even party planners, than advertisers," said Garrick Schmitt, Group Vice President of Experience Planning for leading digital agency Razorfish.[13]

The process TripAdvisor employed while building the Cities I've Visited application presents a new way of thinking in that TripAdvisor didn't know for certain what it would be able to monetize. "Users are challenging publishers, advertisers, and marketers to meet their needs in new, distributed, and largely uncharted territories—many of which have no analog touch points—and to provide services that have no immediate monetization models," indicated Schmitt.[14]

It's also a communication cycle. In this case, if someone within the Cities I've Visited application selects Athens under the category "I'd like to visit," then TripAdvisor has the ability to serve up its top five most popular tours of Athens (which of course are clickable) and take the user directly into a booking process at the appropriate point in time. It's easy to see why this isn't interruption marketing like in days gone past; but it is a value-added part of a useful tool for the user. TripAdvisor is offering value to users in providing a tool to track and brag about where they've gone as well as where they'd like to go, and at the same time, the users are receiving valuable information from TripAdvisor that is directly tied to their particular travel interests. There is no marketing guesswork or marketing laboratory—the users are informing marketers implicitly through their actions.

Companion Credit Union: New Logo

One Australian company, Companion Credit Union, actually turned over the decision on its brand logo to the social community. "The credit union is really owned by the members, and therefore, we decided we should invite them to actively participate in helping us decide," said CEO Ray O'Brien.[15] Of the 12,000 members, 1,000 of them voted. "Many of our current members founded Companion Credit Union, so it only seemed fitting that they would be a part of our new journey and direction," said Companion's marketing manager, Cas Scott.[16]

E-Readers/Tablets

Mobile devices acting as e-book readers (Amazon Kindle, Sony Reader, Apple iPad, etc.) are wildly popular (Kindle is the top-selling product on Amazon), and the fact is that online books offer many of the same advantages as digitized music, newspapers, and magazines. The *New York Times* is available via e-reader for a monthly subscription fee that is drastically less than the traditional paper edition.

It is only a matter of time before we will see advertising and marketing efforts creep into both fiction and nonfiction materials. In fact, as of this writing, you could get the same Amazon Kindle for a lower price if you were willing to have advertisements show up on your device when you weren't reading (akin to a screen saver).

This is virgin territory for marketers. It is a good thing because as the traditional channels of marketing like television, radio, and magazines diminish in effectiveness, marketers need these new marketing outlets to continue to thrive. One way in which marketers, publishers, and authors will come together in relation to e-books is within the content itself. How is this possible without compromising the story? On some levels, this is very simple. Let's say that within a scene of a novel the author describes a hot, dusty day where the main character refreshes himself with an ice-cold Coca-Cola. Authors generally like to describe items specifically so the reader can really visualize them. That is why more often than not they use branded items in their descriptions—instead of "soda," they write "Coca-Cola"; rather than "listening to a music player," they write "listening to an iPod"; and last but not least, they don't write "a stylish Swedish over-the-shoulder baby-carrying device," but keep it short with "BabyBjorn." Because of this, there is tremendous potential for advertisers and authors as e-books continue their rise in popularity.

In the previous example, if there is a mention of BabyBjorn, the company can pay to have that mention become a hyperlink within the e-book's digital format. The benefits of this are that it makes the brand term more pronounced, and if the reader is inclined, he or she can click on the term and either be given more description, branding, and an image, or be taken directly to www.babybjorn.com. Another benefit to BabyBjorn is that the search engine spiders will read its hyperlink, which will help BabyBjorn come up high in the search rankings.

Where in the World Is Bangladesh?

Thinking outside of brands entirely—books often mention a geographic location. With traditional books, curious readers will look up a place like Transylvania with maps or mapping tools to learn where it is. With e-books, this is made simple because it is only one click away, taking you straight to the location on a digital map and providing a benefit to the reader. Think of a particular word in a novel that you may not know the meaning of— say *panoply*. Rather than having to look up the word in the dictionary, the definition would be one click away or you may even be able to mouse over it with the cursor to see a pop-up definition. Both of these can be monetized by the publisher and author. Google currently generates revenue from its mapping application, so it makes sense that a business development deal could be struck whereby Google would be the preferred provider of mapping information within books; in return, the publisher or author would receive a portion of the revenue that Google generates.

Today, Amazon Kindle sales already outpace traditional book sales.

Going back to the scenario of brand product placement within a book, you could argue that if the author is already placing brand terms in the book (e.g., Coke), then why would a company like Coke pay for something that is already there? Coke would want to do this for two reasons: (1) the competition (Pepsi) could swoop in and take this placement, or (2) the placement isn't currently a hyperlink in the e-book. By paying a small sponsorship fee, the company could make it a hyperlink, thus driving traffic and helping improve organic search engine rankings (because search engines reward hyperlinks).

If all of this makes so much sense, why haven't they had this type of product placement in books before now? It wasn't feasible primarily because of tracking. An advertiser wouldn't be able to track the effectiveness of this form of product placement in a hardbound or paperback book. Now, with product placements in e-books, you will be able to see how many people viewed (millions of impressions) along with how many people clicked or moused over the word with their cursors. This is great for advertisers and even better for the authors and publishers, who will now have an additional revenue stream without compromising their content, but rather enhancing it for their readers. It will be interesting to see how advertisers will be charged for these types of placements; the most logical way would probably be a cost-per-thousand-impressions model.

While the transition from both hardcover and paperback to electronic versions will occur, we are at the beginning of this movement. It will not be as rapid or absolute a succession as in other industries (e.g., music, movies). Rather, e-books will be complements or alternatives. Part of this is because there is something more genuine and romantic about curling up with a good printed book. It's not quite the same if you are curling up with your electronic reading device. Another factor is that books are one of the most viral offline items that exist today. Books, especially paperbacks, are disposable — when passed from friend to friend, owners don't really plan to ever see the book again. Also, with today's technology, it is still 10 to 30 percent faster to read something on a piece of paper than it is to read from a computer screen or from a smaller handheld e-book reader.[17] It will be interesting to see if advances in technology for e-readers, tablets, iPads, slates, and so forth eventually help make it faster to read. My guess is they will, and they will soon.

Unlike music and news content, the information within books is not as time sensitive, especially for fiction. The shelf life for a book is much longer than news content or the popularity of a song. A salient example of this is the fact that today middle school kids are still reading *Huckleberry Finn* and *The Catcher in the Rye*. Also, despite the original version of this book being published in 2009, because it uses constructs rather than trends and we update it and provide resources at www.socialnomics.com, over 100 of the top colleges and universities in the world use *Socialnomics* as required reading.

In the foreseeable future, while e-books will be exceedingly popular, they will not be an absolute replacement in the short term like the music, newspaper, and magazine industries have experienced. However, the popularity will be huge, in particular for books like the one you are reading right now. Most likely you are reading this on an e-reader and you are sitting in your robe drinking coffee (okay, hopefully not that second part).

For publishers, there are both pros and cons to the book publishing model being influenced by the rise of e-books. On one hand, publishers potentially save millions of dollars on the physical printing and shipping of inventory, and they would have an additional revenue stream in terms of the advertising via hyperlink placements within the e-books. On the other hand, they are intermediaries, which may not be as crucial a role when an author can easily get his or her content directly to the reading audience. (A good example of this is Google Books allowing authors and publishers to upload their content in PDF format. Google was sued and did lose a court battle because more than one proprietary owner didn't want their content placed on Google Books.) However, look for Apple's iBooks to help fill this void. Expect Apple to make a strong play to put a stranglehold on the publishing industry just like it did on the music industry; its next frontier is TV shows.

Unlike the music and movie industries, the book industry has flourished, even though for hundreds of years there has been a free alternative to purchasing a book—public libraries. It will be interesting to see how the public library model morphs to address e-books. The book industry still thrives in spite of the free availability of the same content at the public library for many reasons: (1) people like to own books; (2) it takes an effort to go to the library, check out a book, and then remember to return it on time; (3) library books have return dates; and (4) there are often long waiting lists for new books. With e-book technology, it is possible that hurdles 2, 3, and 4 from this list will go away entirely. Specifically, there is no need to go to the library, because the content can be wirelessly pushed or downloaded to the e-book device direct from the library. Also, once you have the e-book, you don't have a time limit on when to return it. As for the waiting list for the more popular books, because there is no physical item or inventory (i.e., the book itself), it is limitless; theoretically, everyone in the world can read the book at the same time.

Libraries are beginning to set up licensing agreements for the lending of e-books. So, there may not be limitless inventories and time lines for library e-books. For example, if you want to read *The Girl with the Dragon Tattoo* as an e-book from the library, the library may have the rights to only five e-book copies at a time, and the content may automatically expire from your e-book reader in 30 days. The good news is that inventory will be easier to track (no more lost books), saving the taxpayers some money; libraries will be less costly to maintain. In the long run, the best model would be limitless, eliminating restrictions. Amazon, as part of its Prime program, allows its Prime customers a certain number of free "lent" books during the course of the month. The user has a limited number of days in which to finish reading the book (much like the library model).

The more information that is free and available, the more society benefits. The industry will also need to figure out how an e-book purchase can be passed from one friend to another. This is additional revenue for those in the publishing world, who historically haven't made money from this passing-on tradition. Many reading this right now may be doing so on an e-reader, iPad, tablet, phone, and so forth. Books are strangely social, so there could be new revenue streams for digitally passing a book from one device to the next.

Chapter Five Key Points

1. Consumers are looking to peers for recommendations on products, services, health issues, and more via social media. Only companies that produce great products and services will be part of these conversations; mediocrity will quickly be eliminated. Today, over 90 percent rely on what peers say, while 14 percent rely on advertising.[18] Social commerce and social search are going to be huge in the years to come.

2. Social media's ability to share information helps eliminate different people performing the same tasks (multiple individual redundancies), resulting in a more efficient society.

3. The old adage that you can have only two out of three—cheap, quick, or quality—doesn't hold true within social media. It's possible to have all three.

4. Successful companies in social media function more like entertainment companies, publishers, or party planners than as traditional advertisers.

5. With the increasing popularity of e-books, there will be new digital media placement opportunities for brands. This is very similar to product placement in movies, only this is for books and the placements are clickable and trackable.

6. The most successful social media and mobile applications are those that allow users to brag, compete, or look cool by passing them on.

7. The main threat to Google in the search wars is social search (seeing what one's peers and friends think about products, services, movies, etc.). More and more, products and services will find us via our peer networks (as opposed to us searching for them).

CHAPTER SIX

Death of Social Schizophrenia

If you are Generation X or older, you have spent most of your life in a schizophrenic[1] world. You took on a different role or character depending on where you were and whom you were with. Most of us had at least two personas: a work persona and a nonwork persona. And many of us had several personas: social, work, family, coach, charity, and so on.

Your behavior at an event like Woodstock, Mardi Gras, or Burning Man was very different from your behavior at the office. Al the accountant may be known by his co-workers only as meticulous accountant Al, whereas his bowling pals would know him only as "Al-valanche," because you'd better get out of the way when he is partying, or you could be the next victim of the "Al-valanche."

Even if you believe that life is worse with social media, you cannot deny that social media has forever changed the way in which we live.

In 2008, the University of North Carolina's All-American basketball player Tyler Hansbrough found himself in the middle of a media whirlwind. Hansbrough was a hard-nosed player and the poster child of all that is good about college basketball. Because of his intensity, he was nicknamed Psycho T. This intensity helped him be a high draft pick of the Indiana Pacers of the National Basketball Association (NBA).

One sunny day in Chapel Hill, Hansbrough was hanging out with some friends at a fraternity house off campus. With some encouragement, Hansbrough thought it would be a thrill to launch his 6'10", 260-pound body into the fraternity swimming pool—the thrill part being that he was jumping off the roof of the three-story fraternity house. Now, this type of behavior by college students has been going on for decades. However, on this particular day, one of the observers captured a video of Hansbrough's skydiving act on his smartphone.

Once this video became known to the general media, North Carolina's head basketball coach, Roy Williams, had a difficult decision to make. Should he suspend Hansbrough or not? Because drinking wasn't involved and Hansbrough was a model student-athlete, he made the tough decision not to suspend Hansbrough. Helping Hansbrough's cause was his modus operandi of being intense—after all, Psycho T was just being Psycho T. If this had taken place five years before, Coach Williams and Hansbrough would not have found themselves in such a predicament. Boys would be boys, no one would have known about it, and life would have continued.

Psycho T being Psycho T is a good example of the new world not having as many casual schizophrenics. People are best off being comfortable in their own skin and not pretending to be anything that they aren't. The philosophy of well-known author Marcus Buckingham (*Now Discover Your Strengths*) of playing to your strengths is further reinforced in a social media world. Transparency demands it, and with so much information flow, it is extremely difficult for a person who is well rounded to stand out in this new world.

Without a doubt, it is somewhat daunting to always be on one's best behavior. It is mentally taxing to have fewer avenues to blow off steam or to always maintain a perfect persona. Perhaps Al the accountant is more effective and meticulous at work because outside of work he can let it all go and doesn't have to burden himself with the details.

As a result of preventive and braggadocian behavior, extracurricular activities like music, theater, and organized sports will become even more popular and important because they provide mechanisms of release for people.

There seems to be a place for interactive and virtual worlds, while the names and popularity change over time (Second Life, Sims, Webkinz, FarmVille, etc.). These social games allow users to create fictional personas (often in the form of what is called an avatar—from which the James Cameron movie may have derived inspiration) in computerized virtual worlds.

FarmVille is a good example of how quickly these things can sprout up (forgive the pun). FarmVille at one point had 85 million players. Like many successes, it is simple in nature. You start with a plot of land and your goal is to grow a very successful farm. You meet other farmers (real people playing the game) who can help you on your mission. There is even currency in the game where you can acquire items and use real currency (hard-earned dollars, euros, etc.). FarmVille was not designed to experience decades of popularity; something similar always comes along to replace these types of games. In this instance CityVille came along and replaced it. Then players went on to Angry Birds, Words with Friends, Draw with Friends, and the next fad. People simply enjoy meeting and competing against others online through these easy-to-use gaming mechanisms.

Simulation games (you taking on a different persona or managing a fictitious café) may experience a slight decline in popularity because people may find it difficult to brag about playing a simulated game that replicates life instead of just leading their own lives. Also, these games may be too transparent. A high school teacher can't simply take on the persona of a prostitute specializing in sadomasochism without realizing long-term ramifications when this eventually becomes known. In fact, schools have terminated several teachers for this type of social media behavior. After all, there is a high degree of probability that the teacher could run into one of his or her students within the virtual world as well.

A happy medium may be social video games, which are already wildly popular. If I'm going to spend 60 minutes on the bike at the gym, it's much more exciting if I'm competing against digital avatars of people I know and don't know at other gyms, and even more exciting if there is a celebrity rider like Lance Armstrong who also happens to be on a stationary bike in Austin, Texas, while I'm on one in Cambridge, Massachusetts. Social gaming on the social networks themselves is going to be massive business. In fact, in China, most people join networks in order to game first and meet people second.

While there are downsides to such 24/7 personal openness, overall it's easier to argue that appropriate transparency is a good thing for individuals and society. It is, without question, much cooler to say you are bungee jumping off a remote mountain pass overhang in New Mexico than to update your status with "I'm watching the latest adventure reality series."

Imagine a world that reintroduces people to living their own realities, rather than watching someone else's. Maybe this is why simulation games like Second Life haven't been as wildly successful as many pundits predicted; perhaps people have come to the realization that it is much cooler to lead their own lives. Or perhaps there will always be a place for these types of games and networks when you think about FarmVille, CityVille, and Webkinz.

One of the more overt examples of the downside of not being yourself within social media is the tragic case of Lori Drew and Megan Meier. Lori was concerned that her daughter Sara's former friend, 13-year-old Megan, might be spreading false statements about Sara. So, Lori decided to set up a MySpace account pretending to be an attractive teenage boy named Josh Evans. Josh flirted with Megan, and eventually they became social media friends and developed an online relationship. Once the hook was set, the persona of Josh then started berating Megan through a series of unfriendly comments and nasty remarks. These remarks proved too much for Megan, who had a history of battling depression, and one day she decided to end her life. At the time, Lori Drew, a 49-year-old Missouri mom, faced a possibility of three years in prison and a $300,000 fine for an online harassment campaign that resulted in the suicide of a teenage girl. More laws are being enacted to curtail cyberbullies like Lori Drew.

Even Football Players Need to Calm Down

A University of Texas Longhorns offensive lineman found out the hard way the importance of preventive behavior in social media. The lineman posted a racist update on his Facebook profile just after Barack Obama was elected president of the United States: "all the hunters gather up, we have a n#$%&r in the whitehouse."[2]

Soon after that was posted, Coach Mack Brown kicked the lineman off the team. The lineman was unable to participate in Texas's 2009 bowl game. He posted an apology to anyone his comment had offended, but the damage had already been done:

> *Clearly I have made a mistake and apologized for it and will pay for it. I received it as a text message from an acquaintance and immaturely put it up on Facebook in the light of the election. I'm not racist and apologize for offending you. I grew up on a ranch in a small town where that was a real thing and I need to grow up. I sincerely am sorry for being ignorant in thinking that it would be okay to write that publicly and apologize to you in particular. I have to be more mature than to put the reputation of my team at stake and to spread that kind of hate which I don't even believe in. Once again, I sincerely apologize.*[3]

Meanwhile, on another football team, University of Colorado head coach Dan Hawkins instituted the following rule for his players:

If I request to see your page, you'd better let me in and let me see it. Everybody's kind of got their own standards. I tell them if your mom can see it, and neither you nor she is embarrassed, then it's okay. But if your mom can't look at it, then it's probably not right.[4]

Even the cheerleaders need to learn how to behave correctly in this newly opened society. A New England Patriots professional cheerleader was kicked off the cheerleader squad for inappropriate photo postings on her Facebook page. She and her friends went out on a wild drinking binge. When one of her friends passed out, they decided to write all over the friend's half-naked body. They drew penises and other lewd symbols along with phrases like "I'm a Jew" and swastika symbols. They posted and shared these images of their crazy night with their friends.[5]

As a result of these examples and more, National Football League (NFL) teams started engaging in a controversial practice for the 2009 draft. Player personnel from NFL teams (Packers, Lions, etc.) started creating fake Facebook accounts. Most of these profiles were designed to look like they were those of young, energetic, and attractive females. The purpose was to become friends with potential draft picks so the teams could conduct further research. Historically, NFL companies would spend hundreds of thousands of dollars on background investigations prior to paying a young college kid millions of dollars. This progression into social media subterfuge only makes sense for them. Similar to regular employers, hiring agents are looking for anything that could be viewed as detrimental. In some instances, they have seen drug posts and gambling items on the college player's profile.

The ethical nature of these NFL football teams creating fake profiles to bait 20-year-old athletes can certainly be questioned, but the key message is don't put anything on social media that you don't want the whole world to know about, because eventually, one way or another, the world *will* know about it.

Just like athletic programs, governments around the world are struggling to determine how to handle some social media issues. Twenty-two-year-old Croatian Niksa Klecak was picked up by police and interrogated after starting a Facebook group critical of Prime Minister Ivo Sanader. The group was dubbed "I bet I can find 5,000 people who dislike Sanader."[6] The interrogation drew sharp criticism from Croatia's opposition Social Democrat Party and has inspired a host of copycat Facebook groups.

Just as companies have discovered, perhaps the best tactic is not censorship, but rather to address the problem and have enough good karma produced that it overwhelms and drowns out the negative.

Be the Best at Something, Not Everything

As previously discussed, the transparency and speed of information flow via social media mitigate casual schizophrenic behavior. This is generally a positive result because maintaining different personas is stressful, exhausting, and disingenuous.

The same holds true for corporate behavior in social media. For corporations, trying to be too many things to too many people is costly. Historically, we have seen the "We are the best at everything" messaging come out of many marketing departments. The marketers always start off with high hopes of simply highlighting one message in a 30-second commercial; but by the end of production, they have flooded the spot with numerous messages. The original intent of an advertiser may be to convey the message: "We have been in the business for 45 years." However, the end product is often something similar to: "We have been in the business for 45 years, we have the lowest prices, and we have the largest selection. Our brand name *Perfect* is the most trusted, and you can find us at great retailers like Sam's, Costco, and BJ's."

In a 140-character world, if you want to have a chance at helping the consumer retain a key message and eventually pass it on, it is imperative that you focus on your strengths or particular niche. There is also a need for the continuous flow of information across the entire organization; in particular, it is mission critical for production and marketing to be feeding information back and forth. It's one thing for marketing to respond to consumer complaints; it's an entirely different thing to respond to the customer's complaint, look for trends in product deficiencies, and work closely with production to develop solutions.

The role of a marketer today, and even more so in the future, has less to do with creating 30-second television commercials and guessing what jingle will resonate with prospects, and more to do with having ongoing external conversations with the customers or prospects—while at the same time having internal conversations with operations, customer care, and product development.

In turn, production and development are now less about being behind closed doors in a laboratory and more to do with being connected with marketing; they, too, will have an ongoing dialogue with the customer. Two prime examples of production personnel who have the dual role of product vision and being a public face to the organization are Dave Morin of Facebook and Matt Cutts of Google. At developer conferences, Dave and Matt are almost at the level of rock stars, and they are the faces of their respective organizations in the development community. They aren't behind closed doors trying to figure out the next best thing for their target audience; they are in constant contact with their target audience, and a large part of their role is also marketing. These are two great examples of what marketers will look like in this Socialnomic era.

One Message

Companies that engage in brand marketing have always known it is best to keep the message simple and convey one salient point. Some companies have been able to adhere to this principle, including 7-Up's "Uncola" campaign or FedEx's "When it absolutely positively has to get there overnight" campaign. However, many companies have struggled with this concept. Most often, they get myopic — this product or service is so great we need to get it out there — or they get internal pressure from too many executives trying to get their particular interests across. Companies are lucky if the advertising they create gets remembered at all by the customer, let alone gets the key message across.

So, when a car company crams in that its cars have the best miles per gallon, horsepower, and stereo, and lists all the special promotional lease offers with an accompanying disclaimer, and then adds all the local dealer names at the end of a 30-second commercial, all it is doing is causing mass confusion for the viewing audience. Even when marketing teams know they are supposed to stick to one message, companies often fail to do so because of the pressure of all these different elements and parties involved; too many cooks in the kitchen spoil the broth.

The beauty and curse of a 140-character world is that there is no longer a choice. Tony Blair indicated such at the World Business Forum in New York: "Because of the proliferation and speed of information, people and the press want everything in succinct and easy to digest packages. However, some very complex problems can't be put that way. It is quite an extraordinary challenge."[7]

Whether we like it or not, right or wrong, we have to adapt to communication in succinct and salient sound bites.

From production and strategic positioning standpoints, the beauty is that it forces companies to improve. If your company or product can't definitively state what it stands for and how it differs from the competition in a few short words, then it is time to reevaluate exactly what you are doing. If you don't have a niche position in a marketplace that you are attempting to defend from your competition, and you are trying to be all things to all people, then you are doomed to failure.

This destructive behavior may have taken longer to figure out in the past because marketing mediums allowed advertisers to cram in many different benefits in the hope that so many great things would entice consumers to buy. This was also during a time when customers were more willing to be *spoken to* rather than have a *conversation with*. They may have bought your product based solely on the glitz and glamour of your marketing. This possibility is very limited now that we are living in a world with social media.

The good news is that in this new world order, once you have determined your initial messaging strategy, you have the ability to reevaluate and tweak it for relevancy based on feedback from the marketplace. Because you will be engaging in a conversation with your customer, you will be able to identify and adapt to changing needs much quicker. That's why it's important to ensure that your marketers and production teams are on the same page.

Past Marketer's Philosophy
- It's all about the sex and sizzle of the message and brand imagery.
- It's all about the message; good marketers can sell anything.
- We know what is right for the customer — we are doing the customers a service because they really don't know what they want.
- We develop products and messaging in-house and then disperse them to the public.

Present/Future Marketer's Philosophy
- It's important to listen and respond to customer needs.
- It's all about the product; it's necessary to be in constant communication with all other departments.
- We never know what is exactly right for the customer; that is why we are constantly asking and making adjustments, because we usually don't get it right the first time.

- Take up the motto: Fail fast, fail forward, fail better.
- Often our customers will market the product better than we can; if we can leverage one of their ideas, then it is beneficial to everyone.

Referral Program on Steroids

If you were to ask chief marketing officers (CMOs) of varying businesses, ranging in size from Fortune 500 companies to small businesses, what their top-performing channels or programs are, the majority would indicate that their referred customers are the most valuable. *Top-performing* is defined here in terms of return on investment (cost to acquire said customer) as well as the quality of the customer acquired.

The logical follow-up question for the CMOs is: What is the greatest challenge you face? The response would again focus on referrals, only it would be fixated on the difficulty in obtaining mass volume from this lucrative channel — "How can we get more?"

For the first time, social media enables corporations and marketers to generate this desired mass scale from the existing customer base. It is truly word of mouth on steroids, or word of mouth goes to World of Mouth.

In the 1990s and continuing into the twenty-first century, Jeff Bezos and Amazon.com have done a stellar job of introducing the concept of affinity marketing to millions worldwide. For example, when you purchase a DVD or book from Amazon, Amazon gives real-time suggestions of what you might like based on your own prior purchases.

Millions have found this feature to be very helpful, and it has taken us into an appropriate progression in marketing. However, as many have also learned, there are a few pieces to this program that are suboptimal. For example, suppose you purchase a gift for your four-year-old niece under your own Amazon account. While your niece may enjoy suggestions to buy *My Little Pony* or *American Doll*, you as an adult aren't often in the market for such items.

Much more helpful and useful was Amazon's introduction of the ability to showcase to users: "People who purchased this book also purchased these other ones." Here's where social media comes in and takes this one giant step forward. In the Amazon model just described, you don't know the other people who are referenced. They are an aggregation of thousands of others who happen to have the same purchasing patterns. In other words, there is no personal connection between you and them. The only shared connection is that you *might* share similar buying habits.

In social media, you still have this same aggregate data made available to you by the Amazons and RedEnvelopes of the world: "Here's what the total universe enjoys." But, in social media, it goes significantly deeper to show: "Here's what your specific network enjoys." Within your network, you will begin to identify a handful of friends, possibly more, who seem to have similar tastes and opinions that you can trust. The circle you trust for recommending movies may be entirely different from the circle you trust for restaurant recommendations.

For example, when you see on your favorite social media tool that your friend Angie — who normally purchases and reads romance novels — purchased and started reading a science fiction novel (there are social media applications and widgets that do exactly this), you might scratch your head and think it quite odd that Angie would be reading such a thing. However, Angie's recommendation and write-up on the science fiction book pops up a few days later on your updates, and you are quickly enlightened regarding this oddity:

> For those who know me well, you may be surprised to see that I just completed a science fiction piece. This was quite a diversion from my usual romance novel obsession — but let me tell you it was a refreshing one. Thanks go to my husband, who is an avid sci-fi fan; when he came across this book and read it, he thought I would like it too — and right he was! I loved it. I highly recommend this book and can say it's one of the best I've read in the past three years.

Now, as Angie's good friend who shares very similar tastes when it comes to reading, how likely is it that you are going to want to read this book? My guess is pretty likely. You are definitely more apt to give it a try than if you had seen the *exact same* write-up on Amazon.com by someone you didn't know, someone whom you didn't identify with or trust immediately. With the Amazon Kindle, Amazon allows you to follow other readers and even see their notes and highlights of the book they are reading.

Then there is Angie; she has a reputation to uphold within her network. If it were a blind review process — like Yahoo! Movies — she would be less likely to put as much thought into it as she will for her own network. Spelling a word incorrectly isn't quite as taboo for Angie if it's not going to be knowingly shared with those who know her and are close to her. If users are debating between giving a particular movie three or four stars and the reviewer has identity immunity, studies have shown that he or she is more likely to give four stars. Conversely, if the review is going to friends, reviewers are more likely to be conservative and give it three stars. This is somewhat intuitive because you would never want to be the cause of a friend's bad evening at the show; instead, you would rather underpromise and overdeliver.

Of course, this concept of sharing and reviewing among friends isn't new—book clubs have been around for years. The difference is that book clubs meet once per month and will continue to do so. The need for book clubs doesn't go away; in fact, even book clubs are changing. This book you are currently reading was honored to be the April selection of 12 Books in 12 Months, a book club entirely conducted via social media. I even had a Q&A session over Skype with the club members, and the person who had the best tweet about the book was given a signed copy of the hardcover (ironic, I realize).

With social media, information is shared daily and is about much more than just the single book that was assigned. It also allows others to be involved who can't make it to traditional book clubs for a myriad of reasons: geographical limitations, family commitments, job demands, and so on.

So, what does this change mean for companies exactly? It means that many of their dreams have become realities—"If only we could get more referrals." Well, the referral floodgates have been opened, my friends. However, companies should be careful what they wish for. Great companies that already produce excellent content, products, or services welcome Socialnomics with open arms. While they are not guaranteed continued success, they are certainly positioned for it. Meanwhile, those companies that have survived to date by being great at intermediary games—whether distribution-related, direct mail, brand marketing, lobbying, public relations, or legal rights—have bigger challenges in front of them. Great companies are already adjusting the way they work (e.g., Procter & Gamble cutting 1,600 members of its marketing staff, Doritos outsourcing its Super Bowl ads) to help ensure their continued success.

Intermediaries are becoming less important than they've been in the past, and the rise in power is shifting rapidly to the social graph. This was no more evident than in the 2008 race for the Democratic Party's presidential candidate (more in Chapter Four) where a little-known senator from Illinois was able to defeat one of history's great political organizations—that of Hillary Clinton. This type of victory would have been extremely difficult to architect without the Obama camp having the ability to understand and to leverage the power and advantage that Socialnomics brings. In this instance, the Clinton political organization was the item that had lost some of its power, and that power was transferred to the social graph.

Chapter Six Key Points

1. The transparency and speed of information exchanged within social media mitigate casual schizophrenic behavior. Having both a work personality and a party personality will soon become extinct. People and companies will need to have one essence and be true to that essence.
2. Being well rounded as a company or individual is less beneficial. It's more productive to play to your core strength. This differentiates you from the competition. You need to stand out in order to be outstanding.
3. Companies that produce great products and services rather than companies that simply rely on great messaging will be winners in a Socialnomic world. The social graph is the world's largest and most powerful referral program.
4. Marketers' jobs have changed from creating and pushing to one that requires listening, engaging, and reacting to potential and current customer needs.
5. Fail fast, fail forward, fail better.

CHAPTER SEVEN

Winners and Losers in a 140-Character World

Today there are websites that reduce or make URLs tiny (e.g., bitly, bre.ad) so that people can fit them within their social media postings, which often have character limits. These tools take a URL string of roughly 100 characters and condense it down to 15. This is necessary in today's sound bite world and is a reflection of a societal shift from the languid days of sipping lemonade on the front porch to multitasking in a WiFi-enabled Starbucks. In a world where everything is condensed and hyperaccelerated, who wins and who loses? In this chapter, we explore several case studies that shed light on what it takes to succeed in the world of Socialnomics.

Does ESPN Have ESP?

Some savvy entrepreneurs at ESPN were ahead of the curve in recognizing the different fundamentals of Socialnomics. Their success was the result of innovation and necessity. Fantasy Football's popularity has grown rapidly since its beginnings in the 1980s. As a result, ESPN started to dedicate more of its television programming to discussing pertinent events related to Fantasy Football; but this increased coverage still wasn't enough. Fantasy Football experts Matthew Berry and Nate Ravitz knew that the public hungered for more fantasy data and approached the ABC/ESPN brass. Their plea for more Fantasy Football airtime proved successful.

Although they were not granted airtime or support, they were given the green light to produce their own podcast, *Fantasy Football Today*, which quickly became one of the top 20 most downloaded podcasts within the Apple iTunes store. This was a great achievement, but they were still moonlighting and hadn't produced any revenue that would spark ESPN's attention for more support. This was when they embarked on two very innovative facets and, whether knowingly or not, they were engaging in Socialnomic activity. These two facets were actually making the sponsors part of the show's content and also allowing listeners to help produce some of the content as well.

As a result of its rapid ascent in the iTunes download rankings, *Fantasy Football Today* drew the attention of some savvy big-time marketers. One of its first sponsors was the feature film *Eagle Eye*. This movie featured Shia LaBeouf and was produced by Steven Spielberg. Aside from covering the latest in Fantasy Football, Berry and Ravitz often touch on pop culture, including commenting on the popular 1990s television show *Beverly Hills 90210* as well as the *New 90210*.

The podcasts vary in length from 15 to 30 minutes depending on how much news they have to cover. The varying lengths of the podcasts are an important item to note and a reflection of how our world is changing. Radio and television broadcasts historically attempt to fill an allotted slot of time. That isn't the case with podcasts. If a podcast has only 16 minutes of newsworthy items to cover, then why waste the commentators' and viewers' time trying to fill the slot with subpar content?

The fact that *Fantasy Football Today* was able to secure a sponsor for the podcast wasn't innovative — this was inevitable once it began to attract a vast audience of listeners. We have seen this type of sponsorship in various podcasts. Another good example is a technology podcast, CNET's *Buzz Out Loud* (*BOL*). Recognized as one of the most popular podcasts covering Internet and technology news, it, too, plays up the fact that its segments are of indeterminate length. Its popularity is well deserved because the information is delivered in a concise but humorous fashion and all angles are covered.

Although *BOL* was successful in securing big-name sponsors, including Best Buy, it originally adopted an old-paradigm format when it came to its advertising model. It played a commercial in the beginning, middle, and end of the podcast. Just like in the television world, the commercials were not integrated but rather interruptive; this is disruptive to the listening audience. Worse, for seven months straight, Best Buy played the same exact commercial! Please keep in mind that the podcast listening audience is not made up of casual listeners. People don't simply flip through channels and land on something of interest. This podcast is downloaded daily, so many of its loyal listeners are the same from podcast to podcast.

What a wasted opportunity for Best Buy! It could have taken advantage of the glowing personalities of the hosts (at the time Molly Wood, Tom Merritt, Brian Tong, and Jason Howell) and adjusted the messaging daily by having the hosts read or incorporate the messaging into the show as they saw appropriate. Instead, Best Buy took its terrestrial radio spot and plopped it right in the middle of the show. However, the good news is that CNET was able to learn from this and in 2010 started taking advantage of the colorful personalities and insights of Wood, Merritt, Needleman, Tong, and Howell. Hence, these guys were able to seamlessly work the sponsors in as part of the show, often with tongue-in-cheek references about how the products are used. This helps showcase something else: the talent of these shows getting actively involved with every facet of the production of the show, which ultimately makes it better for both the listening audience and the sponsors.

In fact, the hosts made so much fun of one sponsor's voiceover sounding like a Mafia hit man that the company made all new spots, with each entire spot sounding like a scene out of *The Godfather*. This makes advertising fun, and is a far cry from playing the same commercial for seven months straight. One of the old guard, CBS, purchased CNET and wasn't able to see the opportunities that *BOL* presented; CBS canceled the show in April 2012.

Stop the Charade — Nobody Is Perfect

Let's stay on that thought for a moment and review what ESPN did with their sponsor, *Eagle Eye*. As we mentioned, getting a sponsor for the podcast wasn't innovative; rather, it was the way in which they seamlessly incorporated the advertisements into the show, often in a tongue-in-cheek fashion. Host Matthew Berry was single at the time, and the running joke was that he couldn't get a date.

Occasionally, Berry would even chide himself about his want for female attention. Around the release date of the *Eagle Eye* movie, Berry kept with this shtick and dropped comments like "Even if this movie is terrible, you should go see it to pay homage to Michelle Monaghan's hotness." A comment like that would often lead into a few other comments about what movies she was in and so on. This was all done without disrupting the flow of the football-themed show. Often, these tangents by Berry were about various female celebrities' attractiveness quotient — which wasn't a stretch because the listening audience is 90 percent beer-swilling males. The hosts would even give candid feedback and comments after watching the movie and discussing what they liked and didn't like about the film.

The producers of *Eagle Eye* were also engaging in some basic principles of Socialnomics by allowing the hosts to say what they thought about the movie even if it included negative phrases like "if this movie is terrible." This was a very smart move by the advertisers. By pointing out flaws, you will get more credence from people than when you point out your strengths. If you try to present yourself or your company as always being perfect, then the listening audience will suspect that what you have to say isn't completely true.

In fact, Bazaarvoice, a leading provider of ratings systems, has done studies showing that if a website has two similar products side by side the consumer is more likely to purchase the product with a 4.5-star rating than the product with a 5-star rating. This doesn't make intuitive sense, so the consumers were questioned about their decision. The responses were similar in the sense that they thought the product with the 4.5-star rating was more credible. They also liked the fact that they were able to see what other people didn't like about it and discovered the complaints weren't important or relevant to them. A 5-star rating didn't seem credible to them, because they felt no product can be perfect.

Southwest Airlines realizes it is better off stating, "We only give you peanuts so that our fares cost peanuts," rather than trying to claim that it has both great food and great low airfares.

Certainly a movie is a simple product to incorporate into a show without it being too intrusive. However, the Fantasy Football podcast followed up the movie trailer success with an even greater success — its subsequent sponsor, Charles Schwab. It's difficult to find anything invigorating to say about a financial company, especially during the 2008 financial meltdown, but this podcast was able to deliver the Charles Schwab message brilliantly. The whipping boy on the show was the producer, aptly nicknamed "Pod Vader" (a takeoff on Darth Vader), who was constantly hazed by the hosts for killing the show by virtue of his incompetence. In one of the early podcasts, while they played a robotic-sounding device that answered yes or no to questions, they dubbed the robotic voice "Chuck" because the advertising slogan at the time for Charles

Schwab was "Talk to Chuck." They even had a running joke that Pod Vader was Chuck and that Chuck was Pod Vader.

A typical show during this time went something like this:

Ravitz: Willie Parker is listed as questionable for this week's game, and the *Pittsburgh Gazette* reports that his backup, Maurice Moore, is most likely to start. So if you have Parker, you may want to pick up his backup Moore, because Parker will most likely not be able to play.

Berry: Yes, but the Steelers are going against the Ravens and the top-rated run defense. So, you may be better off picking up Dominic Rhodes of the Colts instead of Parker.

Ravitz: I disagree; **let's ask Chuck**. **Chuck**, don't you feel that Moore is a better choice than Rhodes?

Synthesized voice: No.

Ravitz: Okay, **Chuck** has spoken. Now it's time to read some e-mail from our listeners. This one comes from Fred in St. Louis, and he asks, "Should I trade Roy Williams for Larry Johnson? If it helps my chances of you reading this e-mail on air, I went and signed up for a **Charles Schwab** checking account after hearing you guys say I can earn **3 percent interest**."

Berry: It does help because **Chuck** knows when to **buy low** and **sell high** just like the stock market, and in this case, you should sell Roy Williams high because he isn't going to have any more value than he does right now.

Ravitz: Great job in working in the sponsor.

Berry: Well, I am a company man.

Synthesized voice: **Chuck** says yes. [*Laughter*]

Berry: That was Pod Vader, not **Chuck**, because Pod Vader is **Chuck**.

Pod Vader: No, I am not **Chuck**! [*Laughter in the studio*][1]

This was brilliant and far different from a traditional 30-second radio advertisement because the sponsor and *Fantasy Football Today* realized the format (daily podcast) differs from regular radio advertising — they weren't going to make the same mistake that Best Buy did by running the same spot for seven months straight to the same audience. Instead, creatively incorporating Charles Schwab placement became an integral part of the show without it being intrusive; in fact, you could argue that it enhanced the show by adding a witty element to it. In this case, through creative thinking, the advertiser's involvement actually added content rather than interruption. While we pointed out a mistake made by Best Buy, it quickly learned from its mistake and, enabled by a chief marketing officer (CMO) with a strong love of social media, has pioneered some great social media programs (e.g., Best Buy Blue Shirt employees empowered to answer customer needs on Twitter).

Consumers today, in particular Millennials and Generation Zers, don't want advertisers to shout; they'd rather have conversations and steady ongoing relationships with companies. The callers and e-mailers on the *Fantasy Football Today* show were having fun with the sponsorships by writing them into the show and referencing the sponsors in their e-mails. For example: "I have my **Eagle Eye** on the Packers game this week" and "**Chuck** may know finances, but he was wrong about running back Dominic Rhodes — that chump didn't score a touchdown this week, so I am going to **Chuck** him off my fantasy football team this week."

The most Socialnomic piece of all in regard to this *Fantasy Football Today* podcast example is that the advertising wasn't wrapped around the content, but rather was an integral part of it. This is important because when items are passed virally between individuals using social media tools, if the advertisements are on the front or back end of the valuable content or they are banners or display advertisements that float on the periphery of the content, they are too easily stripped or removed when the content is passed from one person to the next. For example, in a company-sponsored video on YouTube, where banners are to the left and right of the video, only the video will be passed on when the video is shared among those on a social network, since the ads aren't in the video itself. The advertising placement will be eliminated from the string, and the potential viral activity will be lost.

In Chapter Three, we discussed a Diet Coke and Mentos example in which you can see that the Diet Coke items and product placement are the actual content itself. It's important to note the dramatic shift that is being propelled by social media. The world around us is shifting from a model where marketers historically have supported content to a world in which marketers and companies need to create their own content or seamlessly integrate with existing content. Ironically, this harks back to the advent of television, when sponsors helped produce the content; soap operas are aptly named because soap powder companies used to write shows around the use of their products.

In some of their live, televised shows, ESPN hosts and personalities have running on-air dialogue with listeners via interactions on

Twitter. These Twitter sessions are also sponsored by their clients (e.g., "Today's Twitter Board is sponsored by General Motors").

Free Labor

In the *Fantasy Football Today* podcast, it would be painfully difficult to try to find every iteration or mention of "Charles Schwab" or "Chuck," because each mention is actually part of the show — it's not nearly as simple as removing an advertisement that was placed at the front, middle, and end of a broadcast. The second major Socialnomic piece that the football podcasts at ESPN employed was leveraging the audience base to assist with content. As mentioned, these podcasts needed to be produced inexpensively. They weren't getting large financial backing from corporate headquarters; rather, it was sink or swim.

One segment during the week was to report on the various teams across the league. If the producers had employed the principles of the past, they would have started by using and leveraging existing field reporters (e.g., Sal Paolantonio, Adam Shefter, and John Clayton), who would be sent to the various cities and team camps to learn and report back on the particular happenings of those teams. In this scenario, the shows' producers would receive high-level reporting from experts on a few teams during the week. This is an outrageously expensive model because it includes incurring costs for flights, hotels, and transportation, per diem expenses, as well as paying top talent with celebrity-esque salaries easily in the six-figure range. These are costs that the *Fantasy Football Today* podcast could not afford to sustain. As a result, the producers of these podcasts decided to travel down a different path that has resulted in a brilliant revolution in news reporting. Because of its success, we are seeing a shift toward this type of news reporting today.

The producers had people write the show requesting to be the "Super Fan" for their particular team. Many companies attempt to get this level of engagement by giving away a costly contest prize for people who submit their photos with a product, create a video, or write an essay about why they deserve to be a contest winner.

However, this historically popular giveaway or sweepstakes approach can have the opposite effect on people submitting entries because it devalues what you are attempting to do, and a typical response from a potential contestant may be: "Oh, this company needs to bribe us to submit something, and since that prize is of no value to me, I will *not* submit anything for it."

The Tom Sawyer Approach

ESPN decided to engage in a different practice rather than employ a typical sweepstakes model. ESPN didn't give anything away, and it had hundreds of applications from fans expressing heartfelt reasons and arguments about why they should be the Super Fan of their particular NFL team. Keep in mind that if these applicants were selected as a Super Fan, then their responsibilities would include weekly check-ins reporting the current status of their particular team — they would need to know everything about them. Rather than a sweepstakes prize, the winners would actually be put to work!

This is a monumental step toward leveraging the audience base. ESPN's loyal podcast listeners were begging to do free work! This is analogous to when Tom Sawyer was painting the fence and made the chore appear so appealing to those around him that they were hoodwinked into begging Tom to have a chance to paint the fence. Tom Sawyer knew that if his approach was "Ah, come on, if you help me paint this, there is a chance I will buy you some red licorice," it wouldn't be nearly as effective as giving the illusion that painting the fence was fun.

In this ESPN instance, the audience has become Jane the blogger (Chapter One). These are people who have a pressing desire to be heard. They are people who want to be a part of something bigger than themselves. They are also fanatical about their teams, and their teams say something about who they are (similar to brands). A fan of the San Francisco 49ers is more "wine and cheese with a flair for the dramatic," whereas a fan of the Pittsburgh Steelers is more "meat and potatoes, Jerome Bettis, and no nonsense."

ESPN leveraged its worldwide platform to ensure that these Super Fans didn't make competing platforms at the local level. It is a proactive way to look at the old saying "If you can't beat 'em, join 'em." They reversed this old axiom with an approach of "Join 'em before they beat you." Every person today is a competitive media outlet.

During the Super Fan selection process, they even allowed the audience to help determine the criteria for selection. If your suggestion was taken, then you were automatically named a Super Fan. One of the winning suggestions was that each applicant should have to donate a minimum of $25 to the V Foundation for the fight against cancer. So, as part of the application process, submitters were showing receipts to prove that they had in fact donated at least $25.

The producers picked the best and brightest of the bunch to be the delegated Super Fan for each team. There was a San Diego Chargers Super Fan, Detroit Lions Super Fan (bless their hearts), and so on. Whether ESPN knew it or not, they were practicing Socialnomics and utilizing a brilliant strategy that can be summarized by the following seven points:

1. The show garnered hundreds of fans who demonstrated their engagement with the show by sending in applications detailing why they should be a Super Fan. Some of the more humorous entries were read on the air even if they weren't selected as winners.
2. The producers asked their audience what the selection criteria should be and received a recommendation that was better than anything they would have conjured up behind a closed studio door. Specifically, requiring donations to the V Foundation for the fight against cancer as part of the application process was a great contribution for a great cause.
3. They avoided paying reporters and associated travel costs.
4. They were able to report on all 32 teams during the same week.
5. The Super Fans became expert reporters. As team fanatics, they were able to give a fan perspective on what people cared about. They digested all pieces of media just like Jane the blogger about their particular team. They were a little unpolished in delivery, but since it was a podcast and not live, the producers could edit it accordingly to glean the appropriate sound bites.
6. ESPN was proactively helping to avoid competition in the future. These individual Super Fans had more than enough knowledge to do their own podcasts on their particular teams. By proactively asking them to join ESPN, ESPN proactively eliminated some potential competition down the road. Every individual today is a media outlet.
7. These 32 Super Fans also have tremendous reach within the communities and social media tools in which they engage. "Hey, Mom, I know you don't know anything about football, but download this podcast because I'm on it today!"

Point 7 isn't a new construct, but it is very powerful with social media. Local newspapers have used this principle for years. The content of the local newspaper story wasn't half as important as ensuring that it was as crammed with local names—the closer it was to a yellow pages listing, the better. This is a testament to Dale Carnegie's statement that everyone's favorite word in the English language is his or her own name. ESPN realized, just like Dale Carnegie, that if it took on 32 new helpers, those 32 new helpers would be excited to spread the word to their respective social graphs.

While ESPN gets an A, it doesn't get an A+. One thing it will learn in time is that it's difficult for a host like Berry to perform double duty in the Socialnomic age. At the time of this writing, Berry was doing both Fantasy Baseball and Fantasy Football podcasts. Since the respective seasons have crossover, it is virtually impossible for him to be as knowledgeable as the users demand for either baseball or football. Some of these fantasy fans are fanatics of just one sport. If you can't convey to listeners that you are more expert than they are, they will tune out or may even decide that they could do a better podcast! In our new niche world, Berry should focus on just one sport, because his audience and future competition will.

Everybody Wants His or Her 15 Minutes of Fame

Another good example of a company effectively using the Tom Sawyer approach is CNN (iStory and Twitter). CNN anchor Rick Sanchez was an early adopter of harnessing the power of the social graph, and then CNN took it from there long after Sanchez left the network. Recognizing the huge potential of microblogging, Sanchez became an avid user of Twitter early on. Twitter's main function allows users, in 140 characters or less, to update people who are following them about what they are doing by using various interfaces (Twitter website, TweetDeck, Hootsuite, Twitter modules for iGoogle, Facebook, Yahoo!, etc.). Usage ranges from business ("Great article on Southwestern Airlines earnings release can be found here: www.abc.com") to the inane ("Just had my fifth Starbucks Pumpkin Spice Venti!").

Obviously, some of CNN anchors' activities (e.g., "Briefing about Prime Minister David Cameron interview tonight; just learned that he may disclose some new and interesting information about Barack Obama and the BP Oil Spill") are much more interesting than a friend informing you that he is hopped up on pumpkin-flavored Starbucks. Rick Sanchez was probably pleasantly surprised when within a few weeks over 75,000 people were following what he was tweeting. He then discovered it was more important to talk less about himself and more about his upcoming interviews. From there, he started to leverage the Twitter platform to ask thought-provoking questions like: "I'm interviewing Colin Powell tonight. What would you like to know most about Iraq or Iran?" Here is a string of tweets from the 2008 presidential debate between McCain and Obama:

> . . . *if they twittered they'd know how to make the words fit right? (8:17 P.M. October 15 from web)*
>
> . . . *like this . . . put it on joe the plummer, personalize it. way to go mccain (8:11 P.M. October 15 from web)*
>
> . . . *mccain plan, do you rescue everybody, even guy who paid for house he couldn't afford. even . . . flippers? (8:10 P.M. October 15 from web)*
>
> . . . *Okay, i can't dance. my mother is so ashamed, she can. (3:05 P.M. October 15 from web)*
>
> . . . *many blaming palin for Mc-palin slide in polls? is that fair? what u think? (12:43 P.M. October 15 from web)*
>
> . . . *mccain: "doesn't think i have guts to bring up bill ayers" should he? how should obama respond? this could be fun, showdown okay corral. (10:47 A.M. October 15 from web)*[2]

These examples illustrate why social media is disruptive (in a good way) in the entertainment business. CNN is able to have a relationship with millions of people who feel more connected with CNN than they were before CNN started to leverage the Twitter platform. The viewers believe they are helping to produce the show, which in many ways they are. It's no surprise that CNN was rumored at the 2012 SXSW Conference in Austin, Texas, to be considering purchasing social media blog Mashable. This would give CNN an even larger presence in the social media world.

Become a Modern-Day Pied Piper

CNN's Sanchez also started following a large percentage (roughly 32,000) of the people following him. "How can he follow so many people?" you astutely ask. He isn't actually keeping tabs on their tweets unless they relate directly to his questions. He is following these people as a courtesy. The etiquette on Twitter is debatable, but many believe that if people follow you, then you should probably follow them. They will never know if you didn't read one of their tweets! If you don't refollow someone, then you are saying that you have something more important to say than they do, which might not be the impression you wish to convey. The counterargument to this is: If I am a known celebrity or company, am I openly endorsing someone by following him? What happens if that person performs nefarious or lewd actions? Does it reflect poorly on me since I'm following him? This etiquette will flesh itself out in time. If you want to be conservative, then limit whom you follow; if you want to follow everyone who follows you with the hope of developing a fan base, go for it. Many of these decisions boil down to your appetite for risk versus reward.

Getting back to CNN, the next logical progression was to get Twitter followers on the show. Obviously, you can't get hundreds of firefighters, carpenters, tech nerds, teachers, and the like on the show. Or can you?

So, CNN and its producers started asking Twitter followers about their thoughts on various subjects and putting the responses/tweets up on TV during the show on the scrolling byline at the bottom of the screen. This is brilliant as it adds content to the show and encourages CNN followers to watch just so they could see if their comment made the show! Remember the local newspaper philosophy: the closer it is to a phone book full of names, the more possible readers you will attract. The same can be said for the tweets scrolling on CNN.

In a Socialnomic world, companies need to relinquish the total control they have had over the past few centuries and allow users, consumers, viewers, and others to take their rightful ownership. CNN's experiment, which turned into a success, can be summed up in the following tweet from one of its producers:

> *just finished editorial meeting with my group, may have great new video today. will share more shortly. like i say, it's your show. (9:31 A.M. October 21 from web)*[3]

The key line in this tweet (message sent on Twitter) is "like i say, it's your show." Credit should go to CNN for allowing its on-air talent to express themselves on Twitter. These CNN celebrities didn't go through any formal training on Twitter, nor did they sit through public relations and brand courses at CNN on what could be said. Rather, CNN let its talent and producers run with it. Because of the nature of the technology, the brand chiefs and executives couldn't approve every sentence that their employees were tweeting and posting. They had to know that their employees were going to make some mistakes but that they would quickly adjust and move forward. CNN is failing fast, failing forward, and failing better.

Everybody Is Twittering, but Is Anyone Listening?

Whether Ellen DeGeneres, Britney Spears, or Lance Armstrong has 75,000 or 11,750,000 followers, they're all A-listers. People want to hear what they have to say. It's not because of Twitter; it's because these celebrities previously had a fan base.

Now, there will be a few new A-listers that result simply from Twitter or microblogging. However, these will be few and far between.

So, what about the rest of us? If we have 1,500 followers, are any of them really listening? I'd argue that most are not. However, it's still a huge marketing tool, and the nobodies are now the new somebodies for the following reasons.

Twitter and other means of microblogging are free. If a local plumber has 1,500 followers, even if most of them aren't likely to be listening at any given moment, as long as at least one person is, that's all that matters. If that one person has a plumbing issue, the plumber now has a shot at new business, especially if the plumber acquired these followers simply by limiting his Twitter search query to people within a 25-mile radius. For that plumber, that one listener goes from a nobody to a somebody in a hurry. Twitter has enabled geolocation tools so that if a user has it enabled, you are able to see where that tweet came from — this is a huge help for local businesses.

Some salient uses of Twitter:

- Businesses following what is being said about them or their industry — Zappos, JetBlue, Best Buy, Comcast, and so on.
- Celebrity updates — Lance Armstrong tweets about his collarbone. Ellen DeGeneres (@TheEllenShow) has over 11 million followers, and she and her staff often update behind-the-scenes pictures with her guests or she discusses personal issues.
- Real-time updates of news events, especially natural disasters.
- Niche topics, like #MSU, #Kansas, or #Duke basketball during March Madness.
- Tweets for causes, charities, organizations, churches, fundraising, and so on.
- Individuals or companies promoting themselves.
- You name it, you can probably make it happen on Twitter.

Smithsonian Student Travel sent more than 6,000 students to Washington, D.C., for the 2008 presidential inauguration. In the past, it would have been difficult to get major media outlets' attention. However, Twitter made it easy. NPR, MSNBC, and PBS immediately replied to Smithsonian Student Travel's tweets, expressing interest in hearing from middle school students and teachers.

However, two months after that, I typed in #JetBlue, expressing my concern that its in-flight televisions might not work on my particular flight. This was important to me because I selected JetBlue solely for the purpose of watching March Madness on DirectTV. Instead of hearing tweets, I heard crickets chirping. It's cool when companies and even CEOs respond in real time. That was not the case, however, in this particular instance.

In JetBlue's defense, it's somewhat a victim of its own success on Twitter (Morgan Johnston does a fantastic job). People expect the best from JetBlue because it has been one of the pioneers. As a result, more people tweet and follow JetBlue and it's difficult for JetBlue to keep pace. In another instance with JetBlue, there were some massive storms in the Northeast beyond JetBlue's control and its call center was flooded. The average hold time was over an hour. Hence, I turned to Twitter to see what my options were. Unfortunately, they weren't able to respond to these tweets, either, but guess who was: some other people who were in the same situation! My flight was scheduled for Sunday out of the SXSW Conference before it was abruptly canceled. Here are some of the helpful tweets I received:

> @equalman: *Don't bother waiting on hold, the first flight out of Austin Thursday — suggest Houston on Continental*
> @equalman *All flights out Austin and Dallas are booked, you need to buy new ticket via Houston or San Antonio*

While these tweets were not what I wanted to hear, nor did I hear back from JetBlue, they were very helpful. I was able to stop waiting on hold and take appropriate action. There were 15 other tweets like this since so many people were in a similar situation and had already done the vetting process. This helped eliminate redundancy on my part as well as many others' parts. It also helped free up the phone lines and customer service for JetBlue, as there were other fliers like me who hung up once they were informed via other travelers on Twitter.

In another example, I tweeted an interesting article about Travelocity along with #travelocity and indicated that Travelocity was in deep trouble. Here are the responses I received:

@Travelocity: How deep of trouble?

@equalman: Pretty deep as it appears Priceline has the lead and only one or two online travel agents will survive. I love the gnome, so good luck!

@Travelocity: We like Gloria Gaynor;)

It took me a second to get it, but then I was laughing at this witty retort. Gloria Gaynor's famous disco song is "I Will Survive."

As more people join Twitter, this type of one-to-one relationship will be difficult to maintain. Many celebrities like Britney Spears and Kanye West have so-called ghost tweeters.

In the future, instead of getting a witty and salient reply from a CEO or well-informed employee, you'll most likely get an uninspired reply from a call center (tweet center?) in New Delhi—if you're lucky enough to get a response at all. Remember, I received no response to my #JetBlue tweet, whereas I was surprised and delighted by the Travelocity response. Again, to be fair to JetBlue, it is a shining example of a company that is taking social media head-on, and it is being rewarded. It's not a fluke that JetBue has over 1.7 million followers on Twitter whereas its much larger competitors have less than 350,000 followers.

Companies should use Twitter, because the upside is still greater than the downside and it's similar to building a robust prospect and user database that you can message when appropriate. Twitter is becoming a modern-day database.

TV Repeats Mistakes of the Music Industry

During the heyday of Napster, the music industry filed lawsuit after lawsuit about these new file-sharing technologies. While copyrights are important, energy and efforts should have been placed elsewhere. Instead of actions that disenfranchised their customer base (some of the largest numbers of downloaders and sharers were made up of music fanatics), the music industry should have been rejoicing that its distribution, production, and packaging expenses were becoming almost nonexistent!

Music labels could sell direct to customers without the need to pay for packaging, shipping, compact discs, and so on. Some would argue that they didn't embrace the model because of copyright infringement, but the real reason they didn't embrace the model was that they didn't understand it.

By the time they understood the implications of such a runaway hit, it was too late. Apple deftly took a stranglehold of the industry with iTunes. Ironically, the music producers had been giving away free promotional records since the 1950s to radio stations. The music houses understood back then that the more their records got played, the more their sales would increase. Also, think about jukeboxes, a very similar concept. Somehow the music labels lost sight of this construct in the digital era. Television executives could also make the same errors as the record labels and find themselves similarly standing on the outside looking in. Let's take a quick look at some developments.

NBC Earns Fool's Gold in the Olympics

The 2008 Beijing Summer Olympics were the most watched games in Olympic history. The opening ceremony was the biggest television event next to the Super Bowl, reaching 34.2 million American viewers, according to Nielsen Ratings.[4] Michael Phelps's historic swimming captured the nation. The recognition and use of online tools and video by NBC is commendable for that time.

So, did NBC deserve a gold medal for its coverage? On the surface, using old measures, the network reached the podium, but it was awarded only fool's gold. Here's why.

There's This Thing Called the Internet

For one of Phelps's gold medals, NBC showed the action live in every time zone except on the West Coast, which was delayed three hours. Is NBC not aware of a thing called the Internet? NBC failed to do what others had learned long ago: beg, borrow, and make better is the way of digital media.

Too many companies—in this instance, NBC—believe their problems are unique when it comes to the web. However, plenty of other companies have already wrestled with similar issues.

Back in June of the same year, ABC made the right decision by streaming live on the web the Tiger Woods and Rocco Mediate 18-hole playoff to decide the U.S. golf championship. This was in addition to ABC's television coverage. Company web servers cringed, and the country's productivity declined in March Madness–like fashion on that Monday, June 16, but ABC and the Professional Golfers' Association (PGA) were the big winners because they captivated millions of viewers on the web who otherwise would have been lost.

The beauty is that ABC learned from its serendipitous situation in 2008 and leveraged social media fully in the following year (2009). Not only did the network stream live action of the event online, but it also allowed seamless and easy commenting via Twitter, Facebook, and MySpace.

Why didn't NBC do the same thing with its Olympics coverage? Most likely because . . .

Old Metrics Are Deceiving

They were fooling themselves with old metrics. Sure, NBC was happy to show less popular events online, but not precious events like swimming and gymnastics.

Why? Most likely, NBC and its advertisers (Adidas, Samsung, Volkswagen, McDonald's, Coca-Cola, etc.) were judging themselves using old metrics, and that earned them nothing but fool's gold. They were judging success on some archaic Nielsen television rating system. They had the irrational fear that online viewership would cannibalize their normal ratings. However, eyeballs are eyeballs. They would have been better served opening up their online viewership because:

- It's more measurable.
- It has a younger audience.
- Users can't TiVo through commercials.
- Users are willing to give you valuable demographic information like name, age, and gender in return for live online video.
- It increases — not decreases — your total viewership, which means more eyes on advertisements.

Don't Lie to Your Audience

NBC treated viewers with little regard, indicating that swimmer Dara Torres would be up in 14 minutes; 35 minutes later she finally swam her race. Worse, one night NBC indicated Phelps would be on in 32 minutes, and then when the time came, it was four minutes about his eating habits — he wasn't even swimming! Not to mention the whole debacle of computer-generated enhancement of the opening ceremony. As a quick refresher, the network used animation on top of what was occurring at the actual ceremony so the viewer at home had an "enhanced" version of what was actually occurring live.

Dead Air Equals Missed Opportunity

The network got it right showing basketball in the early-morning hours (8 and 10 A.M. EST) online; however, it missed two golden opportunities.

First, there was no option to hear announcers.

Second, and much worse for advertisers, there weren't any advertisements during downtime. So, during basketball timeouts, there was just a wide shot of the court for awkward three-minute intervals. Why didn't the network use this opportunity to give advertisers free placement during this dead air or even have additional web-only advertisers? The technology to pull this off has been around for almost a decade — remember how Mark Cuban became a billionaire when Yahoo! purchased his Broadcast.com?

Worse, for the 2010 Winter Olympic Games in Vancouver, NBC didn't learn from its mistakes. Instead, it took a giant step backward, at least in the United States. In the United States, in order to watch anything online, you needed to prove that you were a paying subscriber of some form of cable, satellite TV, or the like. In countries like Canada, you could watch any event live online. The Canadians are smart; they realize that eyeballs are eyeballs and that an advertising model always works better for the paying client when more people can potentially *see* the advertisements.

For people who are traveling abroad or people at work, sometimes the only way they can watch a particular show or an event is via the Internet. Denying potential viewership doesn't make much long-term business sense.

If a tidal wave is coming, it's better to start swimming with the current. Many people today no longer have landline phones in their homes; this medium has been replaced by the mobile phone. Likewise, more and more households are getting rid of their expensive cable or satellite television subscription fees and relying on web content for their entertainment.

Google Fail

It's potentially understandable that an old-school company like NBC may get some things wrong, but Google didn't exactly turn in a world record Olympics performance either.

When lesser-known athletes burst on the scene, the search engine had a difficult time serving up relevant search results. When the United States' David Neville dove for the finish line in a gallant effort to capture the bronze in the 400-meter race, the search results on Google showed an actor/model by the same name, along with a company that could help you find people's phone numbers.

These poor search results were consistent for many of the athletes, so much so that Yahoo! and MSN attempted to manipulate the results by hand. Google finally threw in the towel and manually pushed news feeds and Wikipedia results to the top of the listings for many of the athletes. More and more people started going straight to Wikipedia; Jamaican runner Usain Bolt's page was updated within seconds of him breaking the record in the 200 meters.

Also, the last-minute nature of the YouTube/NBC deal was laughable. They signed the deal only days before the 2008 Olympics started. This should have been done weeks before; it's not like YouTube was new. It was the established player in the online video market. Since Google owns YouTube, Google and NBC should have placed a sponsored listing within the Google search results for "watch Olympics on YouTube" explaining how the deal didn't cover the United States but was only for those people living outside of the United States. There were many frustrated Americans who thought they could watch Michael Phelps on YouTube and discovered only after several minutes of frustration that this option was available just in selected countries.

That being said, NBC did show some improvements since 2004 (for instance, the Microsoft Silverlight picture quality online was a big advancement in the right direction). However, the network didn't deserve a gold medal for its incorporation of online tools. NBC failed to leverage best practices in regard to combining offline and online content. A bronze medal, or perhaps even a silver medal, was in order. NBC made major strides in 2012, but they still didn't supply enough live access to major events.

TV Shows Viewed through the Internet

It's inevitable that all of our broadcasts will eventually be pushed through the Internet and a majority will be viewed on tablets and iPads. Brand budgets that historically went to television, magazine ads, and outdoor boards are moving to digital channels for three main reasons: (1) the audience has moved there, (2) it's more cost effective, and (3) it's easier to track. What will happen?

In the short term, there will be companies that are able to take advantage of this transition. Just as online travel agent sites like Priceline, Orbitz, Expedia, and Travelocity were able to take advantage of suppliers (hotels, airlines, cruise lines, rental cars) and make a slow progression to web bookings, aggressive conduit companies will be able to deliver what the audience wants. The same holds true for Napster, Limewire, and iTunes jumping on the opportunity made available by the ineptness of the music industry to embrace digital music.

At the beginning of 2008, Jeff Zucker, the boss of NBC Universal, told an audience of TV executives that their biggest challenge was to ensure "that we do not end up trading analog dollars for digital pennies."[5] Zucker understood that the audience was moving online faster than advertisers were, thus leaving media companies in a position of possibly losing advertising revenue and having their inventory devalued if and when they moved online with their television content. In the fourth quarter of 2008, online advertisements in video grew 10.6 percent and went from 2 percent of advertising to 3 percent.[6]

A good example of the use of this medium was also presented during the 2008 presidential election. Candidates don't care about distribution rights or upsetting their offline sponsors. They care only about getting the word out and making it as easy as possible for their users (in this case, potential voters) to access and consume the information. Through their respective websites, each party streamed high-definition convention coverage around the clock. This forced CNN, MSNBC, Fox News, and the like to do the same. The major networks didn't have time to decide if they would allow the public access — they were losing their audience to these other (new) distribution channels. This type of intense competition from unexpected places is a harbinger of the future. Who could have ever guessed that our political parties would be more advanced in terms of online video than our television networks?

The way in which we view broadcasts is also changing. In the political convention example, you had the ability to select various cameras to choose how you wanted to view the process. Specifically, for the Democratic National Convention, you could have selected: (1) national broadcast angle, (2) side camera, (3) backstage, (4) camera focused on Barack Obama, (5) camera focused on Joe Biden, or (6) camera focused on Michelle Obama.

This ties back to braggadocian and preventive behaviors from Chapters Two and Three. For example, if you are Michelle Obama and you are being filmed throughout the entire convention, it's imperative you make certain that you aren't chatting away with your mom during the Speaker of the House's presentation. The upside for the viewer is that it allows for a more intimate relationship with the candidates and their families because viewers can see what they are like off camera.

NBC's *Sunday Night Football* was one of the first to introduce the idea of these various camera angles. They smartly viewed it as a way to capture online viewers, but also as a way to capture their regular television viewers who had laptops open for an enhanced viewing experience. NBC allowed the users to select various angles on the field as well as select cameras that were following star players (like Tom Brady or Peyton Manning). The irony is that whereas NBC didn't excel for the Olympics, the network was extremely progressive when it came to its NFL coverage online.

Applying this concept to content-focused shows like ABC's *The View* could prove to be a further success. Marketers would serve up different product offerings to someone who was viewing via the camera and was fixated on Elisabeth Hasselbeck, versus the viewer who was focused on Whoopi Goldberg.

Adjust Shows Based on Fast-Forward Behavior

Real-time big data helps dictate content: With devices like TiVo and other digital video recorders (DVRs) in the offline world and YouTube analytics, producers of content are able to get real-time feedback about the content of their shows. If ESPN captures the TiVo/DVR information from its *SportsCenter* telecasts and sees that fast-forward or skip rates increase 35 percent during hockey segments, it would behoove the network to possibly cut this segment down or eliminate it altogether. It can make these adjustments in real time.

One entity rose quickly based on its ability to recognize the consumer's demand for online video of traditional programs and movies. The Hulu site at www.hulu.com formally moved from private beta to product launch in March 2008. Analysts, reporters, and bloggers panned the effort as Johnny-come-lately because there were several similar options in the marketplace (e.g., Veoh, Joost) and gave Hulu a limited chance at success because it would be weighed down with its commercially supported advertising model.

By September 2008, Hulu was the sixth most watched video-content provider on the web, with NielsenOnline reporting 142 million streams and 6.3 million unique monthly visitors.[7] Hulu was able to surpass such television giants as Disney, MTV, ESPN, and CNN. Much of its success can be attributed to identifying the need for high-production-quality television shows and movies aggregated in one place on the Internet. Hulu was so successful that in October 2008 YouTube announced that it would start offering more full-length content and original production. In July 2010 YouTube increased the upload capability for users to 15 minutes, equivalent to half a sitcom.

An important part of Hulu's original success was a direct result of its understanding of Socialnomics. Hulu understood that the 8 minutes of advertising generally included in a 30-minute sitcom would not be optimal for the user or for the advertiser. So, Hulu went out of its way to ensure that its 30-minute programs averaged only 2 minutes' worth of commercials. How can 2 minutes' worth be better than 8 minutes' worth of commercials for the advertiser? It was worth more because the recall was much higher.

"The notion that less is more is absolutely playing out on Hulu," Jason Kilar, the chief executive of the site, said. "This is benefiting advertisers as much as it is benefiting users."[8]

According to the Insight Express survey, advertisers saw a 22 percent increase in ad recall and a 28 percent increase in intent to purchase. This caused Hulu's advertising base to grow from 10 to 110, and clients ranged from McDonald's to BlackBerry.[9] "I've been waiting for this for 10 years," said Greg Smith, the chief operating officer of Neo@Ogilvy, an interactive agency of the Ogilvy Group.[10]

In some instances, Hulu users have the ability to select the format in which they receive the advertising. They elect to receive it all in one big chunk — usually movie trailers — or have it spread out in the typical format. The typical format for a 30-minute TV spot starts with a 30-second up-front "brought to you by," a 30-second commercial at the midway point, and then a closing commercial. Another social piece that was pure genius was that Hulu would indicate how long the commercial would be. Users don't have the ability to fast-forward through commercials, but if they know it's only a 30-second commercial break, what are the odds of them getting up from where they are watching? Not likely. The user likes this sense of control, and it echoes avid Internet video fan Mary Alison Wilshire:

> I was watching Mike and Mike on television at the gym, and they went to commercial break for six minutes, then came back and said they would be right back. Well, that was another eight minutes later. A 14-minute commercial break! Also, it's maddening not knowing how long the break will be. At home, I TiVo through all the commercials, but when I watch online, I don't mind the commercials on Hulu because they are so short and they tell me when the show will be back

on. In fact, my husband and I play a game trying to guess who will be the sponsor of The Daily Show.[11]

Jason Kilar of Hulu couldn't agree more: "We think that a modest amount of advertising is the right thing because that's going to drive atypical results for marketers."[12] A survey conducted by ABC also supported this notion — finding that running only one advertisement during a 30-minute program generated an astounding 54 percent recall rate.[13]

The format was well conceived for the user and for the advertiser. Users are appreciative that sponsors are helping to provide them with *free* television in these types of new formats. In a survey conducted by Hulu and Insight Express, 80 percent of the viewers rated their experiences on www.hulu.com as good to excellent.[14] Users are less tolerant of commercials on cable and satellite services because they are already paying over $100 for the service. On sites like Hulu, in contrast, users are most appreciative of the sponsor, because when they hear that the program was brought to them by McDonald's, they know they owe McDonald's some gratitude for making it available online for free. This same message sounds hollow to the viewer via traditional broadcast television.

This is the same concept that television embraced back in the 1950s. However, over time networks kept putting the advertiser ahead of the real client — the viewer. This marginalized the viewer experience, which in turn impaired the advertiser and eventually the broadcaster. Alarm bells should ring when the technology product winner of the year (TiVo) is a direct attempt to circumvent your service offering. Instead of fighting legal battles to stop such technology, advertisers should take the Socialnomic approach of understanding that something in the chain is broken and must be addressed.

Contrast this with a site like Hulu, where 93 percent of respondents to the Insight Express survey (18,000 surveyed) said they felt they were receiving the right amount of advertising for the free content they were enjoying. A large percentage of the sample even expressed that there could be more advertising. An estimated 14.3 million viewed the first Tina Fey "Palin" skit on Hulu, whereas only 10.2 million viewed the September 13, 2008, episode on television. Of course, Hulu's numbers usually benefited from users viewing it more than once. The September 27, 2008, skit attracted 10.1 million views on Hulu and 7.9 million views on television.[15]

Due to the popularity, Hulu actually needed more advertising, not to compensate for lost revenue but to enhance the user experience. Similar to CNET's *Buzz Out Loud* podcast example with Best Buy, it's important for the advertising to stay as fresh as the content. You can't serve up the same ad to the same viewer 20 times. The beauty of it being pumped through the Internet is that sites and broadcasters have insight into how many times a viewer saw an ad, while historically this has been something of a guessing game at best for the television ad community.

The executives of Hulu understood that sites like theirs are just as social as a Wikipedia, Pinterest, or Facebook. That is why they have allowed users to give commercials thumbs-up or thumbs-down ratings.

Hulu's initial success is probably not sustainable, and indications started in mid-2010 that content providers were losing favor and wanted to take back control of their content. However, Hulu and other sites similar to it contribute to moving us toward a more Socialnomic way of viewing our favorite video content from anywhere. So even though Hulu may just be a footnote in history, it's analogous to Napster and Apple pushing the music industry and Priceline, Orbitz, and Expedia doing the same in the travel industry. Disruptive technology may not be sustainable in the short term, but it pushes everyone in the proper direction for the long term. Do you own a landline? When was the last time you purchased a full music album? The television industry is on its way to massive change, and the customer will benefit.

Hulu's success may have been short-lived; but, at a minimum, it understood the customer needs of its space and forced the industry to move in a new direction. As Kevin McGurn, Hulu's Vice President of National Sales, pointed out at an OMMA panel discussion:

> Hulu starts mostly with professionally produced content that already has an audience. But for other content, we use what our editors think is cool, and also what is popular on the site. They aren't always the same. We want to make video as viral as possible. If you think your friends would like a video, we want you to be able to share it. Things on the Web don't have to be an instant success. In fact, they generally aren't, unless they were popular somewhere else first.[16]

Until television moves completely to an à la carte menu served up with the Internet, there will be different variations of workarounds. One such product is Slingbox. Slingbox allows users to access their home-cable-fed programming from anywhere in the world. The device allows travelers to set up a small box in their hotel rooms (or anywhere outside their homes) to be able to watch their regular programs and DVRs from what is being delivered to their homes. This is very convenient for the international traveler who doesn't want to watch a Spanish *novela* or a French cooking show when traveling abroad.

Another item to consider in understanding why TV will quickly move to the cloud is our desire for social interaction. If you are watching a particular game, you will be able to easily inform your social network and invite other fans to join you. You will then have the ability to comment and chat in real time, thereby allowing you to be connected to the tailgate in Columbus, Ohio, even though you are sitting in San Diego, California. Currently, many do this via Twitter. In this instance they may set up a #OSU hashtag on Twitter and people can comment as they watch the game with other Ohio State fans, or, in some instances, trash talk (or is it trash text or trash tweet?) with opposing team fans.

The end winner here will be the consumer because these innovative tools and companies, no matter whether they last, will bring new ideas to the table and change the way that we as consumers have been trained to accept broadcast media.

We started to see a glimpse of the future of TV in April 2009 during CBS's broadcast of the Masters golf tournament. There was online streaming of the event in high definition. It was full coverage for the first two days and then for the last two days you had your choice of four holes to watch. You also had the choice to follow only the lead group. Again, it wasn't quite all the way there, because why wouldn't you show the entire thing? It's all about distributing your product. The more people see your product, the more people see your client's advertising. As technology becomes cheaper and cheaper, it's conceivable that you could follow only the player in whom you are interested. This could have dramatic effects on the ratings. Today, if the player you like is in 15th place, unless his name is Tiger Woods, he most likely will get zero airtime. However, if you are given the choice to follow any player you like, then it truly changes the game.

In many instances, when people are at work the only option they have for watching an event is via the Internet. Also, more and more people are choosing to forgo an expensive monthly cable bill and make do with simply their Internet connection. This should sound oddly reminiscent of a trend that happened about 10 years ago—people started to not have a landline in their house or apartment; rather, they got by with their mobile phone. The same could happen in the television industry.

Most likely we can anticipate some intense legal battles in various governments, because the foreseen problem is that many of the suppliers of cable television are also the suppliers of the Internet connection! If Time Warner, China Telecom, Deutsche Telekom, and Xfinity start to see more and more people cut their $150 monthly cable television bills, they could react by increasing the fee for the Internet connection or set up pricing models to charge per stream — they have attempted this before in some markets. The consumer can only hope that competitors and alternatives for high-speed Internet emerge or that policies are put in place to obstruct cable companies from implementing such policies. This is part of what the net neutrality discussions are all about.

Circling back to the 2009 Masters: On the final two days, CBS showed only four holes. In the near future we will be in a much better place. I would predict that not only will there be full coverage over the Internet, but viewers will be able to select which hole, or which player, they would like to watch. Also, instead of paying for a bundle of channels, if we watch only ESPN, then we would pay $4.99 per month for ESPN (à la carte). ESPN is already testing much of its content online via ESPN3. The power will be in the user's hands, which is where it should be.

Scrabulous — A Fabulous Example

A great example of a situation that companies want to try to avoid involves Hasbro and two entrepreneurs from India. Quickly identifying the potential of the Facebook application platform, two young programmers in India, Rajat and Jayant Agarwalla, thought there might be interest from people playing Scrabble against each other across the globe. They couldn't find an acceptable version of Scrabble to play online, so they decided to create their own. They named it "Scrabulous" as a direct reflection of the game (Scrabble) that they were adapting. Scrabulous co-creator Jayant Agarwalla indicated he sent a letter to Hasbro asking for permission to use the trademarked Scrabble template. He never heard back, and took that as permission to go ahead with his program.

There was more than enough interest, with over 500,000 daily users at its peak. The application became one of the top 10 most used applications on Facebook,[17] and during an interview on CBS's *60 Minutes*, Facebook founder Mark Zuckerberg even mentioned that he enjoyed playing against his grandparents. Speaking of grandparents, it was estimated that 40 percent of the players were over 50 years old, which proves what we've been saying throughout this book — social media is for everyone. Who knew that such an old game would be so enormously popular in this digital age?

When the Agarwalla brothers eventually heard back from Hasbro, they were issued a cease-and-desist letter and a lawsuit was filed against them for copyright violation. At first glance, you could argue that Hasbro/Mattel took the logical route in protecting what they rightfully own by suing Scrabulous for copyright infringement. However, it is apparent that they may have missed the bigger picture and, better yet, the opportunity to capitalize on the existing user base who likely associated Scrabulous with the makers of Scrabble anyway. We can't help but wonder if the legal costs and negative publicity have simply washed away the potential profits that Scrabulous was *freely* providing Hasbro/Mattel. So it would seem that rather than suing the online game's creators, Hasbro could have formed a partnership with them or bought them out.

"But in today's fast-changing social networking environment, Hasbro's lawsuit and its attempt to control its online image may not be the right move," said Peter Fader, co-director of the Wharton Interactive Media Initiative. He believes Hasbro's action was an "incredibly bad business decision." There is no evidence that the Agarwalla brothers were doing "something absolutely disparaging" to the Scrabble brand. In fact, Scrabulous "has been such a fabulously good thing for the Scrabble franchise [that] Hasbro should have been celebrating."[18]

"It is not clear if Hasbro did the right thing by going after Scrabulous," chimed in Kevin Werbach, Wharton professor of legal studies and business ethics. "Many copyright owners today are over-inclusive as they try to assert their rights. The question for Hasbro is whether the benefit they get in terms of direct and indirect revenue from their own Scrabble game exceeds the cost of negative publicity from this action. But it certainly got them a black eye in the online community, although most people who play Scrabble have no idea this has happened."[19]

In the dismantling process, on the morning of July 29, 2008, users were abruptly denied access to the Scrabulous application on Facebook. If positioned correctly, Hasbro could have capitalized and made a strategic move with an introduction of its own Online Scrabble. Had Hasbro been ready to launch its internal electronic Scrabble application, the transition would have been almost seamless to the user, and Hasbro would have continued to profit from the free Scrabulous publicity. Instead, users found that the Hasbro Scrabble application was jammed with glitches and extremely slow to load, and the variety of word selection (the basis of Scrabble) was poor compared to any *Webster's* dictionary.

You could argue that those who really lost out from this ugly episode are both the end users, who were left a little in limbo during the transition, and Hasbro, which had some upset fans as a result of the transition:

> *You didn't have the smarts or initiative to come up with as good a product as the boys did, so your alternative is to mess with the superior product? Do you think that the thousands of folks who were enjoying this superior application will now come running to your inferior product?*[20]

The numbers also took an immediate hit. At the launch of Hasbro's official version of Online Scrabble, the game attracted fewer than 2,000 daily Facebook users compared to the more than half a million players a day worldwide on Scrabulous. Another issue with the new application was that there were various groups holding the rights from country to country. So, for the main Scrabble game, it was no longer a global game, but only for U.S. and Canadian citizens. Mattel owned the rights to many of the other countries. What a great benefit for society: millions of people connecting with others across the globe to play an educational game like Scrabble. The Agarwalla brothers may well have been on their way to a Nobel Peace Prize (admittedly a stretch) before Hasbro spoiled the fun. To be fair, the Agarwalla brothers were pocketing an estimated $25,000 a month from Scrabulous.[21]

According to Wharton's Peter Fader, many companies sue "just because they think they have the right to, instead of pursuing what's in their shareholders' best interests." It is "irrelevant if Hasbro was right or not" in its copyright claims against the backdrop of how Scrabble benefited from Scrabulous, he says. "The downside they have created for themselves and others is a lack of an upside."[22]

Companies "need to move aside from knee-jerk tendencies to bring in legal action," he adds, noting that Hasbro had other options besides suing. "It would have been smart to pay [the Agarwalla brothers] millions of dollars. That would have been minuscule compared to legal fees and their own application development expenses.... Hasbro may have won the battle but it has surely lost the war."[23]

If there is a lesson to be learned from all this, it would be that it is best to weigh your options (like TripAdvisor did with Cities

I've Visited) before jumping in to claim what is rightfully yours. Take advantage of others who have already done the legwork to help you position your brand throughout the social media space. Think strategically before exposing your brand. Hasbro failed to anticipate the speed at which users would react to the abolition of Scrabulous and the introduction of Online Scrabble. It could have favorably capitalized on the work done by the Agarwalla brothers, but instead chose to fight the battle uphill. Behind the scenes it may have tried this, and, to be fair to Hasbro, perhaps the path it chose was the only viable one legally. Whatever the case, all of this translated into the Scrabble name being dragged into unflattering associations: lawsuit, popular application banned, and so forth.

However, Hasbro and Scrabble did eventually make their way through the situation, and kudos to them—Scrabble on Facebook today has over 900,000 monthly users. A question that we may never know the answer to is: could this whole ugly situation have been avoided? Also, it allowed social game maker Zynga to come out with a much more popular Scrabble-type game called Words with Friends. Words with Friends dominated the mobile gaming market for a few years, and it was merely a simpler version of Scrabble. Words with Friends was bumped from its number one spot by OMGPOP's Draw Something. In turn, Zynga purchased OMGPOP for $180 million.

Advertising within Social Networks Is Actually Effective

Because social media lends itself to unobtrusive advertising, that advertising is effective. In a 2008 survey done by Razorfish—"The Razorfish Consumer Experience Report"—76 percent of the 1,006 people surveyed said they didn't mind seeing ads when they logged in to Facebook, MySpace, or other social media sites. Razorfish also found that 40 percent of the respondents said they made purchases after seeing those ads.[24]

Intuitively this makes sense because social media can accomplish things that we weren't necessarily able to do in the past. For example, when my friend changed her status from "in a relationship" to "engaged," she started getting ads for wedding photographers, DJs, and so on. This was information that she didn't necessarily view as advertising, but rather part of the experience—and a helpful part at that.

Smart companies like TripAdvisor understand this technique and approach the market from an outside-looking-in viewpoint rather than from the old inside-looking-out paradigm. Acme Travels was using inside-looking-out thinking and old metrics. Acme incorrectly approached the opportunity of Facebook from the perspective of "How can we grow our database so that we can mail potential customers brochures and send them e-mail?"

The question that companies should ask first is: "What do we have to offer that is unique and valuable to our customers and potential customer base?" Also, engaging in role-playing in which you put yourself in the shoes of your users is always extremely beneficial. As a user, would I take the extra step of giving you my personal information? Only if what the company is offering is valuable enough to me that I choose to share my personal information.

Users generally want to be communicated with through the medium in which you met to begin with. In this example, TripAdvisor knows that they will be communicating through the user's Facebook inbox or Facebook news feed, not via traditional e-mail or brochures. At some point during the relationship, if the user wants to sign up for an e-mail distribution, then TripAdvisor will be more than happy to accommodate them.

A few months after the travel application battle, Acme Travels was discussing a different Facebook tactic, establishing a fan page. A fan page is usually for your company or product home page within Facebook. Facebook users can select a simple "+" symbol, and they are added as fans so they can receive updates in their news feeds for anything going on with that product or service. There was a heated debate about what adjustments should be made to the fan page prior to a large e-mail drop that was going to deploy later that week.

For several weeks, Acme showcased two products on its fan page. The various product managers were arguing about which product should be placed higher on the page and how many outbound links they should have driving to lead forms. This is a classic example of a traditional marketing pitfall: people arguing for months over the color of a car to be featured in an upcoming commercial, or disputing if a URL should be printed as www.company.com or http://www.company.com in the next edition of a magazine ad. Sound familiar? This type of behavior is not strategic and wastes energy because the decisions are not being driven by consumers of the product or service.

Fortunately for Acme, the marketing director sat patiently while the quarreling continued and finally intervened with the following:

We already know what needs to go on top. Italy Vacation Packages has always been on the bottom, which is harder to see and historically this position gets fewer clicks. However, what we have seen is that Italy Vacation Packages has outperformed France Vacation Packages. Our data shows that more people have clicked on Italy Vacation Packages and there are 90 percent more comments and pictures posted about these packages versus the France Vacation Packages. This results in Italy Vacation Packages generating $11.5 million in revenues above France Vacation Packages.

It's not for us to decide; the users have already decided for us. Italy should go to the top of the fan page. Also, we will not have any outbound links to our lead-capture forms on this main page. We don't want to make the same mistake again that we made with the application.

The meeting room went silent when this was expressed. The meeting was over shortly thereafter. In the past, employees alluded to the fact that often meetings had gone on for hours and resulted in a poor decision or even a compromise. With the advent of social media and proper analysis of data, these types of internal discussions and disagreements become fewer and fewer. Business decisions become more about letting the user decide what's important. As discussed at the beginning of this section, this is commonly referred to as outside-looking-in thinking versus the traditional inside-looking-out thinking, and it is becoming necessary with regard to social media.

Content and Conversation Will Drive Awareness — Not Advertising

More and more companies will be developing content in the form of webisodes (five-minute episodes that could be a series), applications, and widgets. Money historically spent on media will be spent to develop and promote this varying content.

Sometimes, this content will be developed from the ground up by the companies themselves—think soap operas on steroids. A good example of this is EF Educational Tours 2009 web series "Life on Tour." It's a story of six students who go on a tour abroad. It's produced by Bunim/Murray Productions, best known for their

MTV "Real World" series. There is no overt marketing placement in the show itself except at the end with a small EF logo. While on the tour abroad, teenagers can chat with the cast members on their Facebook page.

Advertising will be less about social media *campaigns* and more about an ongoing *conversation*.

Other times, the idea or content will already have been produced, and companies will join forces, often with individuals who may go from being a nobody to a somebody overnight because of the power of the social graph.

Don't Put All Your Eggs in One Basket

How do companies know what the next great thing is? How do they avoid missing out on a great opportunity without overexposing themselves? Some argue that given the speed of technology, companies should try everything; they should throw a bunch of small tests out against the proverbial wall and see what sticks. If budgets and resources were not at the forefront of profitability, this would make sense. But with the importance of watching every dollar and companies trying to increase their returns on investments, a more strategic approach should be taken. For example, if your company is about to plunge into social media, it's best to understand fundamentals as they relate to:

- **What** you are doing.
- **Where** you are doing it.
- **Why** you are doing it.
- What **success** looks like.
- What potential **pitfalls** you may encounter.

The best way to look at these five pillars is through an example: summer band camp.

What

Betsy knew that there was a need for a community centered around the summer band camps so that the kids could interact, and Betsy decided that they needed two things in the short term: (1) a group or fan page to attract the kids and (2) a tool or application that would allow the kids to easily connect and interact. The first few months would be a beta release. This was a smart idea that took minimal time to set up. Companies sometimes fall into the trap of trying to make everything perfect before releasing it into the wild.

This harks back to old Procter & Gamble schooling—a model that doesn't work well in social media space because it moves too slowly; the world would pass you by before you got anything out the door (hence one reason why Procter & Gamble reduced its marketing staff by 1,600). If the initial setup costs make sense, it's better to get an idea out the door and run the risk of it failing than not doing anything at all.

The old paradigm of spending 14 months to produce a 30-second television commercial is counterproductive. Customers appreciate the speed at which you deliver innovative products to market and are forgiving with beta sites. Users will go out of their way to help you accelerate the release from beta to full release if they feel the product or service is worthy of the investment (in this case the investment being users' time to provide feedback and insight). Moreover, if users aren't helping you with the beta, you should be appreciative of this silent feedback and understand that they are signaling to you that there is probably not a need for your idea in the marketplace. As a company, not only do you profit from releasing those ideas that your consumers have beta tested, but you also avoid costly up-front fees and development time on ideas that generate a negative return.

This summer band camp project could have easily swelled into a six-month project by having the application pull information from a database to determine where the campers would be assigned at the start of the year. Instead, Betsy's Socialnomic idea pulled the information from the campers themselves to determine where they should be assigned. The campers input data, and the application showed who was in each location based on the input rather than having it pulled from a database. This is an important part of Socialnomics—*companies don't have to do everything*—users/customers are willing to help connect the dots!

Where

Betsy wasn't going to have her campers come to her; rather, she would go to them. She did some quick research on where most of her campers spent their time. Because they were in mostly rural areas and younger (14 to 16 years old), they used several social media tools, but seemed to spend a majority of their time on Facebook, with some campers using MySpace. She didn't know if they would be interested in a community, but figured that her greatest chance for success would be on Facebook. If successful, she would then roll the idea out to other social media sites. She avoided a mistake that many companies fall into: trying to build every possible iteration from the get-go. Betsy believed that an approach of this nature would get her nowhere. She wasn't about to "boil the ocean"; rather, she was going to "eat the elephant one bite at a time."

Why

The reasons for taking this project on were to: (1) keep the kids excited and engaged leading up to camp, (2) have them develop new relationships prior to the camp in an effort to reduce cancellation rates, (3) gain some potential viral exposure by having campers tell their friends about the idea, (4) establish a continued conversation with the campers to gain valuable real-time feedback, and (5) allow past campers the ability to stay connected and provide advice to first-time campers.

Success

So many times companies fail to ask themselves, *"What does success look like?"* It's important for companies to show a united front when it comes to their definition of success; otherwise, the team responsible for implementation may be striving for something that is different from what the executives deem important. In this example, success was going to be measured by (1) how many people joined the group and (2) whether those who added the "meet other campers" application had a lower cancellation rate than those campers who didn't interact with the group beforehand or even download the application.

Notice that success wasn't judged by how many of the campers continued their interactions or comments/postings within the application. Betsy figured that a lot of the kids would meet via the application but would then extend their relationship to other places (e-mail, phone, text, social media mail, etc.). She saw it as analogous to introducing people at a house party and expecting that every time these people interacted it had to be at the same house where the original party was hosted. So many companies want to make sure their customers always return to their Facebook fan page for interactions with each other, but as the preceding sentence points out, that doesn't necessarily make sense. This may be where they met, but it doesn't mean it has to be where they will continue the relationship.

By aggregating all of these campers into one area, Betsy believed she had to watch for two key elements: (1) the competition would find it easier to pick off their high schools, and (2) potential pedophiles might descend on this collection of high school campers. The camp programmers made sure to put in the necessary safeguards to help thwart such activity without strangling growth from legitimate campers.

Pitfalls

Companies that believe in Socialnomics must understand and be willing to unleash control of their brands. Companies that wish to produce a 100 percent fail-safe program in terms of brand and user security are doomed to paralysis. These companies will forever remain in a development phase and miss the opportunity for execution. Companies must exercise social responsibility, and users must also engage in best-practice behavior to ensure user security. Companies should leverage existing platforms such as Pinterest, YouTube, Vimeo, Weibo, Vkontakte, LinkedIn, Facebook, Twitter, and so on, which have already vetted some of the security and privacy gaps. This also shifts any potential liability to reside with the platform, not the advertiser.

In a major socioeconomic shift, individuals are taking responsibility for their own cyberactivity. This started with spam e-mails and viruses, where people quickly learned that they probably don't have an uncle in Nigeria who has willed them $1 million. Then came the savvy and complex phisher sites. These are sites and e-mails that look like an established brand such as FedEx, eBay, or Bank of America. However, users learned to look closely at the URLs and misspellings. If the URL wasn't www.fedex.com, but something unusual like 345262.freshexample.com/fedex, then something definitely appeared *phishy*. In these examples, the major brands take painstaking steps to flush these types of scams out of the system, and in large part are reliant on their online community to alert them of such scams. However, the companies aren't responsible or liable for any loss resulting from these scams.

This isn't new to the world. If a burglar was dressed up like a Maytag repairman, Maytag is not held responsible. It is up to the person at the house to question why the Maytag repairman would be there if no repair service was ordered. Neighborhood watch programs are analogous to today's online safeguarding communities.

So when it comes to pitfalls, companies should be aware of them and attempt to mitigate them, but they shouldn't be paralyzed by them or let them throttle good users' abilities to get what they need from the program.

Second Life Equals Idle Life for Coca-Cola

As worldwide head of interactive marketing at Coca-Cola, [Michael] Donnelly was fascinated by its commercial potential, the way its users could wander through a computer-generated 3-D environment that mimics the mundane world of the flesh. So one day last fall, he downloaded the Second Life software, created an avatar, and set off in search of other brands like his own. American Apparel, Reebok, Scion—the big ones were easy to find, yet something felt wrong: "There was nobody else around." He teleported over to the Aloft Hotel, a virtual prototype for a real-world chain being developed by the owners of the W. It was deserted, almost creepy. "I felt like I was in The Shining."[25]

Donnelly and Coke went ahead and invested some serious dollars into hiring a consulting company to help them get up and running on Second Life. But if it didn't feel right, then why would you go ahead and invest in it?

According to Joseph Plummer, chief research officer at the Advertising Research Foundation:

The simple model they all grew up with—the 30-second spot, delivered through the mass reach of television—is no longer working. And there are two types of people out there: a small group that's experimenting thoughtfully, and a large group that's trying the next thing to come through the door.[26]

Another important piece in this Second Life example is to take a step back and truly assess the potential upside. It's easy to have your vision blurred by hype and propaganda. In this Second Life instance, *Wired* magazine points out what the opportunity really was:

Second Life partisans claim meteoric growth, with the number of "residents," or avatars created, surpassing 7 million in June. There's no question that more and more people are trying Second Life, but that figure turns out to be wildly misleading. For starters, many people make more than one avatar. According to Linden Lab, the company behind Second Life, the number of avatars created by distinct individuals was closer to 4 million. Of those, only about 1 million had logged on in the previous 30 days (the standard measure of Internet traffic), and barely a third of that total had bothered to drop by in the previous week. Most of those who did were from Europe or Asia, leaving a little more than 100,000 Americans per week to be targeted by U.S. marketers.[27]

How do companies find the right balance between launching every possible idea through the door and ensuring they are not missing out on a great opportunity? If you have been paying attention, for success as a company in today's world it is critical to:

- *Leverage the success that is out there.* It doesn't necessarily have to be built from within — swallow the pride pill.
- *Leverage your loyal customers.* Understand that they will help you build and adjust in real time.
- *Don't overinvest.* Build light betas that can quickly be tested and adjusted.
- *Take the time to decide where you will be.* Don't try to be everywhere. Once you decide, move quickly and with a purpose.

Worse than making a Second Life mistake is doing nothing. As Irish poet George Bernard Shaw once said, "A life spent making mistakes is not only more honorable, but more useful than a life spent doing nothing." Even so, there are still a large number of companies that have been slow to embrace and benefit from social media or a particular tool.

As a company, you don't necessarily need to be the *first* to move, so don't feel like you've completely missed the boat if your company hasn't done anything to address a particular tool, say Pinterest or Google+. Sometimes it's prudent to sit back and watch, and to learn from some of the more nimble players in the space. In social media, small businesses are sometimes the best to watch and imitate. Many of them have already waded in and learned some valuable lessons from their successes and their mistakes. Spend some time learning, but don't wait too long, as it's often better to have a fast failure and learning than to miss the opportunity.

Search Engine Optimization for Facebook

Imagine if you were a mortgage lender and could go back in time to 1999 and optimize your home page for the query "low finance rate." Would you do it? Of course you would. Well, the same opportunity exists today with social networks. Let's assume that the owner of Cathy's Creative Mugs (a fictitious small business) wants to post a fan page on Facebook, essentially a company promotional flyer. When prompted by the Facebook interface to name her fan page, she begins to type "Cathy's Creative Mugs," but then realizes she can probably leverage search engine optimization (SEO) best practices here. So instead, she names this page "Coffee Mugs," which is a rich keyword for her industry.

This will help Cathy return searches on "coffee mugs" within Facebook, as well as boost her rankings in the traditional search engines like Google, Yahoo!, and MSN.

In many of the social media pieces, the first few years will be a land grab of opportunity. Just like in the search world, if you were a savvy website back in the late 1990s and ranked high for major keywords like "mortgage loans," "cheap travel," "wedding favors," or the like, you made out like a bandit. If you are one of the savvy movers in social media today, you can set yourself up for some hefty revenue streams down the road. A good case in point is for fan pages on Facebook. There is a fan page for chocolate milk that has over 2 million likes! This type of passion should pique the interest of companies like Nestlé, Hershey's, and Ghirardelli.

While as a company you should learn from your competitors and compatriots, you'd better not take too long to do it — you need to launch and learn. Companies that still think they control whether they do social media or not are terribly mistaken. Companies don't have a choice on *whether* they do social media; they have a choice in how *well* they do it. If you're a large brand, you can rest assured that there are conversations, pages, and applications constantly being developed around your brand and by the community at large. The community is doing social media even if you choose not to.

This is very different from e-mail, search, banner ads, television ads, radio ads, outdoor signs, and so forth. In all those instances, companies had a choice regarding whether to engage. If they didn't want to buy paid search ads or a television spot, that choice was up to the company. With social media, they don't have a choice, because consumers and others will do something around your brand without you.

John Deere Mows Over Facebook

Want proof? Let's take a look at product like a lawn mower. If you performed a search within Facebook in August 2008 for "John Deere," you'd see:

- More than 500 groups dedicated to John Deere.
- More than 10,000 users in the top 10 groups.
- All groups were developed by the John Deere community, not John Deere corporate headquarters.
- John Deere's chief competitor, Caterpillar, had a page in the top 10 listings.
- A group called "John Deere Sucks!!!!" is ranked in the top 10.

This is a great example, because:

- Your users will take ownership in your brand and will *do something* in social networks (both positive and negative) even if your company chooses not to.
- This has huge potential — 10,000 users in the first 10 groups alone — kudos to the power of the John Deere brand.
- Your competition and your users can leverage a recognized trademark to their advantage — unless you hired a few new staffers to dedicate their time to cease-and-desist letters.
- Malicious postings ("John Deere Sucks!!!!") can show up high in the rankings if you don't have more favorable listings to push it down to insignificance.

Who has the power now: John Deere or the person who started the "John Deere Sucks!!!!" group? Just like the person who started the chocolate milk page, in this instance the person has the power. After all, what's to stop this individual from posting a nice static image of a special offer for a competitor like Caterpillar on his site? Money talks, and this could be a cheap purchase for Caterpillar to a highly specialized target audience.

John Deere eventually wised up, got off the proverbial sideline, and started a fan page, which in a two-year time frame grew from 65,000 fans to 1,200,000 fans.

Many of these constructs are similar to SEO best practices. The company that puts in the time will see the payoff.

Sheep without a Shepherd

Another reason companies may decide to do nothing? They don't want to aggregate their hard-earned customers in a public forum because they're afraid the competition will come in and cherry-pick them off.

This might be a valid concern, as many companies crawl and scrape the Internet looking for client names of their competitors so they can poach them through various sales methods. If your fans and enemies in the social networks weren't doing anything without you, then maybe it could be a valid strategy to be safe and not aggregate your clients or fans all in one place. But, as evidenced by the John Deere example, they're out there, mobilizing around your brand. They are far from doing nothing, so you need to join the conversation. Also, if your customers are that easily convinced to move to the competitor, well, then your company has much bigger issues. Perhaps you have failed to build brand equity or to produce a great product or service that a person can't live without or find a suitable replacement for. Hence, your company has much bigger issues to address than your social media efforts being easily viewed by the competition. The beauty of social media is that it will point out your company's flaws; the key question is: how quickly will you address these flaws?

Some of these concepts are difficult to grasp, but when you choose to do nothing, it's analogous to a shepherd (company) watching over a flock of sheep (customers/users). In this analogy, a fence breaks, and the sheep suddenly have access to a new pasture (social media). More than a few wander into this new pasture because it has a lot to offer. The shepherd (company) is uncertain about what to do and decides not to go into this new pasture to find the sheep. What's most likely to occur? The sheep may get eaten by a wolf (competition), or they may get lost (customers frustrated that they can't find what they're looking for). There is no doubt that if the shepherd herds the sheep into a flock, the wolf (competition) has a better idea of where the sheep are.

However, in a flock, even though the sheep are all in one easy-to-find place, perhaps the sheep are less vulnerable because there is safety in numbers and the wolf is less likely to attack. Also, if an attack occurs, the shepherd will be well aware of it and can better prevent it in the future. If the shepherd were to do nothing when the fence broke, the sheep would be getting eaten by wolves, getting lost, and falling off cliffs, and the shepherd wouldn't have a clue until he went out to find them — and by then it would be too late. Even if you decide not to herd your sheep, you should be in the new pasture helping to guide your sheep away from dangerous cliffs and waterfalls.

As a company, you need to be aware of the wolf and proactive to any reaction the wolf may have. There is no question that your competitors will be out culling the web for information that will help give them an advantage (looking for potential customer names, pricing, etc.). Transparency is definitely a two-way street. While it is great for the customer, it is also great for your competition.

As a company, you should also be out sifting for information to give you an advantage. While it may win you new customers, it should also alert you to how the competition is grabbing your information. This will give you ideas on how to safeguard where you can divulge information and where the downside outweighs the benefit. As discussed in another section in this book, if your customers are that easy to pick off, then you don't have a problem with your social media or online strategy; you have a problem with your product.

Making multiple mistakes within social media is far better than doing nothing at all. You don't learn anything by doing nothing.

If you're a large brand, you can rest assured that there are conversations, pages, and applications constantly being developed around your brand and by the community at large. The social community is doing social media even if your company chooses not to. The choice isn't *whether* to do social media; the choice is in how *well* you do it.

Chapter Seven Key Points

1. No person or company is perfect, so it is best to admit your faults, and the public will respect you for it.
2. Advertising historically has been wrapped around the outside of content (i.e., shows, articles); it now needs to be integrated with the content to take advantage of viral opportunities.
3. Companies should leverage the Tom Sawyer approach like CNN and ESPN have, and let fans contribute to their products, shows, or services.
4. Your customers and fans of today are the potential competition of tomorrow. Understand this and proactively avoid letting it happen.
5. Be a digital Dale Carnegie: listen first, sell second.
6. It's better to live a social media life making mistakes than living a social media life doing nothing.
7. Don't forget that search engine optimization (SEO) and social media go hand in hand.

(*continued*)

(continued)

8. Companies don't have a choice in *whether* they do social media; they have a choice in how *well* they do it.
9. Businesses concerned with exposing their clients to competition don't have a social media problem; they have a business/product problem. Why do your customers want to switch?

CHAPTER EIGHT

Next Steps for Companies and the Glass House Generation

I didn't have time to write you a short letter, so I wrote you a long one instead.

— Mark Twain

People have always found extreme value in the brevity of messages. As a result of our ability to have constant connectivity, people believe that immediate, simple, and constant communication matters. These interactions can be one-to-one or open to a broader audience.

The shelf life of conversations has been dramatically shortened. In 2000, when there were only a handful of blogs, a post or article would be commented about for a full week; its half-life would be around three to four days. Today, given the myriad of blogs and the expansion of tools like Twitter and Foursquare, the half-life of conversations has been reduced from days to minutes.

At the simplest of levels, this brevity has been caused by the massive amount of information readily available.

This technology isn't always about the personal and the frivolous; it can be highly leveraged in a time of crisis like a national disaster. The wildfires of San Diego offer a good example of this. Nate Ritter, local to San Diego at the time of the fires, began tweeting about what was happening from "Smoke has completely blocked out the sun" to "300,000 evacuated to relief areas which can be found here." Realizing that it would be most effective to have as many people tweeting about the fires with constant updates, Nate set up the hashtag #sandiegofire that many others quickly picked up. This helped all thoughts and news on Twitter to be organized under #sandiegofire. These tweets worked in concert with other social media tools, from users uploading videos and photos to YouTube and Flickr to Google Maps showing some of the danger zones.

Another example was when two cellular cables were vandalized in San Francisco, knocking out all forms of mobile telecommunication for AT&T users. Many customers kept abreast of updates from AT&T via Twitter #AT&T updates.

Tony Blair, the former prime minister of the United Kingdom, was asked what he found most challenging about his job throughout the span of his tenure as prime minister. He responded:

> *The way in which information is exchanged so quickly has forever changed the way in which people want to consume information. They demand that things be condensed into 20-second sound bites. With complex problems, this is exceedingly difficult, but to be an effective communicator and leader you need to be able to condense complex items down to the core and be able to do this quickly.*[1]

IBM ran some popular television advertisements starting in 2005 highlighting its business services division and juxtaposing long messaging versus short. The ads generally spent the first 25 seconds showing a bombastic and often pompous consultant using big and long buzzwords in lengthy sentences to discuss what a company should deploy as its strategy. The final five seconds usually pulled the rug out from under these suggestions with an intelligent quip, "Can we implement it?" or "How does this make us money?," to which the pompous consultant usually returned a vapid stare or scratched his head.

Karl James Buck, a graduate student at the University of California–Berkeley, found out just how powerful one word can be. Karl was in Mahalla, covering the political unrest in Egypt. One day, things got extremely heated and some of the protestors began throwing Molotov cocktails at government buildings. Afraid they would be arrested, Buck and his translator began to retreat from the area. The police quickly halted their progress. Thinking quickly on his feet, Buck sent out a text to his Twitter network consisting of one word: "arrested." One of his network colleagues was an Egyptian student studying abroad at Berkeley. She, along with several others who received the text, immediately became worried and got into action, contacting local Egyptian authorities and having UC-Berkeley hire local legal counsel.

"The most important thing on my mind was to let someone know where we were so that there would be some record of it . . . so we couldn't [disappear]," Buck said. "As long as someone knew where we were, I felt like they couldn't do their worst because someone, at some point, would be checking in on them."[2] Twitter co-founder Biz Stone knew that this type of platform could be used for larger-purpose items because they had previously tested the technology during earthquakes in the San Francisco area. "James' case is particularly compelling to us because of the simplicity of his message — one word, 'arrested' — and the speed with which the whole scene played out," Stone said. "It highlights the simplicity and value of a real-time communication network that follows you wherever you go."[3]

Power to the People

If power is being transferred more and more to the people via social media mechanisms, what other forms does this take and look like? First, anytime there is a macro shift, a small window of opportunity is unlocked where companies and people can benefit. Most evident are the neophyte companies of the dot-com boom who received good money from venture capitalists. You saw companies go from garage-based start-ups to multimillion-dollar corporations overnight. You also saw people win. At one point, a company called All-Advantage was paying people by the hour so that a bar beneath their browser could scroll ads. And working like the Amway model, if you were able to get more people to use the advertising scroll bar, you received a commission for their viewing as well.

Some people were making thousands of dollars per month just to surf the web. Others were ordering their groceries online and having them delivered by Webvan or Peapod. In grocery stores and at gas stations, some people were paying one-fourth of the normal price because the price was set on Priceline. Yes, at one point in time you could use Priceline to get a great rate on gasoline and groceries.

Eventually many of these ideas failed or were modified. Priceline adjusted its technology to give the user more control when it came to booking hotels, and its stock skyrocketed as a result. Once users felt like they had more control over their own destiny, Priceline surge ahead of its competitors: Orbitz, Hotwire, and

Travelocity. In theory, the idea that All-Advantage embraced was noteworthy — paying consumers for the placement space rather than going through an intermediary (buying outdoor boards, interactive banner placement on highly visited sites, etc.). However, All-Advantage failed miserably at execution. All-Advantage was serving ads based on what users selected as what they were interested in, but it neglected to understand that a user's mere interest does not translate into purchases, so the placement of the advertising alone was not sufficient to justify the spend.

The construct was sound, but the world and technology available just weren't ready for it. The world will be more than ready in the coming years. The reason for reviewing these older examples is that often history repeats itself because nobody listens the first time. In some cases you can take an existing concept like social book marketing (Delicious, Digg, Reddit) and put a new skin on it with great success (Pinterest). In other cases we should avoid introducing a previously failed business model. We will see more than a few business models constructed to take advantage of this fundamental shift caused by social media. Only time will tell what the best model is, but it's interesting to see some models already taking shape.

Customers Get Paid for Their Search Efforts

One shift we may see is that the money previously dispersed to intermediaries is now being redistributed to the companies themselves and to the consumers. A good example of what some programs will resemble is Microsoft's Bing's failed cash-back program. Microsoft announced it would be giving cash back to people who use Bing and subsequently click through and make a purchase. This program was rolled back in May 2010, but the idea could resurface in the near future from either Bing, Facebook, Twitter, or Google.

This program is vaguely analogous to the credit card cash-back programs (e.g., Discover Card) that give cash back.

People often mistake anything on the web as new, when in fact the construct is often not new at all. It is only the delivery mechanism that's new and innovative. Microsoft giving cash back for searches is very similar to a frequent flier/hotel stay program. Let's look at an example:

- Starwood has many hotel properties (W, Sheraton, Westin, etc.) = Microsoft's 700 merchants.

- Users call Starwood reservations = Users search on Bing.
- Starwood gives points for bookings = Microsoft gives cash back for purchases/bookings made via searches on Bing.

What Model Does This Hope to Replace?

This type of model is geared toward augmenting and ultimately replacing the existing paid-search model. The historical paid-search model consisted of:

- Advertiser spends money based on an anticipated return on investment.
- Search agency is typically paid a percentage of the buy.
- Search engine is paid a cost per click based on an auction, resulting in the searchers receiving no payment, even though they are driving all the revenue stream.

As you can see from this model, there are two points where the majority of the money is flowing to intermediaries. A percentage is going to the search agency and a percentage is going to the search engine. Now let's take a look at a cash-back search model.

- Advertiser spends money based on actual return — a sale is completed.
- Search engine receives a percentage of revenue derived.
- Searcher receives a discount or cash back.

The winners and losers in this new model can be strikingly obvious. The consumer is the big winner because he or she is now getting a cheaper product as a result of less wasted money in the middle. Another winner is the advertiser who is spending less to acquire a consumer or purchase, and there is less risk associated with the transaction. In the historical model, the advertisers were paying based on a cost per click in the hope that the click would lead to an action (i.e., purchase of a good or service, subscription, lead). In the new model, advertisers are only paying for action (cost per action).

Another winner of this model is the search engine that deploys it most effectively in an effort to gain market share. Coincidently, the search engine incumbent (e.g., Google) would be the least likely to introduce such a model. By endorsing such a shift, Google could see itself as a potential loser because it currently generates a fair amount of money from the inefficiency of the old model.

However, there is an old saying in Silicon Valley centered around cannibalizing your own revenue; make sure to eat your own lunch before somebody else does.

Because the search engines are paid on a per-click basis, if a customer found exactly what he or she wanted on the first try and was ready to purchase, this would diminish the revenue because the transaction would be completed with just one click. In contrast, if it takes five paid clicks to get that one purchase, the search engine's revenues are five times greater.

The most obvious loser in this potential model is the search engine agency. If search engines are able to handle the entire transaction and they have a vested interest to produce a sale versus a click-through, and if this is performed efficiently, then the intermediary (agency) ceases to add value in the chain, and so ceases to exist. The key and critical piece here is the ability of the search engine to optimize both its best interest and the advertiser's — which should be the same.

Let's take a quick look at this example using vacuum cleaner manufacturer Hoover. (*Note:* This is just an example; it isn't something Hoover actually does or endorses, nor are these numbers real.)

Historical Search Model
- *Advertiser:* Hoover is willing to pay $50 to produce a sale of its $200 vacuum cleaner.
- *Search engine:* Hoover has determined that it takes roughly 15 clicks to produce a sale and therefore is willing to pay the search engine $3 per click ($3 × 15) = $45.
- *Search agency:* The search engine agency charges 11 percent commission, resulting in $5 for this buy going to the search engine.
- *Searcher:* The searcher must pay $200 to purchase the vacuum cleaner.

New Model
- *Advertiser:* Hoover is willing to pay $50 to produce a sale of its $200 vacuum cleaner. In the historical model it paid $50, but in the new model it will pay a net of $40.
- *Search engine:* Hoover has agreed to pay the search engine 10 percent commission of total revenue produced. So in this instance, the search engine will receive $20 for the sale.
- *Search agency:* The search engine agency receives $0 because it is no longer part of the process.

- *Searcher:* The searcher receives $20 cash back if he or she purchases the vacuum cleaner; net cost ($200 − $20) = $180.
- *Result:* **Hoover pays less ($40 instead of $50) and the consumer pays less ($180 instead of $200)**.

Once the new model is multiplied by a larger revenue stream, the gains are enormous.

So you ask, why on earth would a search engine do this? The minority search engine (e.g., Microsoft's Bing) would do so to help differentiate itself by perfecting this model in hopes of capturing more marketing share and in turn more revenue. Competition in the market space breeds innovative ideas that ultimately benefit the end user. In the search engine space, the "it's an auction model" argument doesn't fly, as this example clearly points out. If there is a monopoly in the search engines, the consumer and manufacturer both lose. However, in the previous new model example, Hoover paid less ($40 instead of $50) and the consumer paid less ($180 instead of $200). The reason this is possible is because it eliminates inefficiencies.

Join Them Before They Beat You

Media giant Viacom offers a good example of a company realizing it is better to embrace digital media than to fight it (as the music industry did with music sharing). Viacom was aggressively trying to impose a "no" strategy from the beginning. It was suing YouTube for upwards of $1 billion for allowing users to post copyrighted content through its service. Originally Viacom's strategy was "Let's sue YouTube and block this." However, it quickly realized that would not work. Instead, a better solution is "Let's create a system where content can derive some benefit,"[4] said Forrester Research analyst James McQuivey.

The courts determined that YouTube wasn't responsible for proactively policing content; rather, it was responsible for removing content if the appropriate paperwork or complaint was filed by the copyright owner (e.g., Viacom). This was obviously a laborious process for YouTube to constantly sift through these complaints and rid the site of any violators. Nor was it good for the user, because it meant there was less of the content that the user desired. At the same time, it wasn't good for the copyright owners of the material either because they had to go through the tedious process of finding the violation and then submitting the request through the proper channels to have the content taken down.

YouTube at this point in time had yet to produce a profitable return for its parent company, Google. Realizing that the current "fighting" model wasn't working well for anybody, YouTube came up with a progressive solution. When it received a takedown notice, it would give the copyright owner two options: (1) remove the content or (2) keep the content up but allow YouTube to serve advertising and share in the revenue. YouTube foresaw that if they continued down the path they were on, they'd collectively be beaten. As a result, they employed the strategy of joining them (copyright owners) to their cause. You have probably seen this in action when you are viewing a YouTube video with music. A sleek pop-up message appears that denotes the name of the song and the artist along with a clickable link to purchase the song. This is great for the users, as well, since they can easily make the purchase if they enjoy the song.

After this creative idea from YouTube, Viacom, the owner of Paramount Pictures and MTV networks, decided to take a similar approach with MySpace. One of the more popular activities that MySpace users engaged in (before becoming irrelevant) was passing around video content — often copyrighted video content. MySpace was more than happy to engage in a win-win relationship with Viacom. "Consumers get to share some of the content they want without having it blocked or removed," said Jeff Berman, MySpace's president of sales and marketing at the time. "This is a game changer. It takes us from a world of 'no' to a world of 'yes,' where the audience gets to curate content, express and share it as they choose, while copyright holders are not only respected, they get to make money."[5]

Contrasting this, Warner pulled all of its royalty content off YouTube in a disagreement about how much revenue it should receive from YouTube. Time will tell if this is a poor decision. The odds are it will result in failure because the philosophy of "This is my ball so only I am going to play with it" has failed time and time again on the Internet.

History repeats itself because no one listens the first time. This can truly be said about the strategy the Associated Press (AP) employed in April 2009. If you recall in our Jane the blogger example in Chapter One, some newspapers and traditional writers have had to adapt to these rapidly changing times. Some succeed, while others fail. The AP became fixated on others failing around them and *panic* is the appropriate word to describe what the news agency did next. It went with a "These are my toys and you can't play with them" strategy. This works only if you are the only game in town, which is a rare position to be in.

From our Jane the blogger story and supporting documentation, you can see that the AP is not the only game in town. But what did the AP do? It requested that Google remove its stories from the Google News feed. Now, legally, Google would have been fine saying your request is unreasonable, but they didn't. Google did say your request is unreasonable, but we will remove it if you desire. Sometimes, it's best to take technology out of the question.

This is analogous to a record label in the 1950s asking the world's largest provider of jukeboxes to not put its songs on the jukebox. A hypothetical conversation would go like this:

Jukebox company: We could remove your songs, but then people will not be able to find them and listen to them.

Record label: That's okay — we don't really see any direct revenue from the quarters they put into your machine, so why should users be able to listen to our music?

Jukebox company: At that moment in time, it's the only way they can listen to the song. Even if they own the record, they aren't going to carry their stereo into the bar or dance club. Don't you want people to be exposed to your music? If they like it, don't you think they will come in and buy the record?

Record label: No, these are my toys and you can't play with them.

This is precisely what the AP is doing by asking Google and YouTube to remove its content. While companies that get it are paying millions of dollars in pay-per-click and search engine optimization to rank high in Google, the AP doesn't want this free traffic and exposure. The even bigger kicker is that there was a deal in place where Google was providing some revenue share to the AP. One story in particular went something like this:

AP: You need to pull down that YouTube AP video from your site.

AP affiliate/partner: No, we are an affiliate, a partner of the AP.

AP: It doesn't matter; affiliate, partner, or not, you need to remove that video from your website.

AP affiliate/partner: But we actually got this video from YouTube — someone must have posted it.

AP: Even more reason to pull it down.

AP affiliate/partner: Yes, but you, the AP, are the ones that posted this to YouTube and supplied the <embed> code that allows others to copy and play it on their respective sites. That is what we did. If you, the AP, didn't want to share this video, then why did you post it to YouTube and supply the <embed> code?

AP: Let me get back to you on this, but in the meantime take the video down from your site.

Panic, panic, panic is happening all around us. Companies that keep a level head will be fine and in some instances better off as their competition self-implodes. When dramatic shifts happen, whether financial or digital, great companies don't hide; they do the exact opposite. Great companies attack and double down in the moment of shift and uncertainty.

Don't fall victim to FEAR (false evidence appearing real). FEAR is an acronym borrowed from scuba diving. When things change under 100 feet of water, it's not the most technical diver who is the best off in that situation. It's the diver who doesn't panic and create FEAR (false evidence appearing real). Who in business can remain calm and keep their heads when the environment around them changes rapidly? Who can leverage the changes in their environment to their advantage, rather than be paralyzed by the newness?

Despite the controversial bailouts of 2009, on the technology front government and politicians are not likely to bail out companies that do not implement swift strategies to survive, nor are they willing to step into this sticky mess. President Obama's stance on this was intentionally vague. Following his election, he stated, "We need to update and reform our copyright and patent systems to promote civic discourse, innovation, and investment while ensuring that intellectual property owners are fairly treated."[6]

This is a big step for companies like Viacom; they recognize that they need to embrace social media rather than fight it. One important step to understanding this is realizing that for many companies, revenue streams will be reduced, but at the same time, so will costs. A prime example is on the music side; instead of $5 for a 45 rpm vinyl record (remember those?) you receive $0.99 for a digital download. However, there is also an enormous cost reduction: no costs to produce, ship, store, stock, and so forth.

If you resist embracing the change, you could quickly find yourself in the same declining mode currently being experienced by newspapers, broadcast news, publishers, and the music industry, all of whom to date have failed to embrace and understand this new way of doing business. Isn't it better to have a smaller piece of the pie than no pie at all?

Role of Search

Former Google product guru and Yahoo! CEO Marissa Mayer told the *New York Times* that social search will be a key component in the future of search. Social commerce deserves Google's unbridled attention.

Why are Google, Yahoo!, Baidu (China), Naver (Korea), Yandex (Russia), and Bing interested in social networks? Because social media could eventually dominate the search landscape. This is already evidenced by the social media site YouTube.

YouTube, which for years had been struggling to turn a profit despite being acquired by Google, eventually decided to take a play out of its parent company's playbook, and deployed its own pay-per-click search program. YouTube is the world's second-most-searched site.

It seems logical for YouTube to introduce a model similar to that of Google AdWords (brand name for Google's sponsored ad listings) so that amateur and professional videographers can easily monetize their creative materials. The model is simple: a person who uploads a video has the ability to easily place advertising that complements or is entrenched in the video. The difficulty is pairing up the advertisers to appropriate video content.

For example, companies like Lexus or Puma would not want to damage their respective brands by being associated with amateur videos. This is less of a concern in the Google AdWords model, which is text based; however, Google AdWords too had to work out the kinks several years ago when it ran into issues like an ad being served for Aflac Insurance next to an article discussing a major lawsuit against Aflac. Google worked out the kinks there, and will work out the kinks here as well.

The truly great companies in this model are those that go beyond simply appending advertisements to existing videos. The truly great and innovative marketing minds will roll up their sleeves and get "on the ground" by being nimble and identifying quick wins and reacting adroitly when it comes to developing original content that can be further incorporated into the video.

For example, during the 2008 U.S. presidential election, when the Tina Fey "Palin" spots were popular, a brand like Budweiser could have placed an ad and said, "If there was a Joe Sixpack drinking game for every time the word *maverick* was mentioned, you'd better believe the people playing it would be drinking a Bud." This would have played off the fact that Tina Fey was spoofing Palin for always saying "Joe Sixpack" and "maverick." Again, this is all about becoming part of the content and enhancing the user experience rather than following an interruption model. Dodge did this well in the popular NBC show *The Office* when the audience was asked during the commercial break what the bumper sticker on Dwight's desk read. This is the type of real-time stuff that engages the audience; it's part of the content rather than an interruption to it. Green Mountain coffee also ran a clever outdoor advertising campaign that was along the lines of "Complete this sentence and your response could soon appear here: I'd rather be drinking a coffee . . ." and supplied the number to which you should text your response. In Chicago, Mini-Cooper billboards were reading microchips in Mini-Cooper cars and welcoming the driver by name: *Hello Cindy, welcome to downtown Chicago.*

Originally designed for the visually impaired, the new system of tagging videos (using text to define what's in the video) makes things easy because there are tools that convert web pages into audio descriptions of the page content. These tags make it simple to categorize the web by efficiently determining what the video content contains. Tagging is a huge driver of transparency. If someone is tagged in a video, everyone in the person's network is instantly alerted. The old saying is: "Those who live in glass houses shouldn't throw stones." Well, guess what? With social media, the world is one gigantic glass house. That's why kids growing up today could appropriately be labeled the Glass House Generation.

Also, an enabler for success is for companies to be more open and comfortable in letting go of the ownership and control of their brands. It's not going to be perfect every time, and the end users are smart — they understand that user-generated content is beyond a brand's control. If 90 percent is good and only 10 percent is negative, the positive will overwhelm the negative, and the 10 percent will not cripple your brand reputation. In fact, negative comments help add credibility. Numerous studies have shown that products with zero negative comments are consistently outsold by products that have a few negative comments.

This will be a new approach for some established brands that in the past have often played "not to lose" more so than "to win." Heck, if there isn't 5 to 10 percent negative noise around your brand, then your brand is either irrelevant or not being aggressive enough in the space. TripAdvisor CEO Steve Kaufer states, "The quickest death in this new world is deliberating rather than doing." Fear of failure is crippling to a company or an individual. One needs to fail fast, fail forward, and fail better.

It's no coincidence that TripAdvisor has been one of the first companies to embrace social commerce. For example, it launched the ability for a visitor to their site not only to see the ratings on a certain hotel, but also to see who in their Facebook network (via Facebook Connect) had stayed at that hotel. This is the game changer; this is what Socialnomics is all about: the ability for me to see what my friends and peers think about anything and everything.

This is a monumental difference in mind-set compared to when well-established brands had to be almost 100 percent on message all the time — and rightfully so because it would damage the brand if something was off (e.g., Rolex sponsoring NASCAR). This could still damage a brand today, and steps should be taken to quickly resolve issues when they occur, but if you are producing a ton of noise, or more important, your consumers are producing a ton of noise around your brand, then the few blips along the way will often be drowned out by the rest.

What Happens When the Internet Advertising Structure Collapses?

The foundation and historical model for Internet advertising revenue as we know it today is inherently flawed from a sustainability standpoint. Just as TiVo and digital video recorders were invented to help users avoid having to view advertising on television, tools such as pop-up blockers, spam filters, and banner blockers perform similar functions for Internet users. These Internet tools aren't limited to simply blocking only nefarious advertising activity. People also have a desire to be shielded from legitimate, but highly intrusive, Fortune 500 marketing. Why? For the simple reason that these advertisers still use "push" messaging rather than developing conversations with their users.

In the late 1990s, the hot dot-com start-ups weren't based on advertising revenue models; rather, they were based primarily on e-commerce models, developing steady revenue via transactions. These types of start-ups were the darlings of venture capitalists, who shied away from start-ups that based their revenue solely on advertising models. Then, during the Web 2.0 era, advertising revenue models became all the rage thanks largely to the success of Google.

If you had the eyeballs (people visiting your site), even if you couldn't develop direct advertising relationships (e.g., advertisers paying you to have their marketing materials on your site), you could always have a fail-safe fallback by putting Google search results on your page. This was accomplished via Google's successful AdWords program. The program allows a website owner to place contextual search results from Google on any page, resulting in instant revenue creation. Google serves up ads on a website — for example, American-Novel's site at www.american-novel.com. The ads are related to the site's content. So, for this example to work, the contextual search ads placed on the pages of www.american -novel.com would be related to American authors and American novels. The owners of www.american-novel.com would be paid by Google every time someone clicked on the text ads. For example, if the cost per click for the ad was $4, Google generally would give $2 of this revenue to the owners of www.american-novel.com and put $2 into its own pocket.

This is obviously great for small websites. It also works well for paying advertisers, since they are able to generate more reach outside of just being on www.google.com. This is good for Google as well, as it increases Google's revenue stream (as of January 2009, the AdWords program accounted for roughly 10 percent of Google's revenue).[7]

However, what has been seen over time with sophisticated advertisers and robust tracking tools is that the quality of clicks coming from the AdWords network is much lower than those coming from www.google.com. The clicks weren't resulting in leads or sales.

The AdWords program is still a valuable one, but it will continue on a much smaller scale, and Google has already developed tools to allow advertisers to have more control over which sites the ads are placed on rather than placing the ads on every site in the network. For example, Nike may see that its ads don't perform well on www.american-novel.com and can remove the ads from being served there. While this type of targeting and new tools are good for the advertisers, if Google's revenue from this program dips from 10 percent (current) to 5 percent, that would be significant as it would equate to over $1 billion in revenue being removed from the Internet advertising market. Many companies are dependent on Google's sustained success. For example, the open-source Firefox browser revenues in 2009 were $104 million, with search-related royalties from Google accounting for 88 percent of the total, or $66 million.[8]

Where Have All the Banners Gone?

Does online banner or display advertising get a bad rap? Yes and no. Is banner advertising going away anytime soon? No. Will traditional banner advertising be reduced? Yes. Just like a quarterback on a football team, banner advertising historically was getting too much credit when things were good and too much blame when things went bad. Online banners have better tracking than offline marketing methods like television, radio, outdoor, and the like. Because of this, banners were getting too much of the credit simply from the fact that they could track something. The biggest ruse was the "view-through" sale. Tracking is available to place a cookie (small piece of text) on people's web browsers when they surf the Internet. If a user went to the home page of CNN.com, tracking tools would be able to see that this occurred.

When an advertiser, say 1-800-Flowers, was running a banner ad on the home page of CNN.com, they'd be able to see that a certain number of users had that banner on their screen when they were at CNN. Advertisers did, and sometimes still do, make the assumption that the users saw that banner ad—which in some cases they probably did, and in others they probably did not. The second assumption that advertisers make is that if that some user takes a positive action (buys flowers or gives 1-800-Flowers his or her information), then the advertiser gives credit to the banner for driving that action. In some cases, the banner should be credited for that sale, but in many cases, it should not be. If the banner ads are the only marketing that 1-800-Flowers is running at the time, one can safely assume that the action is most likely a result of the banner campaign.

Since large companies are often running multiple advertising programs, this ultraclean scenario is not too common. In reality, what may occur is that online marketers take credit for sales that may have been driven by other marketing efforts like television, radio, magazines, and so on because the online marketer had the power of robust tracking. Also, this tracking cookie was set for 30 days, so if a user (Will) was on CNN.com and potentially *viewed* the 1-800-Flowers banner—again, there was no confirmation that Will actually saw the ad, just that it was on the page when he visited CNN.com. If Will were to buy flowers in the next 30 days, then that banner marketing would get credit for the sale when, in fact, it was a magazine ad that ultimately drove Will to make the flower purchase.

Marketers became addicted to this perceived success, which led to them buying banners on millions of low-quality pages at very cheap prices and having banners served to millions and millions of people. The odds of someone running across a site in 30 days that didn't place a 1-800-Flowers banner cookie on their browser were very low.

The primary culprits of this were the advertisers and advertising agencies. Essentially three things were occurring:

1. It never dawned on the people managing the campaign that they might be overinflating the effectiveness of their online banner marketing efforts.
2. The managing advertising agency wanted to show the best return to the client and essentially snowballed the client with this type of measurement.
3. The client wanted to show the best return to his or her executives and snowballed the executives with this type of tracking to garner more budget for his or her fiefdom.

We point out these items because too many companies believe that they can have a profitable and healthy online business by simply using the old advertising revenue model. This is no longer the case. New forms of advertising online need to emerge to offset the ones that are currently broken. America Online (AOL) is a great example of this. When AOL decided to get out of the business of supplying dial-up and high-speed Internet connections, the company figured it could survive with just an ad revenue model—but this hasn't worked out very well. Banners and display advertising will still have their place and serve a purpose, but it will be in a much smaller capacity.

Banners and display advertising will also have a place in social media, but it will be much different from the traditional banner approach. One of the huge advantages of social media for advertisers is that social networks can give them insight into a user's demographic (age, geography, occupation, etc.) and psychographic information (hobbies, clubs, networks, desires). In the past, advertisers often had to guess at this type of data. With social media, the users tell advertisers exactly what they have been trying to determine for years.

As people change, the message can change to match their lifestyle. For example, in Facebook if you change your relationship status from "in a relationship" to "engaged," you will start to see relevant advertisements showing photographers, stationery options, and music providers.

A few weeks later, if you make an online purchase of stationery, then these types of advertisements to you would be greatly reduced, if not completely removed. Also, some banners reflect social actions of those in your network. So a company placing a banner to sell lipstick can elect to have a social network to create an ad based on people's behavior around its product. If Kelly is friends with Beth and Beth purchases the lipstick, Kelly will be served a banner with Beth's picture stating, "Beth has just purchased this cherry lipstick." This banner reflecting social actions will be more effective than a generic banner and is an example of the power and progressive nature of social media.

Many companies, both large and small, are doing this very effectively through Facebook's paid ads. It has even been proven that if you know what you are doing within the Facebook interface you can actually target a single individual. While Facebook display ads are effective for what they are, they are still limited. If Facebook is going to be the next Apple or the next Google, it will certainly need to figure out new revenue streams; otherwise, it will go the way of AOL, Yahoo!, Excite, and many others. Facebook will have its place, but it will be much smaller. General Motors, right before Facebook went public with its initial public offering (IPO), indicated it was pulling its advertising from Facebook, since it had been ineffective.

In the general Internet, we have already seen a rapid decrease in the percentage of revenue derived from display and banner advertising. In 2008, the Interactive Advertising Bureau (IAB) reported that search had overtaken display advertising, accounting for 41 percent of the market, whereas display accounted for 34 percent.[9] This is radically different from 2001, when banner advertising dominated the advertising revenue landscape. Could we see the same type of shift from search to social media? Most likely; in the fourth quarter of 2008, PubMatic indicated that the effective price that advertisers were willing to pay for display or banner ads fell 21 percent on average from the second to the third quarter, with the biggest declines coming at small and medium-size sites.[10]

A shift or other form of change needs to occur in order to replace such lost advertising revenue at the macro level. If the gap is not filled, the user will suffer because content companies will vanish and the free content that users have grown accustomed to will be limited or cease to exist. If a new or revised online revenue model is not found to fill this hole, it could have a dramatic effect on the online community and on our economy as a whole.

The good news is that there is a ready willingness and desire by companies to advertise on social media. We are at the start of a digital decade, and the advertising components will be largely shaped by mobile and social media. For example, 75 of the country's top 100 advertisers placed ads on Facebook in 2008, according to the company.[11] Mobile items such as applications and iAds are going to produce huge new revenue streams. For example, today Google Maps is free. However, if Google Maps can't survive on an advertising-based model, most smartphone users would be more than willing to pay $4.99 for a one-time download of an application. The new subscription-based model in terms of magazines and newspapers may more closely reflect one-time application downloads.

Search Engine Results Are Still Prehistoric

Users and advertisers collectively crave more real-time relevancy from search engines. Unfortunately, due to the complexity of crawling the web, this is inherently difficult to achieve in organic results. Why, though, has it taken so long to correct this problem on sponsored search sections?

Why can't an advertiser easily alert users of a winter sale? Search engines are racing furiously to address this shortfall. The first search engine that does so will have a distinct advantage with users and advertisers. Let's look at an example.

Paid Search Relevancy Dilemma

An online travel agency sells hotels, airfare, car rentals, cruises, and so on. Because the business is centered on fulfilling demand, it is spending millions annually on search.

It's tough enough for consumers to differentiate the brands of Priceline, Travelocity, and Expedia in the marketplace. It's even tougher within search engines. A good example: perform a search for "Chicago hotels." There will be 10 sponsored results showing at the top of the page and on the right rail. All the ads are almost identical. They all say "cheap hotels," "best rates," "Chicago hotels," and so on. None of them stand out for the user. Wouldn't it be better for the user and the advertiser if the results were more specific? For example, here's a better ad:

Boutique 5-Star Hotel
- $89 (Normally $299)
- Next to Wrigley Building

The results are infinitely more relevant for the user. In turn, it would produce a greater return for the advertiser. So it's a win-win strategy.

How much greater is the return on investment? We tested this exact scenario within a top-10 travel company that spends around $15 million annually on search. When specific travel deals were dynamically inserted, the click-through rate was *five times greater* than the campaign average. Also, conversions were a whopping 413 percent higher.

If the returns are so great, why isn't everyone doing this? That's where it gets complex.

Tedious, Manual Feeds

Despite what Google will tell you, there isn't a simple way to set up a feed from your database that updates product pricing, specials, sales, and so on. Even if you did, you'd run into the problem of how to automatically generate copy that makes sense. Imagine the opportunity for a search engine that could solve this issue for Target, Foot Locker, Expedia, Home Depot, and so on.

There Must Be New Keywords

Even if you decide to hire cheap labor to upload your sales, travel deals, and so on into the search engines weekly, you'll run into an issue.

Example: Orbitz has a travel deal that is good only for the next week—50 percent off a hotel in Paris. Let's say Orbitz is buying over 100,000 keywords in this campaign. The odds of Orbitz not already buying a relevant travel keyword (e.g., Paris hotel, cheap hotel in Paris) are slim.

Orbitz's campaign keywords are relevant and have built up a history over time. Due to Google's quality score, which essentially gives keywords in a campaign a good reputation over time, you can't quickly infuse new copy into Google's AdWords program. Your incumbent or generic copy that's been running the past several months will almost always win in the short term. Your new copy will have a tough time even being served in the coming week, and if it is, the cost per click is much greater.

Not giving up, Orbitz decides it will pause all the other copy iterations for "Paris hotel" and serve the new sale copy announcing 50 percent off. The problem here is that there is no beneficial quality score. Orbitz would be paying more per click and would lose all the efficiencies gained. There is no easy way for Orbitz to quickly get a sale for a major city listed in search engines that makes sense from a return-on-investment standpoint.

Integration with Third-Party Optimization Tools

We haven't mentioned the complexity of an optimization/bidding tool (most likely via a third-party search agency) that Orbitz is probably employing. Many of the most popular tools in the marketplace today can't react effectively when given a short window of opportunity (less than a week) to make adjustments to existing terms within a current campaign.

Everybody loses: the user (results don't show the sale), search engines (lost potential click revenue), agency (disgruntled client and lost commission), and advertiser (lost leads and sales revenue).

All of these needs seem relatively basic, at least conceptually. Will someone seize the opportunity to fill this obvious void?

Just think, we haven't even mentioned branded images and video within the search results. So, as you can see, we'll soon be looking back at search shaking our heads asking, "How did we ever survive with such a basic model?"

This is where social search will force the acceleration of better search results. One size doesn't fit all. One person who searches for "Paris" may want to know about the capital of France, while another person wants to see photos of the hotel chain heiress. Also, people want to quickly type in semantic queries like "best pizza parlors in downtown Manhattan Beach, California" to get quick results from a Zagat, as well as qualitative results from their social network — this is where things are progressing rapidly.

Oral Communication Skills Decline

If you still don't believe that some traditional interpersonal communication skills may be suffering, then maybe this example will make you a believer. Second Life is a virtual reality application. It's a digitized life that allows you to do anything that you could do in normal life. People develop avatars (digital graphic representations of themselves), sometimes reflecting who they are in real life and other times taking on different personas (a librarian may become a dominatrix). By the time you read this, Second Life may not exist, but there will always be these virtual worlds or virtual games (FarmVille, CityVille, The Simms) in which people engage.

A couple even got divorced over Second Life, and here is how their story goes: Amy Taylor (28) met David Pollard (40) in Second Life, or rather their avatars met each other in Second Life.

Things went swimmingly, but Amy, being cautious, hired a Second Life private investigator (yes, they exist!). This investigator posed as a voluptuous virtual prostitute and tempted David inside Second Life. David resisted the temptation and passed the test with flying colors (a test he was unaware of at the time). Their courtship continued until their marriage. Because they had met in Second Life, they had their marriage ceremony on Second Life (hey, if nothing else, it saved a bunch of money).

Offline they signed the legal documents, and they were officially married. Things were going fine until Amy discovered that David was chatting with another female avatar (not her) and showing genuine affection. Amy was so disgusted with this that she filed for divorce both in Second Life and in the real world.

Is the Journalistic Interview Dead?

More and more interviews will be conducted on video because the cost to entry is much lower. The iPods, phones, and flip cameras are cheap and have the ability to post video clips on social media sites within minutes. The ability to use video Skype over smartphones has changed things as well.

Traditional paper-and-pencil journalism is dying. For articles that will appear in newspapers, magazines, blogs, or online media, the way in which these interviews are conducted has radically changed. In the past, interviews were mostly conducted in person or occasionally on the phone. Now they are generally conducted by the reporter or writer sending a list of questions to the interviewee. The interviewee texts, tweets, e-mails (social network or Web mail), or instant messages back responses. This may seem inherently lazy on the part of the interviewers, but it makes sense on many fronts. It (1) allows the reporter or interviewee to save travel time, (2) saves on the hassle of scheduling a physical time, (3) saves the interviewee prep time, (4) gives the reporter a written record, (5) allows the interviewee to not be misquoted, and (6) offers less chance for the reporter to misreport. I usually am interviewed about 250 times per year, and the only way this is plausible is that much of the correspondence is done electronically. I even have a sheet for my admin that she can send to the reporter with some of the most common questions I receive, along with my answers.

Another big advance is video Skype interviews — so not just the big networks with the studios have this capability. Everyone has this capability and you can even do it from your phone.

The three major downsides to this style are: (1) there is no face-to-face interaction, another highlight on why people's interpersonal communication skills are diminishing; (2) the reporter may miss out on some good information that the interviewee might have divulged in response to a spontaneous question; and (3) there is no chance for the reporter to read body language cues to determine where they've hit a spot and where they can probe further — although with high-definition Skype it does get closer and closer to an in-person conversation.

Mobile Me

According to a study by e-mail marketing firm ExactTarget and the Ball State University Center for Media Design, 77 percent of Internet and mobile phone users ages 15 to 17 use instant messaging, 76 percent use social networking sites, and 70 percent communicate via text messaging.[12]

One of the more popular Apple iPhone applications is called Tracker, but it could have just as easily been called Stalker. This works on the GPS in the phone to locate your friends and tell you exactly where they are. This is similar to Harry Potter's marauder's map. I guess you just need to make sure that this isn't enabled if you are trying to throw a surprise birthday party for some-one. This application is very practical for parents of teenagers — keeping track of where their kids are. Twitter also has the same functionality.

Mobile social media applications like Foursquare and Gowalla have taken this geotargeting even further by allowing you to check in to popular destinations. The way this works is that if you go to a restaurant, you can check in virtually. This alerts all of your friends in Foursquare, as well as your other social media tools (Facebook,

Twitter, etc.), about your whereabouts. This is infinitely helpful when you are at a major conference or at an event like the Super Bowl cheering on your team (many of your other friends will probably have flown in for the game). When you check in to the restaurant, you can also provide tips for other future visitors to the restaurant. For example: "There is no street parking, only $10 valet" or "If you are a healthy eater get the oriental chicken salad not the Santa Fe, as that is served on iceberg lettuce." If you frequent a restaurant more than anyone else on Foursquare, then you receive the title of mayor, and the owner of the restaurant may give you discounts or preferential treatment. Another application that makes it even more progressive is Forecaster. This will alert others in advance if you are going to be in the same city.

These applications are very useful if you are in an unfamiliar airport terminal, as they quickly pull up all the restaurants in the terminal and what other travelers think about them. Yelp and Urbanspoon are particularly helpful in this regard.

Opera Software shows mobile phone Internet access exploding, indicating that during 2008 use of its Min Browser on mobile phones more than tripled — reaching 5 billion page views in October. Opera said, "In many of the Southeast Asian countries the mobile web exists not because it complements existing means of access, but rather because it replaces them."[13]

In 2010, Facebook indicated that 25 percent of its users accessed Facebook via a mobile device, and it believed this trend would continue to increase. Facebook was right; in March 2012 nearly 75 percent of all Android users accessed Facebook via their hand-held devices.[14] As of this writing, social networking is the second most highly utilized mobile Web activity among U.S. Android owners, trailing only search. Facebook even had to note in its Securities and Exchange Commission (SEC) filings how important mobile is to its business in the future:

> We believe this increased usage of Facebook on mobile devices has contributed to the recent trend of our daily active users increasing more rapidly than the increase in the number of ads delivered, states the revised S-1 filing. If users increasingly access Facebook mobile products as a substitute for access through personal computers, and if we are unable to successfully implement monetization strategies for our mobile users, or if we incur excessive expenses in this effort, our financial performance and ability to grow revenue would be negatively affected.[15]

Field of Nightmares: Lufthansa and American Airlines

Lufthansa made this statement about GenFlyLounge.com:

> *GenFlyLounge is a social networking site for Generation Fly and allows you to connect with like-minded travelers. Get the inside information from other travelers you can trust and who share your interests and travel preferences. Explore destinations before you go there. Review, add and rate trips. Join now for free![16]*

While you can applaud Lufthansa for attempting to reach out to the next generation, you could argue that we already have too many social networks and that we don't need another one. Lufthansa and others would be better served developing applications that work with the various forms of social media. It's that age-old cliché: "Fish where the fish are." That is why I affectionately refer to it as the "Field of Nightmares." This is taking creative liberty with the line delivered by a celestial voice in the movie *Field of Dreams:* "If you build it [the baseball field], they will come." In this instance, Field of Nightmares, you may build it and they *won't* come. When companies like Lufthansa decide to build an application/tool/widget that complements social media, the first question they should ask themselves is: "What do we have the ability to develop that is not a poor replication of an existing tool, but is actually useful and places us in the best position to provide relevancy to our audience?" Let's look at a few examples for Lufthansa:

- *Poor idea:* Let's focus on allowing other Lufthansa users to share their thoughts on the best places to travel. This is relevant to Lufthansa's travel base; however, it is a poor idea because there are many companies that already do this better than Lufthansa (Lonely Planet, TripAdvisor, Frommers, etc.).

  One airline that understood there was already enough good general marketing out in the marketplace attacked this same concept, but from a unique (at least unique at the time) angle. Scandinavian Airlines (SAS) desired to establish close ties with its high-profile, high-income demographic group. SAS dedicated social media tools to the gay, lesbian, bisexual, and transgender/transsexual community. Gay staff members of SAS provided recommendations and tips on the best venues, nightlife, and eateries in Sweden and Denmark. SAS also partnered with several organizations and publishers so the site can offer gay maps, gay guides, and an events calendar that is updated daily.

The potential for SAS to be able to market directly to the community of people with the highest propensity to travel is very clear because it found a niche that wasn't being addressed in the general marketplace. Hence, it could truly add value rather than producing a watered-down version of something already existing. This seems pretty logical, yet company after company continues to miss this important concept—always wanting to build inward looking out rather than outward looking in. Build something from the user's viewpoint, not the company's viewpoint.

- *Good idea:* Implement a functionality (wiki) that allows users to see every seat on every plane and allows users to input the pros and cons about each seat. Sites like SeatGuru.com do exactly this, so that is why it is categorized only a *good* idea, not a *great* one. But unlike SeatGuru, this makes it easier for the user because it would be specific to Lufthansa's planes, which may be configured differently than other airlines' planes.

- *Great idea:* Why with today's technology do travelers often run into a situation where the crew runs out of the popular meals? For example, the two choices may be beef or chicken and halfway down the aisle the exasperated flight attendants are out of chicken. Why couldn't it work like a wedding when you make your reservation? Or worse, when airlines sell boxed food and you as a flier are counting on buying one of these delicious (tongue in cheek) boxes on your five-hour flight, but they run out, and the only thing you have to eat is a pack of gum.

This type of social functionality still will not be 100 percent accurate, but it's much better than the system we have in place today. Also, airlines could employ the same concept as trains. Trains do not have "no speaking" or "no cellular phone" sections. Travelers on planes vary by whether they want to talk or they want tranquility. The unsophisticated way to do this is to divide the plane into a predetermined number of seats for each flight. This would not work very well. However, if you develop the right social media application, the work would be done by your travelers, who wouldn't feel it was work at all, and the process would be fluid and variable from flight to flight.

Love connections could occur on flights more often because more single talkers would be aggregated and people who don't want to be annoyed by an incessantly boring talker need not worry. This could potentially give Lufthansa a competitive advantage, but only in the short term—obviously if this was successful it would be replicated by the competition. However, the ultimate success, and it might be difficult to replicate, would be if through social media you were able to attract a particular crowd (e.g., intelligent, professional, singles, attractive) and that helped define your brand—people would actually choose to fly your airline because of the types of people they would encounter on that airline. Airlines have been fighting to distinguish themselves for years, and this could become a reality. This may be taking things a step too far, but you could have the preppy airline, the grunge airline, middle-class airline, blue-collar airline, and so on.

The executives at Budweiser said that they learned some valuable lessons from their failed YouTube rip-off initiative of Bud TV. Let's hope so. They spent $15 million over the first two years alone, and for their efforts, Compete Inc. indicates they don't have enough traffic data to give an accurate reading.[17] They aren't alone, though. We are already seeing such popular sites as Dell.com, AT&T.com, Xbox.com, and Apple.com losing site traffic, but they aren't necessarily losing users! Their customers are just spending more time on social media and getting what they need from the companies there. Although it is a cliché, it's vitally important to fish where the fish are.

Skittles took this to the extreme to showcase a point. For some time during 2009 if you visited www.skittles.com you wouldn't see the regular website. Instead there was a nice, beautiful landing page with an interactive flash navigation box in the upper left. On this box were items like connect, video, photos, info, chat, and news. The beautiful thing was that when you clicked on these links, they didn't take you somewhere on the Skittles site; rather, they took you off the site to social media.

Connect = Skittles Facebook page
Video = Skittles YouTube channel
Photos = Skittles Flickr account
Info = Skittles Wikipedia entry
News = Skittles blog

Skittles was acting as an integration point or hub to great authentic content that existed elsewhere about the company and its products.

The funny thing is that in terms of the Field of Nightmares scenario, this same flawed replication methodology has repeated itself several times (no pun intended) in this relatively short Internet age. Whether it was e-mail, browsers, portals, search, video, and now social media, many companies have believed they would be the starting point rather than an integration point. BellSouth thinking that its users would have a My BellSouth start page (portal) that included weather, sports scores, and stocks is just one example of companies re-creating a poorer version of the wheel (for the record, people just wanted their phone bill from BellSouth integrated into their established portals, MyYahoo!, iGoogle, etc.).

To help avoid making the same mistakes or our clients making the same mistakes, we do a very simple exercise. For the social network example, we have clients write down all the features and functionalities they desire on their site or social network on a transparent piece of acetate. Unbeknownst to them, we have all the features and functionality of the technology industry leader (in this case the leading social network) on a sheet of paper. We take that acetate and lay it over the incumbent listing, and it is pretty powerful. The room usually goes quiet for a few moments, and then we begin discussions on how to appropriately integrate with the leading technology.

Don't build your own Field of Nightmares.

A Truly Interconnected Web?

A key question that remains to be answered (at least at the writing of this book) is about the interconnectivity of the various social media tools. Just like a carmaker doesn't use the same supplier for all of its various parts, but rather selects the best manufacturer for each specialty (e.g., headlights, sunroof, seats), social media providers can't be the best at every functionality (social network, social bookmarks, wikis, video sharing, photo sharing, etc.). Users like the simplicity of one-stop shopping. Corporations do like these walled gardens — these are my toys and nobody else can play! A *walled garden*, with regard to media content, refers to a closed set or exclusive set of information services provided for users (a method of creating a monopoly or securing an information system). This is in contrast to providing consumers access to the open Internet for content and e-commerce.[18] This is primarily due to greed. Three easy-to-grasp examples of walled gardens are the following:

1. AOL's original strategy of containing all of its content exclusively for its Internet subscribers.
2. The ability to get the NFL Game Day Package only if you have DirectTV versus regular cable.

3. Apple iTunes store originally having set pricing at $0.99 even though the music industry would prefer variable pricing (some songs at $0.69, others at $1.26). Apple finally went to the latter model in 2009, so at least some companies are listening and learning.

"It's a race to see who will work better and faster with everyone else," said Charlene Li, founder of consulting company Altimeter Group. "It's recognition that you can't be an island of yourself."[19]

Microsoft Outlook's tied-in contacts, calendar, and e-mail are a good model for how someone will tie up the loose ends of web services.

We've seen this constantly over time, whether it was VHS versus Betamax, Blu-ray versus high-definition DVDs, or having to fill out the same three forms at the doctor's office with the same information every time you visit a different doctor. As for Android versus iPhone, the hope is, due to the open reliance and nature of social media, that this boils down to one seamless connectivity platform. We have seen some willingness to be more open than ever before by Facebook, Google Android, and even Apple allowing programmers access to its systems (via application program interface) to make applications. Apple has struggled with the approval process mandated for any application or iBook to appear in its store. Often these delays are measured in months.

If this type of cooperation were to occur, it would be very beneficial for the user. Today our choices get limited by the platform, provider, or technology we choose to select. Imagine having all of your clothes, shoes, and glasses from one brand versus getting your sunglasses from Oakley, watch from Rolex, and jacket from L.L. Bean. You would hate having to get these items from just one brand or supplier.

Imagine the ability to have only one login! How nice would that be, along with only a few places to visit when we finally reach an uberstate of truly everything being pushed to us rather than us hunting and gathering and putting things into one basket — we would have the basket being constantly filled with suggested information or products from friends we trust! With tools like Facebook Connect and Open ID, we are getting close, as these tools allow you to use your existing Facebook IDs to easily access other sites as well as to have your information follow you.

I have stated all along that I truly feel that in the end game, Facebook and the like will be less of a destination and more of a tool that you use wherever you may happen to be and that it will connect you to other portions of the Web.

— *Natalie Del Conte, CNET TV*

You can already see this with the new thinking that has been put forth by Facebook. In particular, the Facebook Connect product is all about openness. The thought behind Facebook Connect and other such platforms is to allow you to take your friends with you; it's what will result in the emergence of the social web. Instead of trying to hoard all of a user's data, it will be shared on the Discovery Channel site, *San Francisco Chronicle*, Hulu.com, Digg, and so on.

"Everyone is looking for ways to make their Websites more social," said Sheryl Sandberg, Facebook's chief operating officer. "They can build their own social capabilities, but what will be more useful for them is building on top of a social system that people are already wedded to."[20]

This type of open thinking is one of the building blocks of the social commerce items that we discussed previously. Specifically, this allows people to post a restaurant review on OpenTable at www.opentable.com and easily share it with Facebook, Foursquare, Zagat, and others. Before we crown Facebook as a saint, its ultimate goal is to monetize this information for billions of dollars. The proliferation of "Facebook Like" buttons on various websites is so that Facebook has the ability to aggregate this data for social commerce revenue. Now, if only hospitals and dentists could help me out by having only one form to complete.

You Don't Find a Job; It Finds You

Another huge shift in the way we do things, both as individuals and as businesses, is the process of job recruitment. To better understand this shift, we should review the historical practice of job recruiting and job hunting.

For the past 10 years, if you were attempting to recruit talent, you would pay money to post on job boards like Monster, Career-Builder, Hot Jobs, and so on. Or you could hire a recruiting firm or headhunter to assist in the recruitment effort. As you have read and will read throughout this book, intermediaries are removed in most instances as a result of the social web. In the job recruitment market, these are job boards, job fairs, classified advertisements, and job search firms. For the near future, these traditional recruiting avenues will remain but their influence will be greatly reduced, and not too far down the line they will probably vanish altogether, except for very specialized or C-level recruiting. Social networks like Craigslist, LinkedIn, and Plaxo will ultimately take over the recruitment role because they provide more direct and insightful connections between the employer and potential employee. Most likely it will even truncate down to one player; LinkedIn should monopolize this sector for many years to come. It's important to note that, as of this writing, LinkedIn isn't blocked in China, whereas Facebook, Twitter, Google, and YouTube are.

The newfound transparency from social business networks is a godsend for employers. They no longer have to employ a large internal human resources or recruitment staff to perform this type of research, or hire an expensive headhunter. Instead, the potential workforce is already doing this for you, the employer, and they are doing it at much greater depths. Reviewing a resume in the past was part art and part science; it was necessary to read between the lines on a static piece of paper to formulate whether the person deserved a screening call or interview. Now, social business networks supply photos, videos, links showing a person's actual work, 15 to 20 snapshot references, links to blogs or articles the person may be included in, and so on. If a picture can say a thousand words, then a video resume must be in the millions, because there is nothing more helpful than this for a recruiter. Recruiters can quickly screen through potential hires in minutes versus all the guesswork associated with traditional paper resumes (paper resumes will still be a nice complement to video resumes).

LinkedIn is a good place to start because it is a powerful pseudo-monopoly. As of the writing of this book, LinkedIn has almost cornered the market on the social business network. This will be tough to supplant because users already have their rec-ommendations on the site. Unless there is an easy way to port these recommendations to a new business network, it would be a somewhat uncomfortable task for people to solicit their previous references to rewrite what had already been posted for a new social business network (this book covers the importance for all social media tools to be interconnected). Imagine having to call your reference and say, "Morning, Carol, this is Ted. I know I haven't spoken to you in three years, but about that nice comment and thumbs-up you gave me on LinkedIn about four years ago, I was wondering if you wouldn't mind signing up for this new job site, after you get your account, which will take six minutes. Can you then write the exact same thing you did for me previously?" That would obviously be no small order. That being said, the hope is that, as previously stated, LinkedIn also figures out how to make the web more open by allowing your LinkedIn data and recommendations to easily flow and follow you accordingly.

For job seekers, the "always keep your resume updated" paradigm is gone because now it doesn't even scratch the surface of the importance of maintaining updated information, and more important, updated connections. It is essential to constantly update your career progress on social business networks as well as other social media, websites, blogs, and so on. It is also much more than simply updating your paper resumes on these sites. It behooves you to have an updated and professional photograph; also, a list of articles that mention you is helpful.

A link to your own personal and professional website with additional information about you will put you a step ahead of the competition. Any radio or video interviews of you should be easily accessible to augment your video resume. Most important of all is to capture positive feedback and postings from your bosses, peers, partners, and subordinates. In the past, you really needed only one or two solid references from your supervisors.

Previously, once recruiters were able to get potential hires in through the doors, the screening process was difficult at best. It was generally based on a few interviews, a possible call to a reference or two (most likely not), and then your standard background check (this step was also sometimes skipped).

However, that didn't really tell employers the entire story, did it? You could be a superstar adored by your boss, but a recruiter may miss the fact that you are a terrible team player, that you treat your peers and subordinates with little respect, and that as a whole you'd be a detriment to add to an organization that already has good team chemistry. That is why as an individual it is important that you have well-rounded feedback from various divisions and peer groups inside and outside the organization. If you skew too heavily one way or another, it may quickly reveal a weakness to your potential employer.

One of the most important things employers look at today is the person's network itself! If the employer is hiring a bunch of new talent and brings on someone who has a polished network, then the new hire instantly becomes a recruiting asset. It was never possible before to have this type of insight into someone's network. You could assume that candidates were connected with people at their current place of work, but you could never confirm it. Bringing on someone who has 300 well-respected professionals in her network is a tremendous asset to any company because after she is hired, the recruited quickly becomes the recruiter. In other words, as you hire job candidates, look at their potential reach; how many friends and connections do they have? That person's extended digital network is a favorable asset for the hiring company.

What really makes a network like LinkedIn helpful is that it allows users to share their online Rolodexes. Shally Steckerl uses social network LinkedIn (industry leader) to more easily recruit talent for Microsoft and other online companies. Steckerl says:

> With my Rolodex, I had to call any one of these thousand people and say, "Hey, Bob, I'm looking for someone that does this, or I'm looking for someone in this industry, or I'm looking for a job. Who do you know?" With social networking, I don't need to go to Bob directly to find out who Bob's friends are. Or Bob's friends' friends. So, effectively, I have a thousand contacts that could potentially lead me to 100,000; now I have 8,500 contacts that could potentially lead me to 4.5 million.[21]

Echoes Maureen Crawford-Hentz of global lighting company Osram Sylvania, "Social networking technology is absolutely the best thing to happen to recruiting—ever. It's important to load your profile with the right keywords so people like me can find you easily."

It's also important within these social business networks to be constantly building equity. This can be obtained by connecting two people whom you have in your network, posting jobs that you are aware of, giving your peers a thumbs-up, and adding written recommendations next to these approval ratings.

Aside from building equity that can be drawn on later, it's imperative that workers proactively manage their brand, whether or not they are currently in the job market. Employers will perform Google and YouTube searches on a potential recruit's name as well as filter through blogs, Facebook, and Foursquare networks to see what is posted out there. Employers are always looking to mitigate risk. So, even though you may have on your resume a 3.9 grade point average and a 1,300 SAT score (which would equate to a much higher number on the new version of the SAT), this information is immaterial if your Foursquare profile picture is of you holding a beer bong while wearing a jockstrap on your head; good luck in landing that dream job!

While I hope you aren't that stupid, you most likely have some friends who are. So it's important to spot-check what is out there and aggressively ferret out potential career land mines. Job seekers should act like a potential employer and go to the search engines to investigate what shows up when searching for their name. Unflattering items should proactively be removed from the public eye. Part of this search includes confirmation that there aren't any egregious videos out there. Also, if job seekers share a common name with an individual who is less than scrupulous, then the job seeker needs to make certain the employer knows that that person is not the job seeker, but rather someone else with the same name. This due diligence and research can take time, so even if you aren't currently in the job market, it's imperative to keep items inside and outside of your business social networks as buttoned up as possible.

It's also important for individuals to build out their digital business network before they actually need the network. If you haven't communicated with someone in three years, it's much harder to ask that person a favor than if you have been maintaining your network and have been in consistent contact with your social graph. Once you do find yourself in the interview room or via video Skype, it's imperative to show your story rather than simply tell the story. In an old job interview you would tell your story as the candidate. However, today you can literally walk potential employers through your items digitally — showing them versus merely telling them why you are the right person for the job.

Thirteen Virgin airline employees should have heeded this advice before they were let go from the U.K.-based airline for inappropriate behavior on Facebook. The 13 employees formed a group on Facebook and thought it would be a fun joke to insinuate that there were plenty of cockroaches on Virgin's planes and that the passengers were generally chavas. *Chava* is the British equivalent to calling someone a redneck, or more specifically:

> *Chav, Chava or Charva, or Charver is a derogatory term applied to certain young people in Great Britain. The stereotypical view of a chava is an aggressive teen or young adult, of working class background, who wears branded sports and casual clothing (baseball caps are also common). Often fights and engages in petty criminality and are often assumed to be unemployed or in a low paid job.*[22]

Obviously, the competition among airlines is fierce, so Virgin didn't hesitate to quickly fire these employees for what it deemed insubordination. The world has shifted, and whether we like it or not, we are always representing who we are and whether we are on the clock.

Hunters Become the Hunted

The good news for job seekers is that they too also have new and similar powers to check up on a potential employer, thanks in large part to social media. Within these social networks, they have review boards about various employers. And just like in the Kevin Bacon game that uses the famous *Six Degrees of Separation* concept, there is potential that a friend of a friend will have worked for a particular company if a job seeker wants to get the scoop firsthand.

Along those lines, you can readily see if anyone in your social business network is interlinked to the person who may ultimately be your boss in the new job. The ability to check on your potential future boss's background along with what other people are saying about that person is very comforting and useful.

This is also great preparation for the interview. If you know your interviewee is a member of Big Brothers and Big Sisters, you may steer the conversation in that direction. But, even more important, if you are selected for the job, examining the profile of the person who may become your boss will help you decide whether you want to work for this person. Do you think you can learn from this new boss? Do you have the same theories, aspirations, and approach to work and life?

Other social media tools that are popping up are originated by companies like Glassdoor (www.glassdoor.com). Glassdoor was started by Rich Barton, who was also very successful with Expedia and Zillow, both of which opened up information previously not available to end users (for travel and real estate, respectively). Zillow in particular allowed users to go in and change items listed about their houses in wiki format (if there were actually two bathrooms instead of the single bathroom listed, the owner could go in and adjust the data). Glassdoor was started using the concept of "What would happen if someone left the unedited employee survey for the whole company on the printer and it got posted to the web?"

The site mentions what it does: "Glassdoor.com provides a complete, real-time, inside look at what it's really like to work at a company—ratings, reviews, confidence in senior leadership, and salaries—for free." Well, it is free in terms of cash outlay, but the site does require users to share salaries of their current or past positions before they can see salaries that others have posted. The site encourages and demands sharing for the social product to work. Networks like this give the interviewees some power, especially when it comes to salary negotiation, because they can see what others in the same position are currently making.

In the past, information on the ins and outs of companies as well as background on potential bosses was limited, if not nonexistent. In a very short time, social media has eliminated this information deficiency. There are even some web-based recruitment compa-nies sprouting up that are looking at a social commerce model where instead of headhunters getting paid, they actually pay the interviewee money for the opportunity to interview — one such site is called Paidinterviews (www.paidinterviews.com). It will be interesting to see if this represents a wave of the future.

A Better Workplace for Employees and Employers

Generally, this transparency makes for a better work environment for employers and employees. It also can greatly increase produc-tivity in companies because the wrong person is less likely to be put into the wrong job. The number of employees leaving within a year will also be reduced because new recruits will have a better sense of what they are getting into (job, boss, company). Also, once employees are in place, now more than ever before, it's essential that they work well with their peers, subordinates, partners, and bosses because their ability to land their next job will depend on it. Skeletons are no longer in the closet; rather, they are available for everyone to see in social business networks.

Hiring the Internet Generation

Just as the one-way messaging strategy of advertisers is no longer viable in this new age, it no longer works for employers, either. Millennials are used to and want collaboration, but they will not necessarily acknowledge or adhere to traditional lines of authority or chains of command. Soon, many baby boomers in executive-level positions will retire, and there will be an intense talent fight among companies. Companies can give themselves an advantage by under-standing that this new talent has different attitudes, expectations, and skills than the previous generations.

Some people paint members of this under-30 crowd as spoiled or lazy. That is far from the truth. They are just different, and in a lot of positive ways. Work and life balance is much more important to them than it was to their parents, and they desire positions that are able to conform to their lifestyles (e.g., work from home or at odd hours). Company beliefs and values need to align with those of employees. A company mission of simply making as much money as possible turns many members of this generation off. Companies need to contribute to the greater good of society, and have to be part of the social community and causes.

Ironically, though, if another firm offers Millennials more money or a better opportunity, they will go. There is less loyalty; on average, Millennials will have 14 different jobs by the time they are 40 years old. Members of this generation have seen that companies in general aren't loyal to their employees, so why should they in turn be loyal to their employers? They desire to stay at the same company and grow, but they understand this probably isn't going to be a reality. They've also seen that companies may have a strong and robust life span of only 10 to 20 years (e.g., Lycos, Prodigy, Atari, Enron, Circuit City). Fun at work isn't just a *nice-to-have*; it is a *need-to-have*.

Employers need to throw away the old human resources playbook that consisted of hire, train, manage, and retain. This generation wants collaboration in all aspects of their lives, in part because of the social media tools they grew up with and are accustomed to, but especially because work is where they spend the most time.

Showing up at a college campus for a career fair isn't going to get the job done, because it's a whole new world. Online sites now hold 110 million jobs and 20 million unique resumes. Traditional advertising to attract young talent is as good as burning money. As a company, you need to use everything in your arsenal — blogs, podcasts, social media sites, and so on. However, your current staff members are your best recruiters because they are the ones with the networks and referral power. Just as marketing will be more focused on referral programs, the same holds true for recruiting.

Retaining Talent

By using social media tools during the recruitment process, companies have a better chance of maintaining talent because it's more likely to help put the right person in the right position. However, an employer's work is just beginning when the company hires someone. Generation Yers desire constant feedback, and they also evaluate the company from day one. They will not wait around in hopes that things will get better or things will change. There is too much opportunity for them to go to a competitor or even for them to start their own businesses.

Employers are best off exposing new hires to various departments, leaders, and projects. Often the best thing that managers can do is simply get out of the way, because the young talent may be vastly more talented than they are in certain areas (great hire!). So, instead of traditional management and micromanagement, bosses may be more focused on fostering an environment for success.

Just as employees shouldn't burn bridges, employers shouldn't, either. When an employee leaves, it can be bittersweet. But it's important to focus on the sweet versus the bitter because today talent may boomerang back once they see it's not so great out there. It's imperative that employers not take a smug "we told you so" attitude, but rather take pride in knowing that they must be doing something right if this talent is coming back. Often within social networks, people stay engaged with their previous company through specific groups. That's why Yahoo! Alumni and Microsoft Alumni groups on Facebook have 2,300 and 1,600 members, respectively. A study done in Canada of 18- to 34-year-olds showed that the average person had held five full-time jobs by age 27. Rehiring saves money. *Harvard Business Review* indicated it costs roughly half as much to rehire and that rehires are 40 percent more efficient in their first 90 days than new hires,[23] which intuitively makes sense. Plus, they are also less likely to leave again. The key is for your company to embrace this change in the workforce and to learn as much from Generation Y and beyond as these generations do from your company.

Tony Tweets

Tony Hawk is the Michael Jordan of skateboarding. Tony owns more skateboarding titles than anyone in history, and he literally put the sport on the map. After retiring from competitive skateboarding, Tony continued his success in the business world, becoming a global icon from the sale of his video games, clothes, skateboards, and the like.

When Twitter started to grow in popularity, Tony saw an opportunity and seized it. His first foray was to leave a skateboard randomly in a hedge on a street. He sent a note out on Twitter that somewhere along said street was a free skateboard for whoever found it first. This was so successful that he continued doing it, and he saw his followers on Twitter grow to over 2 million. More importantly, he started to see sales grow.

Then Tony started to use Twitter to announce impromptu town events. Tony and some other professional skateboarders would show up at a skateboarding park and ride with the locals. This was so successful that in time Tony realized he couldn't send out the tweet more than an hour in advance; otherwise, there would be so many people that he couldn't physically get through the sea of humanity to actually skate.

Keep in mind that Twitter's initial popularity wasn't with Tony's normal customer base (young adults); rather, it indexed high for business usage for people 35 to 50 years old.

Tony is a great example showcasing that no matter what you do or what you sell, if you are creative, are passionate, and use common sense, you can use social media tools to succeed.

Southwest Is No Ding-a-Ling

As we mentioned previously, we have grown accustomed to the news finding us. We have also grown accustomed to other pieces of information finding us rather than searching for them. Brands and companies that understand this have benefited and will benefit in the future. Southwest Airlines recognized this early on with its Ding Widget. Users place this widget somewhere convenient (desktop, social network, mobile app, etc.). For a user who lives in Nashville, Tennessee, and whose Mom lives in Birmingham, Alabama, the widget will alert them with a "ding" whenever an appropriate airline ticket sale is available. After the first year, the widget hit the 2 million download mark and then went on to generate $150 million in sales.[24] It is estimated that the widget receives upwards of 40 million clicks per year. The cost to develop and maintain such a widget is so low that it is almost at the point of insignificance.

The key with successful widgets like this is for the companies to show restraint in their push messages. Some smart companies have almost adopted a publisher's model. Historically, newspapers and magazines kept their writers in a distinctly different silo than their advertising sales team to ensure that their articles or content were not compromised by pressure from their largest clients.

With successful widgets and applications, some companies go to great lengths and in some extreme cases even turn over how these widgets are messaged to the product team versus the marketing team. In the past, many companies have seen with cost-efficient delivery channels (think e-mail) that marketing will spam the user. With these widgets, if you spam the users (in this example, that would be Southwest sending a general reduced-fare message for 20 cities, none of which are either Nashville or Birmingham), they will be gone.

Speaking of being gone, that is exactly what is happening to some business and personal behaviors. This book highlights that some traditional behaviors, constructs, and principles will continue in this new world, whereas others will not be suitable. Individuals and businesses face new challenges if they are to stay relevant and viable in this new Socialnomic world. Are you up to the challenge?

Chapter Eight Key Points

1. Don't build your own Field of Nightmares by creating or replicating a social network for your company. If you build it, they most likely will *not* come. You are better off connecting to the best-in-class social media tools that exist. You aren't a social media company, so don't attempt to parade as one.
2. Social media is helping to drive the transformation of mobile devices to being the dominant Internet access point instead of computers.
3. The information exchanged in social media in relation to job searching and recruiting has rendered it unrecognizable from the information exchanged 10 years ago. Appropriate matches between employer and employee have increased as a result of this increased information flow.
4. Just as marketing will become more referral based as a result of rapid information exchanges enabled by social media tools, job seeking and recruitment will be more referral based than ever before.
5. The younger generation's interpersonal communication skills are starting to suffer as a result of overdependence on nonverbal and non-face-to-face interactions.
6. Search engine results and the traditional Internet advertising model are antiquated. Social media will push both of these to revolutionize; otherwise, they will see a dramatic decrease in market share.
7. The overall achievement of individuals and companies will be largely dependent on their social media success.
8. Fail fast, fail forward, fail better.
9. Advances in mobile are making for an always connected society. Social consumption will only increase as the mobile consumption devices continue to advance.
10. Proactively build your digital business network before you need it.

CHAPTER NINE

Social Media Rolodex and Resources

As you approach the end of this book, I want to ensure you continue your digital education. By all means, I'd be flattered if you went on to follow my writings, videos, and other exploits. I thought it would also be helpful if I supplied a list of people and resources that I draw inspiration from and look to for ideas, advice, and the opportunity to collaborate with. This is my #FF Twitter shout-out, but in book format!

I hope you find these resources helpful as you continue your digital education. Admittedly the downside to this section is that I'm certain to leave off some very talented people! Feel free to contact me with any I have missed or that you have discovered and I'll augment on www.socialnomics.com. This list is in reverse alphabetical order.

The social media space is constantly changing, so it's important to continue to have the latest news and changes pushed your way. Feel free to refer back to *Socialnomics* often while staying abreast of new findings and trends from the following people and resources.

Dan Zarrella, often called a social media scientist, does a great job of collecting tons of data and making sense of it all by spotting trends. He has insightful findings on which types of tweets have the best chance to be retweeted. He is a product owner at HubSpot and the author of *The Social Media Marketing Book*, *The Facebook Marketing Book*, and *Zarella's Hierarchy of Contagiousness*. @danzarrella

Larry Webber founded one of the world's largest and most successful public relations (PR) companies. He has written five books in the PR/social media space, with his latest being *Sticks & Stones*. @TheLarryWebber

Gary Vaynerchuk is a social media sommelier who has proven that passion + effort + social media = a healthy return. He has helped grow his family wine business from $4 million to $50 million through the use of social media. He is best known for his "Wine Library TV," a series of videos giving insights on wine. He is also the author of *Crush It!* and *The Thank You Economy*. @garyvee

Jamie Turner is coauthor of *How to Make Money with Social Media* and *Go Mobile*. He is also the CEO of the online magazine *The 60 Second Marketer*.

Liz Strauss is an influential noncelebrity blogger helping people to learn. She's been called an idea machine and is the CEO and founder of SOBCon and author of the popular blog at www.successful-blog.com. She likes to provide the human touch. @lizstrauss

Scott Stratten is the president of Un-Marketing.com. He is an expert in viral, social, and authentic marketing, which he calls un-marketing. He has written a book by the same title. @unmarketing

Biz Stone is the cofounder of Twitter. @biz

Brian Solis is a principal analyst at Altimeter Group. His book *Engage* has a foreword from Ashton Kutcher. He is also the author of *The End of Business as Usual*. Solis is co-founder of the Social Media Club and is an original member of the Media 2.0 Workgroup. @briansolis

Mari Smith is a social media business coach. *Fast Company* magazine called her the "Pied Piper of Online." She has intimate insight on social media strategies for small business and is an expert on Facebook. Her smile, Scottish-Canadian accent, and ebullient personality have attracted many fans and followers — she is a great case study in developing one's own brand. Smith combines a good mix of energy and honesty. She is coauthor of *Facebook an Hour per Day*. @MariSmith

Shiv Singh is Avenue A/Razorfish VP and global social media lead. He is also the author of *Social Media Marketing for Dummies*. He is a regular author and contributor to numerous Avenue A/Razorfish white papers and studies on social media. @shivsingh

Clay Shirky is a New York University graduate professor of the Interactive Telecommunications Program (ITP) and one of the world's most requested speakers on social media. @cshirky

Peter Shankman is perhaps best known for founding Help a Reporter Out (HARO), which was acquired by Vocus, Inc. In addition to HARO, he is the founder and CEO of the Geek Factory, Inc., a boutique marketing and PR strategy firm in New York City, with clients worldwide. Shankman is the author of *Can We Do That?! Outrageous PR Stunts That Work and Why Your Company Needs Them* and *Customer Service: New Rules for a Social-Enabled World.* @skydiver

Dharmesh Shah, cofounder of HubSpot, is a very entertaining and informative social media speaker. He is coauthor of the best-selling book *Inbound Marketing.* @dharmesh

David Meerman Scott, marketing strategist and author, was well ahead of the curve in 2007 with his best-selling book, *The New Rules of Marketing & PR.* He appears to have another winner in the book *Inbound Marketing: Get Found Using Google, Social Media, and Blogs* as a contributing author and editor. Scott is very generous with his time and is an active contributor across the web and on the speaking circuit. @dmscott

Dan Schwabel is a personal branding expert and guru of Generation Y in the workforce. Founder of Millennial Branding, he is the number-one international bestselling author of *Me 2.0* and a *TIME/Forbes* columnist.

Mark Schaefer is chieftain of the blog {grow}, college professor, and author of *Return on Influence* and *Tao of Twitter.* @markschaefer

Lon Safko, marketing expert and author of *Social Media Bible* and *Fusion*, has a great understanding of how all the parts of the marketing mix fit or are fused together. @lonsafko

Brian Reich is managing director at little m media. When he is not writing thought-provoking books like *Shift & Reset* and *Media Rules!*, he spends most of his time thinking about the impact technology is having on our society.

Jeremiah Owyang is partner, customer strategy, at Altimeter Group and columnist for *Forbes* CMO Network. He is also a great complement to Charlene Li at the Altimeter Group and excels at interpreting news. As an industry analyst he tells us what it means and is a great reference for the market. @jowyang

Lee Odden is one of 25 online marketing experts featured in Michael Miller's *Online Marketing Heroes*, published by John Wiley & Sons in 2008, and has been cited for his search and social media marketing expertise by the *Economist, U.S. News & World Report*, and *Fortune* magazine. Odden is the CEO of TopRank Online Marketing and author of *Optimize: Win More Customers with Social Media, SEO and Content Marketing.* @LeeOdden

Amber Naslund is director of the community for Radian6. She loves to dissect the collision of community and business within social media. @AmberCadabra

Dave Morin is a former senior platform manager at Facebook. Morin was named one of the "100 Most Creative People in Business" by *Fast Company* in 2009. He is the founder of Path, a popular private social network. @davemorin

Scott Monty is the digital and multimedia communications manager at Ford Motor Company. He practices what he preaches by having ongoing conversations with car buyers and influencers. While he is a marketer rather than an engineer, his new type of thinking and passion has changed the way Ford thinks and is ultimately the reason why Ford is looking more like a Macintosh computer and less like a Model T. Much can be learned from Monty's intelligence, foresight, and fortitude. @scottmonty

Chuck Martin is the CEO of the Mobile Future Institute and director of the Center of Media Research at MediaPost Communications Inc. He has written nine books on mobile marketing, including the popular *The Third Screen*. @chuckmartin1

Amy Jo Martin has over 1.3 million followers on Twitter. She works with Shaquille O'Neal and other professional athletes and franchises. She has hosted a few NFL teams at the Social Media Clubhouse during SXSW. @digitalroyalty

Valeria Maltoni writes a blog, *Conversation Agent*, that is recognized among the world's top online marketing blogs (among the top 25 on *Advertising Age*'s Power 150, as well as three categories in Guy Kawasaki's Alltop). Maltoni was handpicked by *Fast Company* as an expert blogger to write about creating conversations between the marketer and customer. She built one of the first online communities affiliated with the magazine. @ConversationAge

Charlene Li is the founder of Altimeter Group, coauthor of *Groundswell* (along with Josh Bernoff), and author of *Open Leadership*. She is also a great public speaker and has presented frequently at top technology conferences such as Web 2.0 Expo, SXSW, Search Engine Strategies, and the American Society of Association Executives. @charleneli

Dave Kerpen is a very likeable guy. He is the founder of Likeable Media out of New York. His clients include some of the best brands in the world, and Likeable Media helps guide them through the social media waters. Kerpen is also the author of *Likeable Social Media* (McGraw-Hill, 2011), which has been the #1 social media book for too many weeks to count.

Guy Kawasaki is a founding partner at Garage and co-founder of Alltop. Kawasaki describes Alltop as an "online magazine rack." He has written nine books and is always one step ahead of the curve. If you have a chance to read Kawasaki's bio, it is well worth it—a very interesting background (Apple disciple and an avid hockey fan). @GuyKawasaki

Mitch Joel has been dubbed by *Marketing* magazine the "Rock Star of Digital Marketing" and "one of North America's leading digital visionaries." Joel is the author of the book *Six Pixels of Separation* and former board member of the Interactive Advertising Bureau of Canada. @MitchJoel

Brian Halligan is co-founder and CEO of HubSpot. He is also coauthor of *Inbound Marketing*. He is a Sloan Fellow at MIT. @bhalligan

Seth Godin is an award-winning author of too many books to mention. He is always a few years ahead of the curve and is a wonderful storyteller who is able to break down complex issues into very digestible constructs. Godin is the godfather of permission-based marketing.

Paul Gillin was editor-in-chief and executive editor of the technology weekly *Computerworld* for 15 years. His 2007 book *The New Influencers* was awarded a silver medal in the business category by *ForeWord* magazine. @pgillin

Scott Galloway is a clinical associate professor at New York University's Stern School of Business, where he teaches brand and digital strategy to second-year MBA students. He is also the pioneer of the Digital IQ measurement. Galloway founded Red Envelope (NASDAQ: REDE) in 1997 and has served on the board of Gateway Computer (sold to Acer). He is currently on the board of directors of the New York Times Company. @profgalloway

Maggie Fox is founder and CEO of Social Media Group.com, one of the world's largest independent social media agencies. It has been Ford's social media agency since 2007. @maggiefox

Jason Falls is a very honest and funny keynote speaker on social media. He is also the author of *No Bullshit Social Media*. @JasonFalls

Sarah Evans, a self-described "social media freak," initiated and moderates #journchat, the weekly live chat between PR professionals, journalists, and bloggers on Twitter. She is also a guest writer for Mashable. @prsarahevans

Frank Eliason put customer service on the social media map by his pioneering on Twitter with Comcast, and leveraged his success there to become Executive VP of Social Media for Citibank. @comcastcares

Sam Decker has been a thought leader in the social media space since his days at Dell. As the CMO of Austin-based Bazaarvoice, he helped lead the charge on social commerce. He is now CEO of Mass Relevance, one of the few tools to have an integrated partnership with Twitter. @samdecker

Pete Cashmore is founder of Mashable and one of the most followed on Twitter. He is also a contributing editor to CNN. @mashable

Chris Brogan is president at New Marketing Labs. He is recognized as one of the "World's Top Bloggers" (Advertising Age Power 150 Top 10 Blog), and his book *Trust Agents* (coauthor is Julien Smith) reached the *New York Times* best sellers list. He is the author of *Social Media 101* and the co-founder of the PodCamp new media conference series. He takes time to respond to almost everyone who reaches out to him. @chrisbrogan

Josh Bernoff is coauthor of the *BusinessWeek* best-selling book *Groundswell: Winning in a World Transformed by Social Technologies*, and senior vice president, idea development, at Forrester Research. @jbernoff

Jay Baer has founded five companies and spent 15 years running digital marketing agencies. He has worked with the biggest of the big brands. He is the founder of Convince and Convert. @jaybaer

Additional Digital Thought Leaders

Corey Perlman, Louis Gray, Richard Binhammer, Robert Scoble, Lee Aase, Eric Bradlow, Sally Falkow, Don Steele, Julien Smith, Jim Carey, Michael Lazerow, Sarah Hofstetter, Mike Lewis, Mack Collier, Mike Barbeau, Alan Chan, Todd Defren, Tom Gerace, Elizabeth Pigg, Ken Robbins, Richard MacManus, Jon Gibs, Chris Cunningham, Paul Beck, Jesse Stay, Amy Porterfield, Mario Sundar, John Hill, Kip Bodnar, Adam Brown, Justin Levy, Phyllis Khare, Paul Colligan, Andrea Vahl, Rich Brooks, Rick Calvert, Nichole Kelly, Kelly Lester, Ana White, Matt Goddard, Chris Heuer, C. C. Chapman, Chris Penn, Shel Israel, Tamar Weinberg, Morgan Johnston, Tim Washer, Scott Henderson, David Armano, Mark Cattini, Michael Lewis, Nick O'Neil, Mike Stelzner, Sonia Simone, Adam Singer, Jessica Smith, Michael Brito, Geoff Livingston, Mike Volpe, and Wayne Sutton.

Others Who Inspire

Additional luminaries who aren't specific to the digital space, but have helped me and millions of others include Dan and Chip Heath, Malcolm Gladwell, Shawn Achor, Tom Izzo, and Dale Carnegie. Their insights can be applied across any walk of life.

Resources

CNET podcasts
SmartBriefs app
Social Media Today
Mashable
TechCrunch
Silicon Alley Insider
DMNews
BoomTown

Chapter Nine Key Points

1. Use the list of social media experts in this chapter as a reference so that you can continually learn beyond this book.
2. Reach out to the key influencers in your field and start developing those relationships both online and offline.
3. If you want to become an influencer yourself or grow your personal brand, then follow and learn from the luminaries listed in this chapter.

CHAPTER TEN

Social ROI

W e suggest you view these two videos before reading this chapter:

1. Socialnomics Social Media ROI:
   www.youtube.com/watch?v=ypmfs3z8esI
2. Social Media Intern (ROI):
   www.youtube.com/watch?v=auiczd4OUms

Some reading this book are social media geniuses, whereas others are just starting. The interesting part is that no matter where you are in this cycle, there are four easy steps that should always be adhered to and revisited.

Even if your company is a social media trailblazer, it's important to always take a step back and make certain you are following the basics. This is similar to when two college football teams are preparing for the National Championship. In 2010, as Alabama and Texas prepared for the game, Alabama's philosophy was as follows:

"The focus will be on fundamentals and execution, rather than scouting Texas. . . . It's going to be important for us that we get back to where we're physical and aggressive in what we're doing," Alabama Coach Nick Saban said. "That we play with the mental and physical toughness that kind of trademarks our team."[1]

This was very similar to how Texas was striving to achieve excellence:

> *"It's like starting over and having a one-game season," Texas coach Mack Brown said. "So you really have to go back and work on fundamentals."[2]*

These teams were the best in the country; both had perfect records. Yet, they still both felt it was necessary to go back to the fundamentals.

Now, if we are going to replicate a championship-caliber team and practice revisiting the fundamentals, it's important to examine the necessary paths and building blocks an individual or business needs to undertake within social media to have success.

One must wrestle with many complex social media issues. These can be overwhelming. Where to even begin?

Rather than be paralyzed, it's often best to understand that there are four simple, yet critical, steps to social media (see Figure 10.1).

It's easiest to think of it as a stairway (see diagram). If you learn anything, it's that you need to constantly practice the first step: listening. It's the most important step. As showcased in the diagram, the four steps are:

1. *Listen:* Pay attention to your customer and conversations around your brand.
2. *Interact:* Join the conversation.

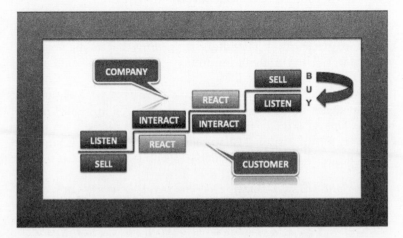

Figure 10.1   Socialnomics: Social Media Escalator

3. *React:* Adjust your product or service based on feedback.
4. *Sell:* If you listen, interact, and react, this will happen with less effort.

Companies often enter the social media fray and jump straight to step 4, selling. This is the worst thing you can do, and it won't be effective.

You need to start with step 1, which is listening. Without listening, the other three steps won't achieve any degree of success. As many have said before me, there's a reason we have two ears and one mouth.

After listening, you then have the appropriate baseline and credibility to join the conversation. Imagine if you were at a housewarming party and walked up to a group of people who were already engaged in a conversation and said, "I'm not sure what you are talking about, but here is what I want to talk about." This is socially unacceptable behavior in the offline world. Yet we also need to remember it's socially unacceptable behavior in a digital world as well. You don't want to be that person at the housewarming party, and you don't want to be that person or company in the digital social sphere.

Many embrace the listening and interacting correctly, but then they commit a terrible crime. They fail to do anything (react) based on the suggestions and information gathered. If 90 percent of the people complain about a certain aspect of your product or service, it's imperative that this issue is resolved, and resolved promptly. If 90 percent of the conversation is centered around certain aspects of the product or service that people love, then it's imperative that this information is placed in the appropriate hands (PR, production, sales, customer service, etc.) — *"Let's make sure we do more of this! Everyone loves it."*

We won't touch very much here on selling, because if you do the first three steps well (listen, interact, react), then the selling will happen with a proper push here and a prod there.

Notice in the diagram that the steps for the customer then happen in the reverse order of the steps for the company. This is *huge*. It's these steps that the customer takes within social media that give an exponential return (good or bad). (Please note that although we use the label "company" in the diagram, this could easily be a charitable organization, political party, small business, or something else.)

To make the framework easier to grasp, you can consider the following customer actions as steps 5, 6, 7, and 8. This is where the magic can really happen.

5. *Listen:* The customer buys the product or service from the selling company. The customer's first step is to *listen* for what to expect from the product or service (important expectation setting here). What is the value that will be delivered? This also may involve reading instructions or a manual.
6. *Interact:* The customer will then *interact* with the new product or service (e.g., use the product or service).
7. *React:* During or after this interaction, the customer will *react* according to his or her experience (good/neutral/bad).
8. *Sell:* The consumer's reaction to the product or service will determine if the consumer *sells* for or against the company or product. Keep in mind if it's a negative reaction, you still have a chance to correct the situation by *interacting* and *reacting*.

As a company, if you appropriately engage in the four steps, the stairs in the diagram act more like an escalator than a traditional stairway (i.e., social media escalator). It will create a positive motion, which, with the appropriate effort, will continue to take your product or service to the top. And that is the true beauty of social commerce.

The best strategy in social media is a simple one; in life and social media speed and simplicity win. Always remind yourself of the fundamentals.

What We Can Learn from *Footloose*

As of the writing of this book, it is a common practice for companies and organizations to ban social media in the workplace or office—one study indicates 54 percent of companies block social media. It reminds me of the 1984 movie *Footloose*, where a town banned rock music until Kevin Bacon's character helped save the day.

In today's version, instead of starring Kevin Bacon, perhaps either Jack Dorsey (co-founder of Twitter and Square) or Mark Zuckerberg (founder of Facebook) could star in the lead role. Just as we now look back on the ban in *Footloose* as being rather silly, the same will likely apply to these social media bans that companies and organizations now employ.

USA Today reported that as of the fourth quarter of 2009 54 percent of companies completely blocked Facebook, whereas another 35 percent applied some limitations. That leaves only 11 percent that don't put restrictions on Facebook in the workplace.

Why does this feel like déjà vu? It is. Web mail (Yahoo!, Hotmail, AOL, etc.) used to be banned in the workplace. A few years before that, companies banned the Internet or e-commerce sites at the workplace.

And it's not just companies that placed these types of bans; teachers often ban mobile phones in the classroom as well. Is this the right thing to do?

Banning social media at work is:

- Analogous to banning the Internet.
- Analogous to banning the phone because you might make a personal phone call.
- Analogous to banning paper and pens because an employee might take a note that isn't related to work.
- Potentially a signal to workers and future recruits that your company just doesn't get it.

Wasting Time on Social Media Actually Makes You More Productive

"People who do surf the Internet for fun at work — within a reasonable limit of less than 20 percent of their total time in the office — are more productive by about 9 percent than those who don't," according to Dr. Brent Coker, from the department of management and marketing at the University of Melbourne, Australia.

Before we dive back into the workplace, the teacher example is an interesting dilemma to review. Some phones have such high-pitched ringers that teachers can't hear them but the students' younger ears can hear them. But is this really a technology issue, question, or problem? Or is it a historic problem that teachers have been wrestling with since the first school opened?

Whether students are whispering, daydreaming, sleeping, passing a note, doodling, or sending a text, it's all the same thing: the teacher isn't reaching them. Recently, Lee Scott, Walmart's chairman, said for his first four years on the job he was looking for new critics, when all along he should have been looking to produce a better product or store experience.

Capturing students' attention has been historically difficult. The teacher's task isn't an enivable one. However, the really good teachers have been able to overcome the hurdles presented before them.

If you ban today's technology, does it solve the problem? Probably not. Also, texting is probably less intrusive than whispering or passing notes, as it doesn't affect the others in the room as much.

Also, good students might suffer, as they may be potentially looking up something on their mobile browsers that the teacher is covering either to fact-check or to see if something visual clicks with their brains in a way that's better for them than how the teacher is attempting to explain it. Or, if they have already grasped the concept, why shouldn't they be able to learn something else new and exciting at their fingertips?

Some teachers may benefit by leveraging this technology in the classroom; students have grown up with technology. Rather than being lectured at, they're used to dynamic interaction with various technologies and sources to provide possible answers.

It also depends on the age of the student. This is applied more easily to college students than, say, middle school students, where anything that could possibly distract attention from the teacher isn't good. (It's also another reason why our teachers should be paid more, as it's one of the most difficult jobs around, and now teachers have the added challenge of keeping abreast of new technology.)

Company Restrictions on Social Media

Banning social media could send the wrong message to employees and potential recruits that a company doesn't get it. Also, how can companies learn what to do in social media if they aren't allowing their employees to even use the tools?

All new tools have a learning curve. When people started using phones in the workplace, they had to be educated not to make 30 minutes' worth of personal calls, call internationally, or speak too loud.

More recently, when e-mail was introduced, classes were held in workplaces on tonality of e-mails, not replying to all, not wasting much of the workday on e-mail, and so forth. With social media, similar instruction and guidance should be given to the workforce. For example, Facebook or Skype instant messaging (IM) chatting or Google+ hangouts with your friends may not be the best use of your time, and will make it difficult for you to achieve your goals; nor is it wise to status update "Glad I'm out of the jail I call work for today."

An employee either produces desired results or doesn't. If one employee reads Wikipedia during her break time but produces 40 sales per week and another employee reads books outside during his break but produces only 15 sales per week, which employee would you keep? If you're in the business of making money, you'd keep the one producing 40 sales per week and let her read Wikipedia.

"Short and unobtrusive breaks, such as a quick surf of the Internet, enable the mind to rest itself, leading to a higher total net concentration for a day's work and, as a result, increased productivity," Dr. Coker of the University of Melbourne said.

Some employees might benefit from having social media in the workplace. If you're in outbound sales for home insurance, it would be helpful to receive a tweet from a friend in California indicating that the wildfires have taken a sharp turn toward Orange County or from a Midwestern friend that the telephone lines are out in Minneapolis, or to see a user-generated picture or video of the fires taking place that includes a geolocator on them.

Or think about sales in general. What are two of the top rules of sales? *Listen* and *know the customer*.

Google isn't so great at supplying real-time results, but social media certainly is (there's a reason why deals were struck among Bing, Twitter, Google, and Facebook). So, if I'm a salesperson about to make a phone call, tools like Technorati, LinkedIn, Twitter Trends, and Wikipedia are helpful for figuring out what is being said about this prospect or the prospect's company. Why would you ban tools that are valuable to your workforce?

One possible answer is that management doesn't trust workers not to abuse the sites for other reasons. Is that a social media issue? I'd argue it's a workforce issue.

Also, whether you're at work or in the classroom, when you treat people like kids by not trusting them, expect them to behave like kids. Is that what you want?

Do you think Apple or Google bans people from these sites? Their stocks were up 140 percent and 79 percent, respectively, early in 2010. They must be laughing out in Silicon Valley.

Occasionally, some bans make sense. For example, a university that bans downloading music on its network because of bandwidth issues is reasonable. Other bans (like those in *Footloose*) are just silly.

Don't ban social media. In the near future we'll look back and wonder, "Remember when we used to ban social media? What were we thinking?" Don't be a dinosaur; they became extinct.

Social Media Return on Investment (ROI)

A big question out there these days is: What is the ROI of social media? Or the ever-popular: How do I measure the ROI of social media? Often an appropriate retort to this question is: "What's the ROI of your phone?" Other times it's not appropriate to respond with this answer, which, if done in the wrong tone or place, can win you a free punch in the face. Often the simplest response to this question is: "The ROI of social media is that in five years your company will still exist."

Then there are the naysayers who adamantly proclaim: "We aren't doing social media because there isn't any ROI." Again, it's important to stress for companies, organizations, churches, and the like: There is not a choice in *whether* to do social media; the choice is in how *well* you do it. Some companies and marketers are becoming paralyzed with attempting to determine the ROI of social media by incorrectly using inappropriate tools and measurements. Or as Gary Vaynerchuk eloquently puts it: "It's like asking what's the ROI of your mother."

To borrow from the conductor of the Boston Philharmonic Orchestra, Benjamin Zander,

> There are those in life who sit in the back row with their arms folded, judging and complaining. Then there are those who sit in the front row with a vision, and they are spending their energy on making that vision a reality.

When Google search exploded onto the scene, what did the good companies do? The good companies immediately started buying pay-per-click advertisements to help drive sales.

What did the great companies do? They also jumped with both feet into the pay-per-click arena, but they further realized that 70 percent of the clicks happened outside of the paid listings. The majority of the clicks were in the free, organic, and natural listings rather than the sponsored listings. In order to rank high organically, the great companies realized that some search engine optimization (SEO) principles needed to be applied.

SEO has come a long way, but even today a CEO may view it as black magic and it's often tough to calculate a *hard* ROI for it; it can take years, not weeks, to see the fruits of the labor. However, great companies didn't sit back with their arms folded saying we aren't doing SEO until you prove an ROI. Great companies went on the attack, since they recognized that these major shifts present opportunities that don't come along often. Great companies went full speed ahead attacking keywords like "home mortgages," "cheap travel," and "black dress," and they derived tremendous revenue. Some even adjusted their business models entirely. They had a vision.

To borrow a line from New York University Professor Scott Galloway, social media is not checkers; it's chess (I believe he credits the line to Denzel Washington in the movie *Training Day*).

Social media is something the likes of which we haven't seen before (just like SEO before it, but with greater impact). As a result, I prefer to ask, "What does or will success look like?" rather than "What's the ROI?"

After all, why are we trying to measure social media like a traditional channel? Social media touches every facet of business, and it should be viewed more as an extension of good business ethics—which, if done properly, will harvest sales down the line. Co-chairman Alex Bogusky of Crispin Porter & Bogusky puts it best when he states:

> *You can't buy attention anymore. Having a huge budget doesn't mean anything in social media. . . . The old media paradigm was* pay to play. *Now you get back what you authentically put in. You've got to be willing to play to play.*

If your executives are stubbornly set on tracking metrics like a traditional ROI, you can do it. On the following page are some points to ponder. However, I would caution you that even though you can measure certain aspects of social media this way, I strongly argue that you are *greatly* underserving your current and future efforts by not understanding that social media touches every aspect of your company and isn't a simple ROI formula for your marketing department.

Before going into a list of ROI examples, one that I love is from General Mills. General Mills placed codes on packs of its Green Giant frozen vegetables that consumers could redeem for Farm Cash on FarmVille. (FarmVille is a social gaming tool produced by Zynga that had close to 100 million users in 2010.) General Mills is actually able to track whether Green Giant sales index higher for the packages containing the Farm Cash codes.

Convenience store 7-Eleven did a similar thing with some of its products. For example, buyers of certain flavors of ice cream were rewarded with a Neapolitan cow (quite difficult to get) in FarmVille. "People are asking, 'How do I know what the ROI is on these social media programs?' and in this case, we can definitely track directly to sales on our registers," said 7-Eleven marketing manager Evan Brody.[3] These are two quick and creative examples of how you can track a hard ROI using social media. Here are 22 more quick statistics relevant to ROI:

1. Gary Vaynerchuk grew his family business from $4 million to $50 million using social media.[4] Gary's eccentric personality and offbeat oenophile knowledge have proven a natural path to success with his Wine TV Library.[5]

2. Vaynerchuk found firsthand that $15,000 in direct mail = 200 new customers; $7,500 Billboard = 300 new customers; $0 Twitter = 1,800 new customers.[6]

3. A Wetpaint/Altimeter study found that companies that are both deeply and widely engaged in social media significantly surpass their peers in both revenues and profits. The study also found that company sales with the highest levels of social media activity grew on average by 18 percent, while those companies with the least amount of social activity saw their sales decline 6 percent.[7]

4. Lenovo was able to achieve cost savings by a 20 percent reduction in call center activity as customers go to community websites for answers.[8]

5. Burger King's Whopper Sacrifice Facebook program incentivized users to give up 10 of their Facebook friends in return for a free Whopper. The estimated investment for this program was less than $50,000, yet Burger King received 32 million media impressions, which, roughly estimated, equals greater than $400,000 in press/media value.[9] To put this in context, this is somewhat like reaching the entire populations of 19 states[10] (this doesn't account for unique versus repeat visitors, etc.).

6. BlendTec increased its sales five times by running the often humorous "Will It Blend?" videos on YouTube, blending everything from an iPhone to a sneaker.[11]

7. Dell sold $3,000,000 worth of computers on Twitter.[12]

8. To put things into perspective, only 18 percent of traditional TV campaigns generate a positive return on investment.[13] This is where the majority of media dollars reside today. I don't believe the majority of media dollars will reside here for much longer.

9. "You can't just say it. You have to get the people to say it to each other," says James Farley, CMO of Ford Motor Company. The automaker seems to know what it is doing,

especially with Scott Monty leading the social media charge. By giving away 100 Ford Fiestas to influential bloggers, the carmaker made 37 percent of Generation Y aware of the Ford Fiesta before its launch in the United States. Is it any wonder why 25 percent of Ford's marketing has been shifted to digital or social media initiatives?[14] Ford was the only U.S. auto company that didn't take a government loan.

10. Naked Pizza, a New Orleans Pizzeria that specializes in healthy pizzas, set a one-day sales record using social media. In fact, 68 percent of its sales came from people "calling in from Twitter"; 85 percent of its new customers were from Twitter.[15] So, yes, social media does work for small businesses. Feel free to have a bottle of Vaynerchuk wine with your pizza.

11. Volkswagen went 100 percent mobile for the launch of its GTI in 2009.[16] The reason I mention this is that mobile drives social media usage and social media usage drives mobile. More and more, we will see most social media usage on mobile devices, tablets, and iPads.

12. Tweets for a Cause sent out a tweet from Atlanta to encourage support of Susan G. Komen for the Cure. As a result of retweets from such notables as @mashable, @G_man, @zaibatsu, and others, the Atlanta chapter site received 11,000 visitors in 24 hours. This was an initiative by ResponseMine Interactive.[17]

13. Intuit introduced "Live Community" into its TurboTax® products two years ago. Due in part to the resulting word of mouth, Intuit has seen unit sales increase 30 percent each year and has now integrated "Live Community" into other products like QuickBooks and Quicken. "Live Community" allows customers to ask other customers questions, which has proved beneficial both to the customer and to Intuit. In some instances, the customer can answer questions that Intuit isn't allowed to answer because of regulatory restrictions.[18]

14. Software company Genius.com reports that 24 percent of its social media leads convert to sales opportunities.[19]

15. During Barack Obama's rise to the White House, he garnered 5 million fans on social media and 5.4 million clicked on an "I voted for Obama" Facebook button. Most importantly, this resulted in 3 million online Shepard Fairey Obama "Hope" image donors contributing $500 million in

fund-raising. An astounding 92 percent of the donations were in increments of less than $100.[20]

16. The University of Texas M.D. Anderson Cancer Center witnessed a 9.5 percent increase in registrations by using social media.[21]

17. Web host provider Moonfruit more than recouped its $15,000 social media investment as its website traffic soared 300 percent while correspondingly sales increased 20 percent. Moonfruit also saw a huge lift in its organic search engine rankings, getting on the first page for the term "free website builder."[22]

18. eBay found that participants in online communities spend 54 percent more money.[23]

19. "Think of Twitter as the canary in the coal mine." — Morgan Johnston, JetBlue.[24]

20. Seventy-one percent of companies plan to increase investments in social media by an average of 40 percent because of: (1) low-cost marketing, (2) getting traction, and (3) we have to do it.[25]

21. "Our head of social media is the customer." — Quote from unknown source at McDonald's.

22. An Old Spice Guy social media campaign increased sales 107 percent over one month and 55 percent over three months in 2010.[26]

To point 9: Ford may want to rekindle its old slogan "Have You Driven a Ford Lately?" With Alan Mulally spearheading the way, Ford has made great strides in changing its image as a truck-only company in the United States. It's hard not to like Mulally's passion and enthusiasm. I was fortunate to be a keynote speaker along with him at a private nontech event. In fact, it was a room full of CEOs; I was floored by how much he discussed social media and technology. Then he was onstage as a keynote speaker at the Consumer Electronics Show (CES) in Las Vegas. This in itself is a tremendous step in the right direction for an automaker — these CES speaking slots are generally reserved for the Steve Jobses of the world. While at Boeing, Mulally had helped design the digital cockpit, and now he is doing the same with Ford. Some of the more exciting features are:

- Ability to stream Pandora Radio.
- MyFord Touch is an iPhone-like customizable touch screen that replaces your typical radio dials.

- Ability to have text and tweets read aloud to you via Ford's Sync technology.
- Ability to send text or tweets via voice command.

Mulally also has a vision of changing dealer showrooms into an experience more akin to an Apple store. Rather than having giant lots filled with hundreds of cars (and weeds), the vision is a clean, open dealership with showcase cars where users can interact via technology and order cars suited to their needs.

What is striking about Ford has to do with the ROI of social media that many ask about. With the great work of Alan Mulally, James Farley, and Scott Monty at Ford, there is something that can't be measured: a cultural change. Progressive thinking from the top down causes this cultural change to happen both internally and externally. The revitalization of Ford is much more than social media and technology; social media and technology are playing a huge part not only in terms of the bottom line, but also in the perception and culture of Ford, which is often the bottom line of tomorrow. So, perhaps a more important question is: What is the ROI on a positive cultural change?

Eye-Opening Statistics

Here are 37 statistics and other facts about social media:

1. Over 50 percent of the world's population is under 30 years of age.
2. Some 96 percent of them have joined a social network.
3. Facebook tops Google for weekly traffic in the United States.
4. Social media has overtaken pornography as the #1 activity on the web.
5. One out of five couples married in the United States met via social media.
6. Years to reach 50 million users: radio, 38; TV, 13; Internet, 4; iPod, 3.
7. Facebook added over 200 million users in less than a year.
8. iPhone applications hit 1 billion in nine months.
9. If Facebook were a country, it would be the world's third largest, ahead of the United States and behind only China and India.
10. Weibo (equivalent to Twitter) dominates China.
11. A 2009 U.S. Department of Education study revealed that on average, online students outperformed those receiving face-to-face instruction.

12. About 80 percent of companies use social media for recruitment; 95 percent of these are using LinkedIn.
13. Generations Y and Z consider e-mail passé — some universities have stopped distributing e-mail accounts.
14. Instead, universities are distributing e-readers, iPads, and tablets.
15. What happens in Vegas stays on YouTube, Flickr, Twitter, Facebook . . .
16. The #2 largest search engine in the world is YouTube.
17. Every minute, 48 hours of video are uploaded to YouTube.
18. Wikipedia has over 15 million articles. Studies show it's as accurate as the *Encyclopædia Britannica*. Some 78 percent of these articles are non-English.
19. There are over 200,000,000 blogs.
20. Because of the speed in which social media enables communication, word of mouth now becomes World of Mouth.
21. If you were paid $1 for every time an article was posted on Wikipedia, you would earn $1,712.32 per hour.
22. About 25 percent of search results for the world's top 20 largest brands are links to user-generated content.
23. Some 34 percent of bloggers post opinions about products and brands.
24. Do you like what they are saying about your brand? You'd better!
25. People care more about how their social graph ranks products and services than how Google ranks them.
26. Over 90 percent of consumers trust peer recommendations.
27. Only 14 percent trust advertisements.
28. Only 18 percent of traditional TV campaigns generate a positive ROI.
29. About 90 percent of people who can TiVo ads do so.
30. Kindle e-books now outsell hardcover books.
31. Of the 25 largest newspapers, 24 are experiencing record declines in circulation.
32. We no longer search for the news; the news finds us.
33. We will no longer search for products and services; they will find us via social media.
34. Social media isn't a fad; it's a fundamental shift in the way we communicate.
35. Successful companies in social media act more like Dale Carnegie and less like *Mad Men*: listening first, selling second.

36. The ROI of social media is that your business will still exist in five years.

37. ComScore indicates that Russia has the most engaged social media audience, with visitors spending 6.6 hours and viewing 1,307 pages per visitor per month. Vkontakte.ru is the #1 social network.

These statistics tell the story: social media isn't a fad; it's a fundamental shift in the way we communicate. Please feel free to share with any nonbelievers!

All sources for this data can be found at: http://www .socialnomics.net/2010/05/05/social-media-revolution-2-refresh/.

Chapter Ten Key Points

1. You can get to an ROI using social media for certain aspects and campaigns. In fact, you can track it better than more traditional forms of media like outdoor, sports sponsorships, TV, and print.
2. Don't hyperfocus on short-term ROI as you will miss 90 percent of the bigger opportunity long-term.
3. In some long-term respects, asking what's the ROI of social media is like asking what's the ROI of your phone.
4. Culture, not content, is often king when it comes to your overall social success.

CHAPTER ELEVEN

Social Success Secrets (Give Them to Me Now!)

Some of you may have read all the previous chapters, while others, more anxious, just jumped to this chapter. Starting with this chapter and continuing to the end of the book, we are going to get into the brass tacks of proven ways to achieve success within digital, social, and mobile media.

Therefore, we are going to jump around a little, but each bit will be digestible and actionable. Make it a habit to sprinkle one or two of these suggestions into your daily activities and you will be well on your way to success! Many of these suggestions I've been able to glean over the past four years as I've traveled the world for book signings, consulting, and giving keynote speeches. I've been fortunate to have had engagements with Starbucks, Coach, Cartier, M&M Mars, the University of Texas, Google, ADP, IBM, the National Guard, NASA, Nokia, Raytheon, and Facebook, as well as many nonprofits and small businesses.

Top Opportunities Missed by Most (But Not If You Read This!)

Opportunity: Retention of Existing Customers

Companies pay too much attention to the vocal negative minority and often miss serving their best customers.

For example:

@happycustomer tweets: "I love Company ABC, couldn't live without their products."
@unhappynoncustomer tweets: "Just was on hold with Company ABC for 10 minutes... hung up #frustrated."

If these were tweeted around the same time, who do you think will get responded to first? That's right, 9 out of 10 companies (based on my experience) will respond to @unhappynoncustomer. The reason is simple. Most companies don't fire employees for not responding to or for going above and beyond their duty for a happy customer. But they do fire employees who don't respond to an unhappy customer, or in this case an unhappy potential customer.

If a company is going to have success within this digital decade and those beyond, it often needs to start with a cultural shift within the company. Part of this revolves around what employees are rewarded for. If you were the social media marketing manager or customer service rep responsible for managing the Twitter account of Company ABC, you would respond to the negative customer first as well. You don't want to get fired.

However, what a miserable existence to have a job where your only incentive is not to get fired. The great companies enable their employees to surprise and delight customers. At Zappos the employees of course respond to upset customers or potential customers, but they also go out of their way to surprise and delight existing customers (often by having their shipments expedited at no additional fee or sending a handwritten note).

Ironically, companies are always harping on a return on investment (ROI) of social media, and it is staring us right in the face. According to *The Value of an Existing Customer* by Ethan Bloch, the cost to acquire a new customer is six to seven times higher than to maintain an existing one.[1] Yet, in the preceding example, how many companies would respond to the negative prospect (not yet a customer) first? Also, I'm sure you've been in an after-hours meeting or an emergency weekend meeting to discuss something negative that has happened to the company and how it's going to be handled. But how many emergency meetings have you been in where everyone was distraught that you weren't reaching out to all of your satisfied and happy customers?

The same research further shows us that our attrition rates of customers can reach 50 percent over five years[2] if our communication remains dormant. Imagine losing half of your customer base over five years simply because you weren't giving them any love. And it's so easy to give people digital bouquets by the click of a like button, posting "U Rock!," or sending a digital discount code. A digital bouquet is similar to surprising someone with roses in the offline world—it is simply publicly showing someone digitally that you care.

So we've looked at the downside of not paying attention to our best customers (losing 50 percent). What's the upside? The upside is that your profits can increase up to 95 percent, and that can come from increasing your retention rates by as little as 5 percent![3] The 2012 American Express® Global Customer Service Barometer also found that consumers who have used social media for service wield the greatest amount of influence. According to the survey, a user of social media is likely to tell 42 other people about a positive experience. This is more than four times the amount of influence of a person who hasn't used social media for customer service.[4] The stakes are high. The ROI is there, yet culturally we are all fixated on the negative minority. I'm not advocating that we ignore an unhappy prospect. In fact, the same American Express study showed that 55 percent walked away from an intended purchase because of a poor customer service experience.

I'm simply imploring you to avoid the common mistake of believing that your social media strategy and success begins and ends with responding to negative posts. Nobody would set up a strategy as such, but if days go by and that is the focus, the people working in the trenches will slowly move to a defensive behavior of avoiding being fired.

If you were to use an offline analogy, how many of us would take the suggestion box at a restaurant, invite all the patrons into the bathroom, and flush all the suggestion cards down the toilet? That sounds ludicrous! Yet this is exactly what many companies do every day digitally. They don't surprise and delight their best customers. The ROI is right there: 84 percent say positive customer experiences and word of mouth have helped their brands and businesses grow.[5]

Opportunity: Listening Reports

At this point many companies understand the basic building blocks of social media success that we've covered in the earlier chapters, specifically: Listen > Interact > React > Sell. And many of us have set up the correct social media listening platforms so that we can properly accomplish this. Yet almost every company fails at the last mile when it comes to listening.

Businesses fail to produce a summarized listening report. This should be a one- to two-page report that is given to the small business owner or to the CEO, as well as to the rest of the company. This is invaluable information; it's the pulse of your customer or client. As mentioned, social media touches every part of your organization. This executive summary or listening report is the glue that will help keep businesses and organizations on the same page.

So then you may rightly ask: if this is so important, why doesn't every business do it? Because it's hard work! Whether you use Radian6, Omniture, IBM, Lithium, Sysomos, Alterian SM2, or Beevolve, none of these can fully tabulate this last mile for you. These executive summaries should answer four questions:

1. What are the top items that clients/customers are loving about your brand, organization, or products and services?
2. What are the top complaints or disgruntled themes around your brand, organization, or products and services?
3. What are some practical suggestions that can help you do more of #1 and mitigate #2?
4. What is the time line to get #3 done with a start date of today?

As you can see, no computer system can provide these answers, at least not at the writing of this book. The fact that a robot can't do this for you is a good thing. It allows you to stand out from the competition, if you are putting these reports together, and acting on them, and your competition is not putting forth the same effort (believe me, from visiting over 100 companies all over the world, most are not!).

Also, if you are the one putting these reports together, you automatically will get constant exposure to the executives of the company and will be an integral linchpin to all moving parts and departments. You will be an all-star.

I'd also suggest you do the exact same reports for a few of your competitors as well as a company you aspire to be more like. (Choose one other than Apple — come on, be original! Besides, Apple to this point hasn't fully engaged on social media. Perhaps this will change with the new leadership.)

One should also do a similar report for their employees. Historically, this had to be collected by human resources sending out a survey; then it would take them a few months to tabulate the results. Well, we don't have the luxury of a few months anymore. As previously discussed, the Generation Y workforce has no issue moving from one company to the next. So, it's imperative that companies harness the big data available to them to help keep their proverbial finger on the pulse of their employees' well-being. This type of information is priceless. In fact, Daniel Goleman, a Harvard PhD and author of *Emotional Intelligence*, indicates that

> one of the most important abilities of an executive is the ability to read the team's emotional intelligence.

This data can help you better assess the climate of your organization.

For business-to-business (B2B) companies, I suggest you do these reports for your clients' customers. For example, if you are Intel and you sell chips to Dell, Apple, and Samsung, you will want to keep tabs on how consumers feel about the speed and reliability of their new devices. Or if you sell soupspoons to Tim Horton's in Canada, you will want to see if there are ever any complaints or suggestions about the spoons digitally. For example, someone might post on Facebook:

> Anyone else hate this Tim Horton soupspoon? Just spilled on my dress again! Argh!

This may seem like a pretty innocuous post, but if 87 people hit the "like" button on Facebook or add their own comments, then this becomes an opportunity for the soupspoon manufacturer to improve its product. It's a chance to be proactive before its client, Tim Horton's, either asks for a change or switches to another supplier (please note I'm just using Tim Horton's as an example — enjoy their breakfast if you are ever in Canada or other parts of the world).

Opportunity: Always Ask, "What Is the Social Play?"

As we've discussed at length in this book, social media touches every facet of the business (customer service, product development, crisis management, recruitment, marketing, public relations, employee satisfaction, and beyond). Yet so many companies fail to ask, "What is the social play?" Instead, many do isolated social media campaigns. This is the exact opposite of what you should be doing. Instead, you should be leveraging existing programs and ensuring that social media is the glue that connects every facet of the business.

In 2011, more than 50 percent of the companies that ran Super Bowl commercials failed to ask, "What is the social play?" As a result more than 50 percent of the companies did not have their commercials on YouTube after the commercials ran on national television. What a missed opportunity! What frustration for those who were looking for the advertisements and couldn't find them. Opportunistic bloggers seized the opportunity, and when an ad wasn't available they'd creatively download it from TV or film it and post it on their YouTube channels. Effectively, these bloggers were getting traffic that the brands should have been getting, simply because these companies failed to ask, "What is the social play?"

Other companies, like Volkswagen, were savvy enough. Not only did VW have its ad posted in time for the game, but VW posted it on February 2, four days before the game on the 6th. This helped create buzz leading up to the game as well as helping VW schedule interviews on the morning talk shows following the game. Also, the child actor who played Darth Vader was from Children's Hospital, so this was also a feel-good story for media outlets to cover. Reporters also loved the fact that the child actor had not even seen the movie *Star Wars*. So, instead of having the chief marketing officer of Volkswagen on this broadcast, the company was able to have the child actor and his mom. Within 48 hours of the game, the commercial had already had over 30 million views on YouTube (talk about extending your exposure!).

By asking what is the social play, Volkswagen was able to create momentum well beyond the Super Bowl. "There was a lot of really positive momentum that went on up until the late summer when we launched Passat and then Beetle," said Tim Mahoney, the German automaker's top product and marketing executive for the United States. Volkswagen's sales increased 26 percent for the year.[6] As of the writing of this book, the Darth Vader commercial has had over 53 million views on YouTube.

Leslie Berland, Senior VP, Digital Partnerships and Development, American Express (AmEx), understands the importance of making sure everyone at the company is thinking differently and digitally. Berland made it a point when coming onboard to AmEx that social media wasn't "just about PR and conversations. We look at these platforms as business-development opportunities." When AmEx decided to offer card members exclusive access to Bon Jovi concert tickets, Berland was able to convince executives with the company to also promote the program on Twitter. (Historically, the company would have marketed the program by calling the VIPs directly or mailing them newsletters.[7]) Did Twitter work?

> We'd only been on Twitter for two days, but we pushed out one tweet, and within three hours, the entire thing was sold out. **We had never before seen results that fast.** These proof point moments (around social and digital) get leadership to believe and say, "Okay, now this could be bigger."[8]

When you align all facets of the business and use social media (your customers and prospects) as the glue, success is not only possible, but probable.

I'm sure that some reading this are scratching their heads and wondering, if companies can't even remember to post their commercials on YouTube, what else is being missed on a day-to-day basis? Get in the habit and be that person who always asks, "What is the social play?" This often is a cultural shift for many companies, so it may take some time, but even if you are simply ordering bagels for a morning meeting, get in the habit of always asking the question.

Chapter Eleven Key Points

1. Don't make the mistake of catering to just your disgruntled customers or prospects. Give your happiest customers a digital hug. It's six or seven times more expensive to acquire a new customer than it is to retain an existing one. Profits can increase 5 percent to 95 percent by improving your customer retention rates by as little as 5 percent.[9] A person is likely to tell 42 other people about a positive experience.
2. Develop and constantly update a two-page executive listening report for your brand, and do the same for your top competitors.
3. Always ask, "What is the social play?"
4. Don't do social campaigns; let social media serve as the glue that helps connect everything.

CHAPTER TWELVE

Blogging:
What Works

Many organizations and individuals use blogs to express themselves, advance their brands, drive traffic, and produce sales. As a result, blogs continue to grow. From 2006 to 2011 the sheer volume of blogs grew from 36 million to 181 million.[1] Interestingly, about one in three bloggers are moms.[2] Here are nine quick wins and lasting concepts for anyone who wants to run a successful blog. They have helped Socialnomics.com become a top 10 blog, according to *PC Mag.*

1. *Commitment:* Blogs are free like a puppy, not free like a beer. In order for them to grow strong and healthy, they require time and care. The commitment is dependent on many factors (amount of posts, authors, skill set of bloggers), but you can anticipate a 30- to 90-minute commitment per day to run a successful blog.
2. *Consistency:* Unless you are someone like Bono and whatever you do or think will be of interest to people, you will need to pick a general content strategy for your blog. Is your blog going to center on politics or on police chase scenes? How specialized is your blog going to be—general politics or Republican female senators? Are you going to focus on breaking the news or reporting on the news? The more specific and consistent your content, the better chance your blog has at success. Remember, you are competing with

close to 200 million other blogs! You need to stand out in order to be outstanding.

3. *Audience:* You should not be writing for everyone. As you begin, determine the audience you are writing for. Then, as you progress, you should continually check your blog analytics, subscriber data, and audience surveys to determine who your audience truly is. More often than not, you will be surprised at your findings. Write posts tailored to your audience; this sounds simple, but remember that simplicity wins. Also, so many people forget about their most important asset: their audience!

4. *Momentum marketing:* Take advantage of stories that spring onto the scene and how they relate to your audience. For example, if a new term like "tiger blood" becomes a trendy topic (it did), be creative about how you can ride the momentum. If you have a foodie blog, you may want to write a post on a recipe for a Tiger Bloody Mary or comment on the Charlie Sheen–inspired Tiger Blood energy drink (sadly, this is a real product). If your company is a research company, then a post that discusses the differences between human blood and tiger blood would be appropriate. Many people will be doing searches for tiger blood on Google, so by riding the momentum, you can dramatically increase your traffic. Our Socialnomics.com traffic spiked during the royal wedding because we were focusing on all the social media that was being used to cover the wedding. Soon in the search engines we ranked high for "Pippa Middleton."

5. *Findable:* Once you have a blog, make sure you post it on all your existing assets so people can find it. For example, use a tool like WiseStamp (www.wisestamp.com) to have a nice-looking image that links to your blog. Make sure you use RSS feeds so users can subscribe to your RSS. E-mail is still a top-performing digital marketing tool, so allow users to sign up in newsletter fashion on your blog. Capture their e-mail addresses for future mailings outside of your newsletter feed as well (make sure they opt in for this). On your Twitter, LinkedIn, and Facebook accounts, in the profile section make sure that you have a link to your blog. The links from your profiles can drive tons of traffic!

6. *Sharable:* So many blogs make it difficult for users to easily share their content. Ensure that you use a social widget that allows readers to easily share on their personal Facebook, Twitter, LinkedIn, and other social accounts. AddThis is the

most used widget, and it provides code to easily copy and paste into your blog (www.addthis.com/).

7. *Searchable:* The number one driver of traffic to blogs is still search engines, yet so many blogs forget to properly optimize their posts. This is so important that I go into more depth on it in the next few pages (Blog SEO).

8. *Mobile:* When you are ready, also make sure your blog is easy to find on mobile devices. We suggest making a mobile app similar to Mashable, Huffington Post, SmartBriefs, or TechCrunch.

9. *Contributors:* As your blog gains momentum, you may have the ability to recruit others to write posts. This is huge. Some blogs require the writer to post only original content. I disagree with this for the most part. While it would be nice to be the only blog that has a particular post, I also understand that writers want to develop their own brand as well. Remember that these columnists are volunteers — so treat them as such. When your blog becomes very successful, then you will have people lining up to contribute to the blog (e.g., Mashable, Huffington Post).

Content That Works

What follow are general rules of thumb, but it's imperative that you always are analyzing what your audience likes and gravitates toward. Analyze: What posts are most retweeted? Which ones are shared on Facebook? What time of day seems to work best for your posts?

Posts That Generally Work

- *Curation:* There are tons of good content already out there. While it's a hotly debated topic, if done properly, curation of content can be very valuable for your blog audience. Curation is simply collecting content from a variety of sources and delivering it in an organized fashion for your readers. One often "mashes up" this content. Often you may add your own twist to the content you have compiled. It is important to properly source and give credit to where the content originated. Not only is this the right thing to do, but it will also actually drive more eyeballs to your blog. The people who created the content are always looking for their name, so they will come check out your post (see more on vanity baiting later).

- *Top lists:* People love lists, and bloggers are no exception. Personally, I like to use an odd number so that (1) it sticks out in people's minds; (2) it's easier to own in the search space since everyone uses top 10, top 20, or top 100; and (3) it's easier for you to track success on Twitter, Facebook, and beyond if you use a unique number. *Tip:* If you are going to have a list beyond 10, then I highly suggest keeping the description of each item in the list short.
- *Statistics:* Everyone is always trying to find a particular data point. However, often these statistics are difficult to find. Do your audience a favor by finding these "wow" statistics and aggregating them into one post—for example, 11 Shocking Medical Statistics (see how I used an unusual number?).
- *Infographics, short and interesting videos:* I suggest you start with other videos, and once you get a sense of what your audience likes, then you may make an investment into producing your own.
- *Case studies:* Whatever your blog topic covers, people want to hear about success stories. How did someone become a top chef? What company has had success in mobile marketing? How has a university used LinkedIn to recruit? What school has integrated iPads into the classroom successfully? How did a charity raise a million dollars over the weekend?

  When you do successful case studies, be sure to write in the following fashion: Situation > Action > Result > Learning. A good rule of thumb for percentage allocation given to each section would be:
  - Situation (10 percent of the post = what was the issue/challenge faced).
  - Action (25 percent = the action taken to resolve the issue).
  - Result (30 percent = the return on investment or result of action taken).
  - Learning (35 percent = tangible takeaways/learning for the reader).
- *Vanity bait:* The more company names or people names you can include in a post, the better. This is called vanity baiting. Companies and individuals will often digitally search for where they are mentioned and will come to your post that mentions them. If they like your post, then they will blast it out to their social connections and also link to your post, helping to drive additional traffic.

Often the best people to vanity bait are those who are influential but don't get a ton of mentions. For example, if you mention Robert Scobel, he is already quite famous, gets tons of mentions, and probably will not have time to read your post or link to it. The same holds true of big brands like Nike, Home Depot, and General Motors. Try to focus on the up-and-coming personalities and brands. They will be more honored by the mentions and more likely to take action that helps your cause.

- *Hot topics:* Use tools like Alltop.com, StumbleUpon, Twitter Trends, Google Trends, and Yahoo! Buzz Index to determine what stories are breaking out. This is your opportunity as a blogger to ride the momentum of something greater than yourself (momentum marketing). Be creative in figuring out how you can write a post that appropriately incorporates a trending event that is also relevant to your audience. If your blog discusses politics and it's the week of the Super Bowl, you can discuss how the winner of the game might affect some of the elections or what political ads will be broadcast during the telecast.
- *Video:* If you see a video you like on YouTube or Vimeo that is relevant to your audience, make sure you share it on your blog. It's as simple as hitting the "share" button on YouTube next to the video and copy + past the <embed> code onto your blog. Add a few lines of text on why you posted the video, and you have a post in 5 to 10 minutes!
- *Photos:* Photos can drive a tremendous amount of traffic by people looking for images via search engines. Also, they make the article much more enjoyable for your readers. Do you like reading a long string of text? No! (Sadly, I wish this book could have incorporated more images and video; in the future my books most certainly will!) If you have a particularly great image you've posted, make sure that you post and pin the image on places like Pinterest.

Top Three Blog Platforms

- *WordPress:* WordPress is a free, open source blogging platform and content management system. It is used by some of the top bloggers in the world, as well as by some large brands like

CNN, Mashable, Ford, eBay, and Yahoo! Part of its popularity is that there are many free plug-ins, widgets, and themes. There is a strong community of WordPress bloggers, making it easy to get your questions answered. Wordpress.com is the free version that allows you to have everything hosted and backed up by WordPress for free. It is the choice of many individual bloggers.

Wordpress.org, in turn, is free blogging software that you pay to host and back up yourself. Many of the top bloggers and big companies use Wordpress.org as it allows for more control and flexibility. However, it is more expensive and complex. We use Wordpress.org for Socialnomics.com. My suggestion is to do what I did — start with Wordpress.com or Tumblr, and if you outgrow them, you can always move over to Wordpress.org.

- *Tumblr:* Tumblr is a popular blogging platform that continues to grow in popularity — 58 million blogs as of this writing. It is the most modern of the three platforms mentioned here. As such, many Generation Y bloggers use this software as their blogging platform of choice. You can literally be up and running in only a few minutes. Companies like American Express, *Rolling Stone*, and IBM also use Tumblr for some of their blog needs.
- *Blogger:* Because of its simplicity and templates, Blogger has been the choice of many bloggers for more than a decade. Many beginners prefer it for its ease of use and integration with some Google components (it was acquired by Google in 2003). It was started by Evan Williams, one of the founders of Twitter. If you have your own domain name (e.g., www.purpleicecream.com), it allows you to use this for free.

Blog Search Engine Optimization (SEO)

It's important for your blog articles to gain traction within search engines, as they are more likely to be read and shared on social networks. Following are just a quick few tips to help you succeed. The two biggest mistakes that bloggers make is (1) they don't spend enough time and effort on making sure the entire post is optimized for SEO (images, title tags, keyword rich text, use of headers and bold for major keywords), and (2) they use generic keywords instead of getting specific (*election* vs. *2016 Republican National Convention*). Figures 12.1 and 12.2 are two quick screen

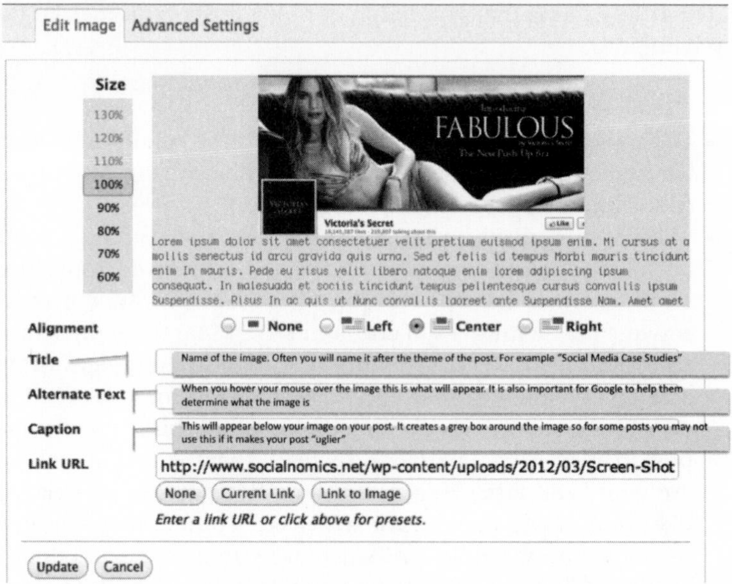

Figure 12.1 Optimizing Fields for Search Engines in WordPress

Figure 12.2 Example of Proper Search Engine Optimization
of a Blog Post

shots taken from the WordPress editor to show how you would optimize an image in a post. Optimizing images is important, as a blog can receive thousands of visits from a Google or Bing image search. Many blogs (even some of the top blogs) fail to put in the necessary search engine optimization techniques.

Other key items that will help your blog posts rank high in the search engines:

- Create compelling content.
- Consistently sprinkle your two to three main keywords throughout your post and in prime places (top left of the first sentence, subheaders, images, etc.).
- Make your posts easy to share on social media with "chicklets"—little social media icons from free tools that allow users to easily share on Facebook, pin on Pinterest, retweet on Twitter, YouTube, and more. Search engines rank factor these social components very high in their algorithms.
- Selectively share. While you make it easier for your readers to socially share, you personally shouldn't blast your every post to every social network. Instead, share what you believe are your best posts. Hence, if you do five posts in a week you may only share one or two with your connections via your personal social media accounts. Over time, you will benefit, as your followers will understand that the items you send out are of the upmost quality and relevance. Hence, they are more likely to click on them.
- Put your main keyword in the title of the post.
- Provide a Google Sitemap: Google appreciates when you give them an easy-to-view layout of your site. Most of the top blog platforms have a Google XML Sitemap plugin (think of plugins like apps on your smartphone, but for blogs) that does all of this easily for you.
- Put links to related posts on the bottom of each article. This not only helps your reader, but also provides a guide for search engines.
- Optimize your blog URL structure. In other words, make your hyperlinks look pretty. Instead of a link looking like: www.socialnomics.com/?page_id=4, it should look like: www.socialnomics.com/social-media-case-studies. This will give the search engines a lot of useful information. In order to do this look for the permalink tools in the blog platform you choose.

For more in-depth tactics on blogging, I highly recommend the books *Inbound Marketing* by Brian Halligan and Dharmesh Shah (John Wiley & Sons, 2010) and *Content Rules* by Ann Handley and C. C. Chapman (John Wiley & Sons, 2010).

Chapter Twelve Key Points

Achieve retweets and grow your personal brand via these blogging suggestions:

1. Post case studies, statistics, surveys, stories.
2. Keep it short — stories under 400 words, videos under two minutes.
3. A reader only cares about an opinion if it is based on fact.
4. Don't bury the headline.
5. The content of a case study should be: situation 10 percent, action 20 percent, and result 70 percent; results should be in hard numbers.
6. Credibility is based on properly editing, crediting, and vetting your stories — don't take shortcuts.
7. Become an expert in a sector of digital marketing (education, law, pharmaceutical, health, auto, etc.).
8. Infographics, videos, and images are what people crave — create them.
9. Curating existing stories is valuable; if you see an amazing story, summarize, curate, and credit.
10. Immediately and professionally respond to comments.
11. We all have unique access to something or someone; leverage yours.

CHAPTER THIRTEEN

100+ Social Media Tools

Social media is in a constant state of flux, so to help us keep up with it all we need to use tools.

DailyTekk at dailytekk.com does an incredible job of keeping an extensive and updated social media tools list. I use their list and descriptions while adding a few of my thoughts and favorites (check for updates at http://bit.ly/100-social-media-tools).

Random, Must-See Social Media Tools

1. Bazaarvoice – Social commerce platform for ratings and reviews. (See Figure 13.1.)
2. HubSpot – Inbound marketing; a marketing hub for small business (*equalman fave).
3. Awe.sm – Analytics for social media.
4. TweetReach – How far did your tweet travel?
5. Contaxio – Contact management for your social networks.
6. PostPost – Awesome stuff gets lost on Twitter. Strip-search your time line.
7. SocialScope – A mobile inbox for your social networks.
8. NutshellMail – Delivers a social media summary to your e-mail inbox.
9. Amplicate – Find out what people love and hate on social media.

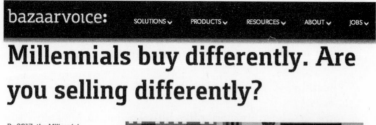

Figure 13.1 Bazaarvoice

10. Bottlenose – A smarter way to surf the stream.
11. AddShoppers – Share rewards, measure results, add shoppers.
12. GroupTweet – Create a more dynamic Twitter account with multiple authors.
13. HowSociable – Measure your brand magnitude.
14. North Social – Quickly create and manage Facebook pages.
15. BrandMyMail – Include live social content in your Gmail e-mails.
16. CardMunch – LinkedIn app scans business cards to your contacts (*equalman fave).
17. Social Mention – Real-time social media search and analysis.
18. FeedMagnet – Social curation for websites and events.
19. TabJuice – Ultimate e-commerce solution for Facebook (100 percent free).
20. Conversocial – Deliver great customer service in Facebook and Twitter.
21. Bitly Enterprise – Short URL branding, real-time alerts, monitoring, and more.
22. PeopleBrowsr – Social analytics for marketers.
23. Needium – Social media lead generation.

24. Crowdspoke – Find relevant content to share with customers and fans.
25. The Archivist – Save and analyze tweets.
26. MyLikes – Publishers promote your content through social networks.
27. Postling – Provides small businesses with social media tools.
28. Bre.ad – URL shortener like bitly with customizable Toasts (*equalman fave).
29. Evernote – Never lose a random thought again—all stored in the cloud.
30. Eventbrite – Online tool for events and selling tickets (*equalman fave).

Marketing

1. Shoutlet – Enterprise social marketing platform.
2. Awareness, Inc. – Publish, manage, measure, engage (*equalman fave).
3. Unified – The world's first social operating platform; enterprise marketing.
4. EventBrite – Perfect for any event—even handles tickets. (See Figure 13.2.)
5. EngageSciences – The fastest-growing European social marketing vendor.
6. LocalResponse – Helps marketers respond to real-time consumer intent.
7. GraphScience – Leverage the social graph. Optimize Facebook marketing.

Figure 13.2   EventBrite

8. GoChime – Reach the people who are a perfect fit for your products.
9. Adly – Celebrity endorsements in social media.
10. Hy.ly – From fans to leads. Facebook presence, contents, and more.
11. SocMetrics – Engage influencers.
12. MarketMeSuite – Your free social inbox. End-to-end social marketing.
13. Fanplayr – Social game marketing.
14. Memelabs – Branded Facebook contests and much more.
15. PowerVoice – Advertisers harness a consumer-to-consumer platform.
16. Lithium – Social community and marketing solutions.
17. Syncapse – Social media marketing, measurement, and management.
18. Vitrue – Helps you utilize social communities for business.
19. Adotomi – Performance marketing for social media.
20. Zoniz – Full-service social marketing management platform.
21. Argyle Social – Data-driven social media marketing software.
22. Buddy Media – Offers a social enterprise marketing suite.
23. Extole – Consumer-to-consumer social marketing.
24. BuzzParadise – International network of social media advertising.
25. Zuberance – Energize your brand advocates.
26. Involver – A social marketing platform and more.
27. Silentale – Market and customer insights for Facebook page data.
28. SocialTwist – Acquire new customers using social referrals.
29. eCairn – Social media marketing solutions for marketing agencies.
30. Bazaarvoice – Ratings and social commerce software (*equalman fave).

Monitoring and Intelligence

1. Netvibes – Social media monitoring, analytics, and alerts dashboard.
2. Brandwatch – Social media monitoring tools.
3. ThinkUp – Free open source social media insights platform.
4. DataSift – Unlock insights from historical Twitter data.
5. Odimax – Actionable intelligence for social media marketing.

6. GlobalWebIndex – Provides data on users of your web presence.
7. Attentio – See what the world is saying about your brand.
8. Traackr – Find the influencers who matter to you.
9. Unmetric – The social benchmarking company.
10. LiveWorld – Moderation, community programming, and actionable insight.
11. PeerIndex – Understand your influence across social media.
12. Jive – Social media monitoring and much more.
13. ethority – Social media intelligence.
14. CliMet – Maintain your brand's reputation on Facebook and YouTube.
15. YourBuzz – Get the buzz on your business (American Express OPEN).
16. Eqentia – Enterprise content curation, monitoring, and republishing.
17. Sentiment Metrics – Social media monitoring, measurement, and engagement.
18. MutualMind – Intelligently monitor, analyze, and engage.
19. Appinions – Discover and engage leading influencers on any topic.
20. Social Fixation – Apps, automation, awesomeness.
21. Digimind – Competitive intelligence and online reputation monitoring.
22. StepRep – Listen to what people are saying about your brand online.
23. Trackur – Social media monitoring made easy.
24. CustomScoop – Online news clipping and social media monitoring.
25. Beevolve – Comprehensive and affordable social media monitoring.
26. Visible – Social media monitoring, analytics, and engagement.
27. Sysomos – Social media monitoring tools for business.

Social CRM

1. Radian6 – Social media monitoring and engagement, social CRM.
2. Sprout Social – Social media management, Twitter tools, social CRM.

3. Spredfast – Social CRM and enterprise marketing.
4. Nimble – Social CRM simplified. Turn communities into customers.
5. Sprinklr – Social CRM, enterprise social media dashboard.

Management

1. HootSuite – Dashboard for Twitter, Facebook, LinkedIn (*equalman fave).
2. SocialFlow – Optimized publisher for Facebook and Twitter.
3. UberVU – The intelligent social media dashboard.
4. Tracx – An end-to-end social media management system.
5. This moment – Engage everyone, everywhere, easily.
6. Hearsay Social – Enterprise social media software.
7. Sendible – Social media marketing, monitoring, and management.
8. Pluck – Integrated social media solutions from Demand Media.
9. SocialVolt – Social media management software.
10. Engage121 – Social media management that enables customer relationships.
11. Parature – Personalized approach to web-based customer service and help desk software.
12. Tweetdeck – Dashboard for teams using Twitter and Facebook.

Blogs and Websites

1. The Future Buzz – Digital marketing and social media blog.
2. SocialTimes.com – Your social media source.
3. Social Media Today – News, strategy, tools, and techniques.
4. Mashable – Social media news and tips.
5. Socialnomics – Insights from brands and experts on the why and how of social media.
6. Social Media Explorer – A blog about social media marketing.
7. Social Fresh – The business of social media.
8. The Social Media Marketing Blog – Marketing insights from Scott Monty.

9. Chris Brogan – Learn how human business works beyond social media.
10. Brian Solis – Defining the convergence of media and influence.
11. Britopian – Discussing the latest in social business.
12. Social Media Examiner – Help businesses discover how to best use social media.
13. Michael Hyatt – Christian slant on leadership, productivity, publishing, and social media.

Agencies

1. Likeable Media – Dave Kerpen's agency (top clients Neutrogena, Verizon).
2. Banyan Branch – Social media strategy, engagement, analysis, and more.
3. Converseon – Social strategy and analytics agency.
4. Brickfish – Viral map software (top clients Redbox, Lemonhead).
5. Splashcube – Social media marketing and training.
6. WannaBeeSocial – Southwest Airlines of social media agencies (caters to small businesses).
7. Webtrends – Social, mobile, and web analytics and tools.
8. iStrategyLabs – Experimental social media marketing and more.

Other/Miscellaneous

1. Klout – Discover a person's influence via their Klout score. (See Figure 13.3.)
2. ShopVisible – Social commerce solution.
3. Yammer – The enterprise social network.
4. Gigya – Social login, social plug-ins, analytics, gamifaction, and more.
5. TrustYou – Social media monitoring for the hospitality industry.
6. Cyfe – All-in-one business dashboard and real-time monitoring.
7. Janrain – Social login, social profile storage, game mechanics, analytics.

Figure 13.3   Klout

8. BzzAgent – A word-of-mouth marketing company.
9. IZEA – Connects social media publishers with advertisers.
10. Lotame – Data and audience management platform.
11. OneDesk – Connect employees, partners, and customers.
12. SocialVibe – Engagement marketing.
13. TwentyFeet – Social media monitoring and ego-tracking.
14. Timehop – What were you doing one year ago today?
15. Refollow – Discover, manage, and protect your Twitter social circle.

Also keep an eye out for IBM's Smarter Commerce team, who are doing some incredible things.

CHAPTER FOURTEEN

Making Viral Videos

My social media video series, as of the writing of this revision, is still the most viewed social media series in the world. The first video, "Social Media Revolution," is the one that truly changed the game from me; and I've been able to fail and learn over the years with online video.

www.youtube.com/watch?v=x0EnhXn5boM

One of the top questions I receive after giving a keynote speech on Socialnomics or digital leadership is: "How can we make a viral video?" But that, you see, is the wrong question to ask. If you go into video production with the end goal of making a viral video, you are certain to fail. The correct question is always: "What kind of video can we produce that will provide value to the viewer?" The viewer makes things go viral, not you, the producer. There are some things we can do as producers to help give our videos a chance to go viral, which I discuss in this chapter, but you always must start with the viewer in mind. Again, when it comes to our digital world, we always need to think outward looking in, rather than our historic *Mad Men* approach of inward looking out.

Another question I am often asked is: "What compelled you to make the first 'Social Media Revolution' video?" The reason I produced the first video was simply as a tool to help explain social media, especially to small business owners and executives who weren't digital natives. As laughable as it seems now, not everyone really understood the power of social media. This was at a time when MySpace (remember them?) was bigger than Facebook. Many brushed off social media as simply being "something that teenagers do." In short, I was having a difficult time convincing people that social media was the next big thing for everyone. So, I decided to do two things: write the first version of this book and produce a video.

I'd seen a great video called "Shift Happens," produced by Karl Fisch and Scott McLeod, on changes in education. I decided that I needed to make something like this, but completely centered on social media. I've produced many videos since this time, and even own my own production arm (Equalman Productions) — developing videos for some of the top brands in the world.

What follow are some key learnings. I put the first video on a YouTube channel labeled Socialnomics09 rather than Socialnomics. The reason was that I wanted to test to see if it would work properly before putting it onto my main YouTube channel. Well, did it work! I received hundreds of thousands of views in days. The problem this created was that I needed to keep it on this channel (Socialnomics09). YouTube will not allow you to move videos and their views to another channel — the number of views will start at 0 rather than at 200,000. Hence, I've been stuck with putting all my videos on Socialnomics09. I've since discovered that this has happened to many people I know. So, my first piece of advice is to test everything on your main channel, because viral can truly happen overnight and you don't want to be pinned to a test channel.

"Going viral" is not a strategy. However, here are five key steps you can take to give your videos a chance at going viral:

1. *Good music:* Unless your video is of a cute baby or an extraordinary kitten, the music you select will be critical to its success. In various countries, YouTube's Content ID program allows you to use copyrighted music. As a quid pro quo, a pop-up window will display during your video listing the song title and artist and allowing users to click through to purchase the song. YouTube and the music label then share the revenue from the sale.

   My advice is to find successful viral videos that are similar to the one you want to produce, and determine what music they are using. You may seriously consider using the same music, as it has proven to be successful and the music owner isn't blocking it.

Keep in mind that your idea will not be new — as of the writing of this book, every minute there are 48 hours of video being uploaded to YouTube. Review videos similar to what you want to do, and take note of what is working and not working for these particular videos.

Note: YouTube's Content ID program can be a bit frustrating, since often music labels and musicians can change their minds on when and where their music can be used. Hence, you may have three videos that use the same music and they all have 4 million views, but then one day one of them has an error message saying the music is owned by EMI. Also, they may not work in every country. Hence, if you truly want to play it safe, either go through the steps of obtaining the rights or, for most, use royalty-free music.

2. *Short and sweet:* Definitely keep your video to under five minutes, preferably to a minute or less. In *Enchantment*, author Guy Kawasaki displayed data from research firm Visible Measures showing that 19.4 percent of viewers abandoned a video within the first 10 seconds, and by 60 seconds 44 percent had stopped watching. Lead with your most eye-popping content to gain and hold viewer attention. Don't build to a crescendo that may never be viewed.

3. *Viewer is king:* Only viewers make videos go viral. Yet, often we produce videos from the vantage point of what we want to get out of them. This approach is wrong. We need to constantly ask: Am I providing something of value for viewers? What do they want to get out of it? If you have to include your brand, then make the mention short and preferably at the end of the video.

4. *Other purpose:* Don't produce a video simply hoping that it goes viral. Produce a video with a clear purpose in mind. For example, you may produce a video for your sales team so that they can use it when they present to the board. If it goes viral because you adhered to the first three suggestions, it's a bonus! If it doesn't go viral, no problem; it is still a great tool being used by your team.

5. *Share:* When people ask for your original file so they can use it in their presentations or for other purposes, share it. Sure, there will be a few who do so with malicious intent, but they will be in the minority. The majority will be adding distribution points and beacons for your great work. They may make the video into something cooler than you ever dreamed of as well. Also, understand that YouTube data

shows that videos often require a taste-maker to provide the crucial tipping point. In a well-known TED talk, YouTube showcased several popular videos that were dormant for months until a tastemaker like Jimmy Kimmel blasted it out to his legion of followers.

Guided by these five maxims, I produced several videos explaining the power of social media. Viewers pushed these viral, becoming the world's most viewed social media videos.

Chapter Fourteen Key Point

1. Making a viral video is not a sound strategy — making a video that provides value to the viewer is.

CHAPTER FIFTEEN

Social Media for B2B

Many business-to-business (B2B) companies are struggling with what their social media strategy should be. Unfortunately, executives often incorrectly believe that social media isn't applicable for their B2B company. Rather, they think it's something reserved for business-to-consumer (B2C) companies.

This is flawed thinking. Many of the same social media principles we preach for B2C companies also apply to B2B companies. Some tactics and philosophies, however, need to be adjusted accordingly to address idiosyncrasies particular to the B2B space. One quick difference is that the volume of interaction is often less: 32 percent of B2B companies engage with social media on a daily basis, whereas 52 percent of B2C companies engage on a daily basis.[1]

Here are a few social media B2B musings that will hopefully help clear things up and explain why we see that over 90 percent of B2B companies actively participate on Facebook.[2]

Phil Mershon of *SocialMediaExaminer* conducted an extensive survey that uncovered where B2B companies experience digital success:[3]

- *Over 56 percent of B2B marketers acquired new business partnerships through social media (compared to 45 percent of B2C marketers).*
- *Nearly 60 percent of B2B marketers saw improved search rankings from their social efforts (compared to 50 percent of B2C marketers).*

- *B2B marketers are more able to gather marketplace insights from their social efforts (nearly 69 percent versus 60 percent of B2C marketers).*
- *The one area where B2B marketers significantly lag behind their B2C counterparts is in developing a loyal fan base; 63 percent of B2C marketers found social media helped them develop loyal fans, compared to only 53 percent of B2B marketers.*
- *B2B marketers are more likely to use search engine optimization (SEO) (67 percent versus 62 percent of B2C marketers).*
- *Event marketing is more used (68 percent of B2B versus 60 percent of B2C).*
- *B2B firms use webinars more than twice as much as B2C companies (28 percent versus 12 percent).*

B2B Customer Relationships Are Often Fewer and Stronger Than B2C Relationships

The key word here is *stronger*. Social media tools like LinkedIn can only strengthen these relationships and complement — not replace — the necessary face-to-face, interpersonal communication.

B2C companies can have purely digital relationships with their customers and often have to do so as a result of the pure volume of customers. However, what social media has allowed for B2C companies (closer engagements and real-time digital conversations with customers) can also be leveraged in the B2B world.

While B2C companies can, and for practical purposes often must, have purely digital interaction with customers, it's still important for B2B companies to use social media tools as a complement and not a replacement for face-to-face interactions.

B2C Company Clients Often Aren't Competitors

I'm usually not in competition with my neighbors when they buy the same iPhone that I purchased (well, maybe a status symbol competition). However, the clients of B2B companies are often in competition with each other. Two local ice creams shops may buy their plastic spoons from the same supplier.

Because of this dynamic, a B2B company needs to be careful with respect to giving different clients different deals or offers. One needs to understand that this deal information has a better chance of getting out in this transparent world than it did in the past.

Social media doesn't have the same impact on every business. I've always said there is a scale of 1 to 10 on how much social and digital media can impact your business. If you are Starbucks, your potential is a 10; if your company sells stealth bombers to the government, your potential is probably a 1 or a 2. The key to remember is that it is *never zero*. So if your potential is a 4, you need to reach that potential.

If you supply stealth bombers to governments, then the likelihood of sales dramatically increasing as a result of social media is probably marginal and, due to security reasons, the amount of interesting content that can be disclosed to the public may be slim.

However, opinion groups potentially formed within social media around the government's decisions to purchase more or fewer stealth bombers, tweets on the subject, or flattering/ unflattering information on Wikipedia could influence decisions. This is your potential, and even if it is only a 1 or a 2 you want to make sure you are achieving your potential.

Listen First

This is a major maxim for B2C companies in social media, and it's just as important in the B2B realm. Each B2B industry uses social media differently, so it's important to determine not only where the conversations are taking place, but what the conversations are about. Many tools can help a company collect this conversational data (including Radian6 and Filtrbox).

You will be able to better determine the needs of your most important clients by listening. Good B2B companies have always listened to their clients. Great B2B companies have always taken it one step further and listened to their competitors' clients.

The explosion of social media has made this downstream listening much more practical and real-time. If your company provides a component like the gorilla glass for an Android phone, it's important to listen to end users' likes and dislikes — that way you can stay ahead of the game and you aren't solely dependent on your buyer's secondhand information. You can even help provide some of this information to your buyer and become an even more valued partner. For example, on the original iPhones, women were having a more difficult time typing on the screen because their fingers are generally colder than men's. This is biologically based. Women generally store their body temperature in the core, which is great for babies. However, the extremities, like toes and fingers, receive less warmth. Since the iPhone is heat sensitive to the touch, women were having a more difficult time than men getting the touchscreen to work. Hence, moving forward, it may behoove Apple and its B2B partners to have more engineers on the team who are female (probably a good blanket statement for all technology companies).

Once you're close to mastering this type of social media listening skill, the next step is to listen to your competitors' clients. Discerning noticeable customer gaps will ultimately put you in a position to fill these gaps and win new business as a result.

Tips for B2B Social Success

Here are 15 tips for B2B social success:

1. Face-to-face interaction cannot be replaced or replicated. However, use digital tools to augment your personal meetings and further strengthen the relationship.
2. If your clients are willing, promote case studies about them. Make sure you reach out to industry blogs to share these case studies. Also look to general blog outlets as well to share these stories: CNN.com, Mashable, Smart Briefs, Huffington Post, among others. There is a general void of good B2B case studies, so these outlets will often promote them. In return you will gain more exposure and have a pleased client.
3. Digitally listen for your client's customers' online conversations. What do they enjoy? What do they hate?
4. Create — or better yet, curate (compile/summarize) — content that is specific to your clients' and prospects' niche. (See the Vocus Case Study in Chapter Sixteen.)
5. Share industry articles and blog posts via social networks (Twitter, Pinterest, LinkedIn, Facebook).
6. When you make a mistake, this is your chance to be *flawsome*[4] — own up to your mistakes and then correct them. FedEx has found when it makes a mistake and fixes the problem that the client is more likely to repeat than a general client who never experienced a problem in the first place. This is what being flawsome as a company is all about. Mistakes are simply opportunities to exceed a client's expectations.
7. Share lots of relevant photos; this is simple, but powerful.
8. Don't forget about mobile, as many of your client executives will be consuming content on the go.

9. If not a proprietary risk, share exclusive, behind-the-scenes content.

10. Be responsive to fans' and disgruntled clients' requests, inquiries, and posts.

11. Don't hesitate to take some items offline when necessary.

12. Hold industry and offline meetings and events. Use digital tools before, during, and after to help promote and continue the conversation.

13. Develop partnerships with your clients, other organizations, and yes, sometimes even your competition. Collectively promote one another's events and content.

14. Use industry keywords in your company Twitter bio.

15. Make sure you know how to align and track success: nearly 30 percent of B2B marketers are not tracking the impact of social media programs on sales.[5]

So B2B can learn from B2C and B2C can learn from B2B. Let's take a closer look at some social media case studies in the next chapter.

CHAPTER SIXTEEN

Case Studies

Often the best way to achieve success in the digital space is to review where others have failed or succeeded. With that, what follow are a few case studies that should prove helpful.

SafeNet Security Systems[1]

B2B

Situation: SafeNet is the country's third largest supplier of security systems. One of the things it does is help put the "s" into "https://."

Action: SafeNet started a group on LinkedIn to encourage discussions and idea sharing among those in the Information Security Community. (See Figure 16.1.)

Result: SafeNet's director of product marketing, Holger Schulze (@HolgerSchulze), started the LinkedIn group as his own experiment. In fact he started two groups; one that had SafeNet in the title of the group and one that was called the Information Security Community. The group with SafeNet in the group name didn't attract many members, so he turned it into something that could be used internally by the company.

(continued)

(continued)

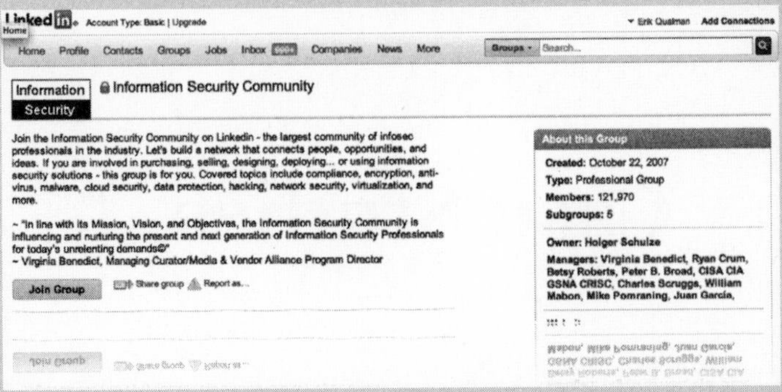

Figure 16.1   SafeNet

Not deterred, he turned his attention to the Information Security Community. In a little over two years the group has grown to over 120,000 members. More importantly, the group is producing $1 million annually in additional revenue to SafeNet.

There are four members of SafeNet, from various divisions (marketing, systems, engineering, product management), each spending a few hours a week interacting with and managing the community.

Learning: SafeNet didn't have success with its first group, but this didn't stop it (remember: fail fast, fail forward, fail better). People join groups because of topics and an eagerness to learn. They don't join groups to hear about companies. They want insights from personnel within companies, but not general messaging from companies. Holger Schulze has since been promoted from director to vice president.

Success: $1 million in revenue; increased brand awareness.

Tools

1. Marketbright marketing automation software.
2. Community managers reporting individuals they introduce to SafeNet sales and staff.
3. Salesforce.com.
4. LinkedIn.

Personnel: Four members from different departments.

Grand Rapids, Michigan, "American Pie"

Community Outreach

Situation: After *Newsweek* published an article calling it a "dying city," the people and businesses of Grand Rapids, Michigan, were in a strong state of disagreement. A trio of residents in this west Michigan city decided they would get the word out that, to the contrary, their city was flourishing.

Action: They took to the streets, literally. The storyboarded idea was to put together a lip-synch video that showcased the beautiful downtown of Grand Rapids and its cultural multitude of enthusiastic citizens.

They solicited local businesses for financial and resource support, ending up with over 20 sponsors of varying participation levels, covering the $40,000 production budget. The final video involved a shutdown of the downtown of Grand Rapids and roughly 5,000 people lip-synching to a cover of Don McLean's "American Pie."

Results

- The video went viral, reaching 4.2 million views on YouTube in the first four months. It cracked the top 10 for most viewed video in the world on May 28, 2011,[2] including hundreds of thousands of Facebook likes/shares to date. Also, the project received huge coverage across traditional media outlets and blogs, greatly increasing the message and reach.
- Expert movie critic Roger Ebert called it "The Greatest Music Video Ever Made."
- It set a world record for the largest music lip dub of all time.
- A very conservative estimate would put the total media impressions at roughly 15 million to date when you add in the video views, articles, social reach, and blogs. Utilizing an average cost per thousand (CPM) of $20, you could easily say they received roughly $300,000 worth of media impact on their $40,000 investment (15M * $20/1,000 = $300,000). And keep in mind that the final video is over nine minutes long—that is a lot of 30-second commercials.

(continued)

(*continued*)

The global reach and impact of this campaign resulted in its creators (Jeffrey Barrett, Rob Bliss, and Scott Erickson) forming a new agency entitled Status Creative.

Key Learnings

- Reach and exposure in social media can be achieved with much less investment than traditional media or Internet display ads.
- Creative and entertaining executions are in demand by consumers and will be rewarded by being shared within the social sphere.
- Community outreach can be powerful; there are masses of proud citizens who are willing to contribute for a town, a product, or an industry.

Link to final video: http://www.socialnomics.net/2011/09/28/social-media-case-study-grand-rapids-lip-dub/
Making of the video: http://www.youtube.com/watch?v=5mEfDka4w6M

Insert Gamer

B2C

Situation: Insert Gamer was looking to further penetrate into the social media arena and build its Internet gaming network (IGN). Specifically, it wanted to significantly increase its Facebook fan base with qualified consumers.

Action: Insert Gamer started by placing ads on its competitors' Facebook pages, driving users to the Insert Gamer page. The new visitors were then prompted to take an optional survey. Insert Gamer was able to gather pertinent demographic information from its competitive conquests: age, household income, gender, primary game consoles, and annual game purchases. Of the 50,000 visitors, just under half took the survey. The company then whittled the number down to 8,000

(*continued*)

(continued)

based on the target customer, one who made more than five game purchases annually.

The next step was to figure out how the company could most efficiently and effectively get more of its target customers to become fans of its Facebook page. It focused on Facebook's Edge Rank algorithm. This algorithm essentially figures out the top news that shows in each user's Facebook page, analogous to showing up at the top of someone's e-mail or being placed in someone's spam folder. You might think that the ideal target Facebook user is someone with tons of friends. However, your messaging is most likely going to be lost in the myriad of posts those users must sift through. Instead, Insert Gamer focused on users with fewer than 300 friends and 30 pages to ensure there was less noise. It also focused on users who had good connectivity; that is, they had shared at least one game page with friends. Last, Insert Gamer focused on the user's engagement (at least once a month) and the user's affinity for the brand (recently touched).

Based on these criteria, Insert Gamer was now down to a target segment of 2,500 from the original target group of 8,000. The company could now target ads more efficiently and effectively across Facebook based solely on the behaviors and similar actions of the new target group. For example, Insert Gamer now knew that followers of Monster Energy and Portal 2 were roughly 20 times more likely to fall into the target consumer group than other fan pages.

Result: Insert Gamer attracted an additional 509,000 fans in 120 days. Over 60 percent of these fans buy more than five games per year; this is the inverse of the data Insert Gamer gathered from targeting its competitor's fans. This increase in 509,000 fans represents roughly $76 million in buying power [509,000 fans × 60% = 305,400 fans × $250 (rough estimate cost per game $50 × 5 games) = $76,350,000]. On top of that, Insert Gamer's Facebook page gets 645 percent more engagement, an 811 percent higher comment rate per post, and 394 percent higher "like" rate per post than the competition.

(continued)

(continued)

Key Learnings

- Include an optional survey to gather important demographic data from your visitors.
- Identify the ideal customer based on purchasing and user behavior: engagement, connectivity, and brand affinity.
- Targeting is important: Message to where your ideal customers are. Spending $20,000 in advertising will be the equivalent of spending $60,000.

Metrics and some information in this case study are as presented at the iStrategy Atlanta Conference on September 13, 2011, by Jeff French, LoudDoor cofounder and CEO.

Vocus Public Relations Software[3]

Category: B2B

Situation: Vocus clients are public relations (PR) professionals and firms. The PR professionals use Vocus software and tools to help them manage various campaigns. Vocus wanted to provide thought leadership in the industry to increase its brand awareness and cachet.

Action: Vocus started posting and sending articles relevant to those in the public relations field. The primary outlets used in PR are Twitter, LinkedIn, and Facebook. (See Figure 16.2).

Result: Vocus originally produced most of the content internally. However, this was time consuming. Also, the company started seeing better results from providing bite-sized content that the Vocus people didn't produce themselves; rather, they compiled and summarized news stories and editorials for their audience.

Learning: Vocus discovered that showcasing too much of its own content turned clients and prospects off. It took the company some testing and learning, but eventually it found a nice balance between original Vocus content and curated content. Vocus was later acquired by HubSpot.

(continued)

(continued)

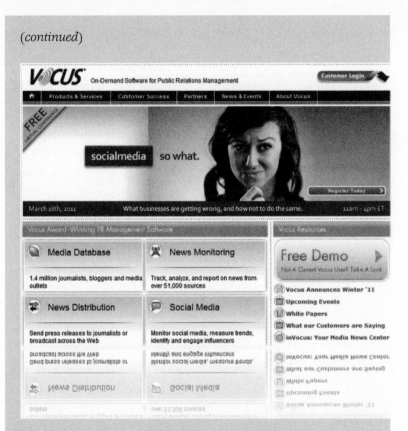

Figure 16.2 Vocus

Success: $500 million in revenue; increased thought leadership.

Tools
1. Vocus lead tracker.
2. Salesforce.com.
3. Facebook.
4. Twitter.
5. LinkedIn.

Personnel: Internal writing and creative staff.

Hoodie Allen Music

B2C

Situation: Two college buddies, both big music fans, decide to collaborate on one last music project before becoming working stiffs. Both were graduating seniors with corporate job offers waiting for them. For RJ Ferguson and Steven "Hoodie Allen" Markowitz, what came next was completely unexpected.

Action: They released their song free online; it was titled "You Are Not a Robot." They targeted music bloggers who were active on the Hype Machine (www.hypem.com), a collection of music bloggers that aggregated MP3s via blog posts. Users were then able to rate the tracks based on a top 100 type format. "You Are Not a Robot" made a meteoric rise to number one. They received 60,000 listens overnight, trackable since the song was being hosted in the SoundCloud.

Since they had seen such great success, they decided to continue at it in their spare time. They went to work at their corporate gigs but collaborated on a full-length mix tape titled "Pep Rally" on evenings and weekends. Some of the actions they took:

- Built a web page with one-click access to download the music. They utilized their own independent server to ensure that massive amounts of site traffic would not crash the web page (including bandwidth to allow for faster downloads of songs) and provided prominent social media links to ensure ease of sharing.
- Identified bloggers with a large social influence and sent them each a personalized e-mail with some information on the project and directions to the newly built web page.
- Developed a Hoodie Allen Facebook account (not a fan page). They utilized Social Mention (www.socialmention .com) to listen and then Hoodie engaged with those who showed interest in the music materials now circling the web, usually in the form of a hello, friend request, or thank you.
- Interacted with their fans and followers. By responding to as many posts and tweets as possible, they were able to connect on a personal level with fans.

(continued)

(*continued*)

Result: In the following months, "Pep Rally" was downloaded in excess of 500,000 times. Hoodie Allen was offered (and accepted) a contract with the Morris Agency to be his booking agent. He now shares the same booking agent as Kanye West. They recently released "Leap Year" as their second independent album, utilizing a similar approach to "Pep Rally" but have included video content on YouTube as a way to augment the impact, as well as e-mailing tracks out to influential vloggers.

Hoodie Allen now performs upwards of 15 times a month, selling out at venues across the country. The corporate day job? History.

Key Learnings

- Peers are 10 times more influential than someone trying to sell to you. Harness the power of those with a passion for your industry.
- Target those already separated into a group (music bloggers in this instance). Relevant content is still king.
- Listen to and engage with your consumers, especially those with a large social influence. Connection and interaction are key.
- Provide easy access to your product; often follow the one-click rule.

Check out Hoodie Allen's music at www.hoodieallen.com. Special thanks to Scott Shelton, owner at http://WaitingTo Explode.com for helping provide some insights into this social media success story.

Audi

B2C

Situation: Audi had the first Super Bowl commercial to feature a Twitter hashtag (#Progressls). In edition to pushing the

(*continued*)

(continued)

hashtag on TV, Audi purchased a Promoted Trend ad from Twitter, and it hired Klout, a start-up firm that combs through Twitter and Facebook in search of the most influential people online. Audi has a full-time team monitoring its presence on social media sites, it is constantly posting new content, and it has even held special events for the most devoted members of the online Audisphere.

www.youtube.com/watch?v=3snyXTNmFm8&feature=player_embedded>

Action: Klout helped Audi find more than 1,100 people to reach out to about the campaign—200 of them received an Audi travel mug and flashlight. Klout's Audiphiles tweeted more than 12,000 times about the hashtag, creating a viral chain of Audi-related chatter online. The company then chose the best tweets containing #ProgressIs; the winner, @jetsetbrunette, won a trip to California to test-drive some Audis, and she also got to choose a charity to which Audi donated $25,000.

Result: The company will readily admit that it doesn't know the exact return on investment. "Today the equation to measure that doesn't exist," says Doug Clark, Audi of America's general manager for social media and customer engagement. However, Clark did point to a study by Visibli, a social-marketing analytics company, which recently found that Audi has the most "engaged" fans of any entity on Facebook.

Audi's more than 3 million fans apparently are devoted to pushing the brand forward. Most savvy marketers know that social media is a longer-term play of building relationships with customers. Just as organic search engine optimization was a long-term play 10 years ago, the smart companies that do social media well today will see nontrackable returns in the years to come.

For more details on this, please read the great article at Fast Company by Farhad Manjoo ("Does Social Media Have a Return on Investment?," June 22, 2011).

EMD Serono (Merck)

Regulated Industry

Situation: EMD Serono, a division of Merck and a leading manufacturer in the biopharmaceutical arena, had a new drug to bring to market and wanted to begin establishing a brand presence. The drug was to help fight multiple sclerosis (MS), and the objective was to increase registrations prior to the future release date. EMD Serono hired Greater Than One to help spread its brand and messaging in an effort to own the MS community. They were able to secure legal and regulatory buy-in on the front end. Since this was not an approved drug at this point, they could have faced regulatory fines.

Action: Greater Than One decided that the content and reach of bloggers would be a very effective and efficient way to obtain massive reach and get the message to the MS community. They started by doing a social media scan for bloggers that focused on MS. They found and video interviewed 20 active bloggers they felt had good, positive content and, furthermore, were dealing with MS in their everyday lives.

From those 20 initially interviewed, Greater Than One found five of them who would help with their endeavor. But Greater Than One was not just interested in them blogging about the new EMD Serono drug; they were interested in them video blogging about it (vlogging for short). Words can be powerful, but not nearly as powerful as video. So Greater Than One armed each of the five vloggers with a video camera to post videos on their blog and in the social space.

Sufferers from MS just want to lead a normal life, so the strategy behind the vlogging was not that MS is something you conquer, but something you learn to live with in order to lead a normal life. The vloggers started spreading their message across YouTube, blogs, Twitter, and Facebook, driving those interested in additional information to HowIfightMS.com. Greater Than One also helped to provide content topics that were top of mind in the MS community.

(continued)

(*continued*)

They were also successful in having cross-agency integration of the digital and offline agencies. Working in tandem, there was sharing of all creative and brand assets to ensure consistent messaging. They were diligent in working with their database and vendor team to ensure proper back-end data capture. They had quarterly reviews to provide readouts on the data to further react and evolve their strategy based on what was working and what was not.

Result: They were able to tap into 70 percent of the MS population. They met their objectives of building brand presence and were successful in receiving thousands of preregistrations for the new drug. They've had thousands upon thousands of YouTube views and have received 14 awards to date for the campaign.

Key Learnings

- For regulated industries, ensure you have the proper front-end approvals to avoid fines.
- Vlogging can be a more powerful medium for messaging than blogging.
- Do a social media scan and focus on those who have a natural passion or are invested in your product or service; the results will be much more impactful than someone just working for a paycheck.
- Ensure you are properly capturing the data on the back end. Have regular readouts to adjust focus to what is working and what is not to maximize the efficiencies and effectiveness of your campaign.

Data in this case study was obtained at the iStrategy Atlanta Conference, September 14, 2011, as presented by Elizabeth Apelles, Greater Than One CEO and co-founder.

Other Top Social Brands and Organizations

- Burberry
- Four Seasons
- Red Box
- Zappos
- Red Cross
- Caterpillar
- Quicken Loans
- Starbucks
- West Elm
- Oreo

CHAPTER SEVENTEEN

Social Analytics: Big Data and Beyond

Corporations, small businesses, and organizations exhaust exorbitant amounts of manpower and money to ensure their social media presence is the best it can be. Yet, more often than not, much of the potential from these efforts isn't fully realized. An underinvestment in, or a misunderstanding of, social analytics causes these missed opportunities.

According to Satmetrix, a customer service software provider, only 49 percent of companies it surveyed worldwide in January 2012 tracked and followed up on customer feedback on social media, while 28 percent did neither of these.[1]

Most believe that social analytics is merely listening to what is being said on social media. While those who have read the earlier chapters of this book understand this is a critical first step, it is simply that: a first step. The purpose of this chapter is to help organizations move beyond simply listening to social media chatter. Organizations that are able to move beyond just listening will have a definitive advantage over their competition. Even those organizations that simply improve their listening capabilities will see dramatic results.

To move beyond basic listening, organizations will require more robust analytical tools to properly analyze the data to produce actionable insights. The investment in these tools is worth it, as these actionable insights will enable real-time decisions that will help propel the business forward.

Those that don't invest in social analytics will struggle, and the gap between the two (those companies that invest versus those that do not) will widen as more dollars migrate to digital and big data continues to grow. Big data refers to the enormous amounts of data that are difficult to analyze using common database management tools.

A key driver of big data is the prolific use of social media by users. Every time a user sends a message on Twitter or posts to Facebook, the user is contributing to big data. This big data is important as, among other things, it contains valuable customer thoughts, trends, and preferences. Hence, in order to achieve the insights and advantages that can come from big data, organizations will need to better mine social media content and conversations. Cracking this code will require the right combination of talent, culture, and analytical tools. This often isn't easy:

- Over 70 percent of executives feel they can't properly leverage data insights.
- Over 50 percent of organizations struggle to make real-time decisions based on digital marketing data.[2]

Analyzing social data is not just about whether a Facebook update receives a "like" or if a Twitter post enjoys a retweet. One must go further into the discovery of how the content, conversation, and engagement impacts your customers and business. In turn, it will inform and impact not only marketing strategies, but also business strategies as a whole.

Organizations need to use what the public is saying about them to their advantage. Being able to bring together various conversations/posts (e.g., blogs, forums, Facebook, Twitter) and put structure around them to build better customer segmentations and profiles, understand customer interests and role in influencing others, predict why a customer or client might leave the company, identify potential locations for a disease outbreak, and beyond.

The business challenges marketers face with social analytics include knowing what factors to measure, how to measure, and how to analyze the data that comes out of these measurements. From there, one needs to determine how to properly utilize this analysis to predict future customer behaviors, outcomes of marketing initiatives, and changing or developing trends in the marketplace.

Social networks help brands connect on a deeper level with their audience and the information the audience shares through them via apps, status updates, likes, comments, check-ins, and the

like. Here's a picture of how social media has invaded consumers'
lives and how it affects their purchase decisions:

- There are 5 billion mobile phone connections per year, globally.
- There are nearly a billion users of Facebook.
- About 45 percent of consumers ask friends for advice before
  purchasing.
- Some 64 percent of consumers make a first purchase because
  of a digital experience.[3]

Some brands receive a few mentions a day, whereas others like
Dell may receive up to and above 25,000.

Brands need to listen to what the public is saying. The question
is: to what level? Resources are always a pending factor, and
companies like Dell luckily have the resources to listen closely.
Dell has the social media strategist and analysts' ideal setting — a
Listening Command Center. Other companies like Quicken Loans
and Gatorade have similar listening centers.

These brands realize the advantage of information and how
it can help to make better business decisions based on consumer
wants, likes, and needs. For Dell, "the goal is to embrace social
media as an organization and as an integral part of the workday."
Dell makes it part of the company's culture — it's not just a "nice to
have"; it's an expectation ingrained within each employee.

When you have this level of commitment, listening becomes
part of the regular business day, and not an add-on. The brand
realizes the need to leverage this listening in order to respond to its
audience and target market on a deeper and more connected level.[4]
Social analytics is analogous to the world's largest focus group. If
an organization listens properly, it can dramatically assist crisis
management, recruiting, product development, public relations,
strategy, and word of mouth.

Listening consists of a few different facets, but to keep it
simple, foremost are the five Ws: who, what, where, when, and,
most importantly, why.

1. *Who:* It is important to determine who is speaking about you,
   whether that individual is a member of your target audience
   or an extension of that audience. Most importantly, are any
   of those individuals influencers in your category? Identifying
   the influencers, such as bloggers who receive thousands of
   views and comments per post, is essential in order to get the

word out about your product/service and brand. As most brands have noted, it is no longer what the brand says, but what the advocates of the brand share about its integrity and quality.

2. *What:* Once the "who" has been narrowed down, focus on "what" those people are saying. Are the comments negative? Positive? Neutral? It is important to respond, comment, and stay within that conversation in order to steer it in the direction in which your brand would like to be perceived. Otherwise, your brand could become a seat warmer on the bench, giving the chance for your competition to weigh in.

3. *Where:* Next up is "where" are these conversations happening with these potential influencers? Are they on Facebook, YouTube, LinkedIn, forums, blog posts, Twitter, or another network you aren't on yet? The key is to be present and engage actively where members of your audience are already talking about your brand. If they are on a network where your brand can't compete well, then steer your audience toward other networks where they can hear more about your product/service and your expertise in that category.

4. *When:* Another important aspect of listening is knowing "when" your audience is talking about your brand and when they're most active. It's not just about the particular time of day or the day of the week—although those are still very important. It's about the content you put out, the events, the holidays, and so on. For example, is your audience more active when it is the holiday season and when you have promotions? Or is it when there is a special event your brand is hosting?

   It is significant to note these peaks and dips in action from your audience in order to determine when your brand can do more, or where it should back out due to lack of interaction from the audience.

   One particularly important aspect about when is the ability to tie this back to the where and who. One person may be more likely to communicate more through social channels on the weekend because of a hectic work schedule, while another person may be a stay-at-home parent and communicates more during the week.

   The platform used may also have different nuances. URL-shortening platform bitly's data showed that the best time to garner the most clicks on Twitter is by posting between 1 and 3 P.M. EDT Monday through Thursday. For Facebook, the data was even more specific: post on Wednesdays at 3 P.M. EDT.[5]

While this research gives one a general guideline, every customer base will be different; the key is to determine, via data analysis, your specific customers' nuances and habits. Knowing this allows you to interact with your customers and clients at times when they are most receptive to an interaction.

5. *Why:* The "why" is the most important, and the hardest to obtain. This requires more social analytics, such as deeper analysis into specific events, times, and reactions — rather than just observational listening. Determining why your audience does what it does, and how your brand can strengthen its bond with that audience and especially those influencers, is where you receive significant return on investment (ROI).[6]

Listening properly appears as simple as monitoring one's Facebook wall posts and mentions and replies on Twitter, yet it goes well beyond this. As stated by Deepak Advani, Vice President of Business Analytics at IBM:

> *Customers tell us a great deal in their different types of interactions with companies. The use of analytics . . . can help business leaders to identify what's important to different customers, pinpoint the next best action, and follow through with the appropriate response that resonates with customers.[7]*

In order to get started and identify what's important, it helps to have a dashboard and monitoring system. This dashboard should suit your specific organization's needs to listen more closely. Monitoring tools have many variations, but the essential requirements are:

- Easy-to-use dashboard.
- Keyword-based search.
- Real-time.
- Ability to do everything in-house.
- Support from vendors.
- Multiple language support (if appropriate).
- Multiple social platform listening capability.
- Alerts.
- Analysis reports.

Some may require more support from vendors, depending on team size and needs, but these are the priority items to consider when evaluating listening and monitoring tools. There should be an emphasis placed on the third requirement, "real-time," because the longer the data sits and the longer it takes to analyze, the less value it will have.[8]

Imagine customers online at the point of their buying decision; if you can get them a 10 percent coupon via Twitter that incentivizes them to select your product over a competitors' product, that is extremely valuable. But if you send this coupon five minutes too late, it's essentially worthless.

Social media can assist organizations in deepening relationships with customers via efficient and effective communication channels. This efficiency often decreases the cost to influence existing customers and acquire new ones.[9] The key is deeper levels of listening, better response and interaction with the brand's audience, as well as assisting to gauge the level of reaction needed for business decisions.

In addition, monitoring helps brands predict what certain social scenarios will be in the future depending on the parameters involved. These predictions have many factors involved, such as big data — which is not just another buzzword. Big data is about cutting through the clutter of information and the uncertainty that comes along with it and developing new strategies from that information. The problem is: how can businesses utilize all of their data, analyze it, and transform that into useful and valuable information? That's where reaction and prediction processes come into play in social analytics.[10]

Big data — data that makes social analysts' hearts race — helps businesses understand how to predict their next steps in marketing and business in order to excel in their business goals. The tough part is encountered in the insurmountable amount of data that is being added every single second through tweets, likes, comments, videos, posts, and more. This data is the key basis to understanding competitors' strengths and weaknesses and also assists in determining new ways of productivity growth, innovation, consumer sentiment, and more.[11]

For example, in 2010, 1.8 trillion gigabytes of data were generated and the big data market size was $3.2 billion.[12] This size is an indication to marketers of the untapped opportunities and the insights that await. Furthermore, it will not slow down anytime soon; it is growing exponentially.

IBM conducted a survey to determine what chief marketing officers (CMOs) are facing as business and marketing challenges. Data — specifically how to utilize big data — was at the top of marketers' list of challenges.[13] Leading companies realize that big data can unlock significant value, helping make information transparent and usable.[14] These companies focus on both social media and predictive analysis solutions to analyze the following considerations:

1. *Understand and anticipate customer behavior better;*
2. *Adapt supply chain based on customer demand and orchestrate interactions between trading partners and suppliers;*
3. *Market, sell, and fulfill the right product and service, at the right price, right time, and right place;*
4. *Provide flawless service to customers by predicting their needs, engaging them, and sustaining relationships.*

If other companies can get at the core of this analysis and focus on these considerations, they will be on the correct path of analysis and adaptation of those results to their business values and endeavors.[15]

For example, if the mentions on Facebook and Twitter go up, is there a correlation to sales? Another example of analysis is intent of purchase versus already purchased. If a consumer "likes" a Facebook page and is perusing accessories to an already purchased laptop, the consumer has an affinity to a certain type of brand and a certain money bracket. The types of items people "like" — the brands they Tweet to or about, the places they vacation, the cars they own — help brands decide on what these consumers will or will not buy in the future due to their income brackets as well as their loyalties to certain brand types and categories. Analysis such as this helps to get a 360-degree view of perceptions in order to give the consumers what they really want, and companies' social listening is the key to this endeavor.[16]

Social media behavior from our customer can help predict a person's willingness to purchase and whether they will attempt to influence others.

Forrester data indicates that Facebook fans of Best Buy were more likely to purchase something than non-fans. Specifically, in the last 12 months, 79 percent of Best Buy Facebook fans bought an item, while only 41 percent on non-fans purchased something. The research also showed that a Best Buy Facebook fan was 5.3 times more likely to purchase something and to recommend Best Buy (74 percent) compared to non-fans 38 percent. This type of behavior seems to apply to other brands as well. If you live near a Walmart it doubles your odds of buying there, but if you "like"

Walmart on Facebook you are four times more likely to buy there than the average person.[17] It's not just limited to business, either; the Boston Police Department and the Criminal Justice System in Orange County, California, sift through the massive amounts of collected data to help them predict, disrupt, and prevent criminal, terrorist, and fraudulent activities.

The tricky part is that data is always evolving, and a great example of this is mobile data. According to Barry Hurd, "Mobile Data = Social Data = Customer Data = Demographic Data."[18] Basically, social analytics is not just about what consumers interact with on their computers, but more and more about what they do on social networks via mobile as well. This raises another good point. Social media tools will constantly evolve. The MySpace of today will be the Facebook of tomorrow. It's important for organizations to understand this and to ensure that the analytics tools they invest in are flexible versus being tied to only certain platforms (e.g., Facebook, Twitter). Also, if your customers are on only two or three of the social media platforms, don't overinvest in a tool that can handle a hundred platforms. Similarly, if you are with a large corporation and start small (i.e., monitoring two or three major platforms), be certain that your analytic tools have the capability to grow as you grow. This also includes various program access points (e.g., smartphones, tablets).

For example, during the World Cup a leading sport shoe producer analyzed real-time messages on social media through both regular outlets as well as mobile. It followed how comments evolved through the course of the time period and tried to understand the sentiment behind each story of the consumer. The marketing team was then able to fine-tune its sponsorship activities on a closer to real-time basis, and to "dynamically reprioritize TV advertisement themes and product launch strategies" accordingly.[19]

Similar to this shoe brand, it is important to consider the story and sentiment behind a consumer action online. This is even more significant now with check-in apps, including Foursquare, which integrate with other social networks such as Facebook and Twitter. Additionally, brands also have to consider the second screen when it comes to television watching and interacting on a tablet or smartphone at the same time. So the question is: how can analysts continue to learn more and stay on top of all this data? Discovering how data analysis is helping business decisions can take multiple forms. General forms of data mining can help simplify and summarize the data so it is easier to understand and utilize.

For example, social analytics was used to help predict the opening box office success of *The Lion King 3D*. Specifically, social media commentary from Twitter, Facebook, and blogs was used to determine how much buzz was building around the film to help predict how much money it would make on its opening weekend. The predictions from social analytics were, on average, 13 percent off from actual box office performance, compared to 17 percent for traditional prediction models.

A more reactive use of data is to access digital video recording (DVR) habits of users. For example, if ESPN can see that 90 percent of users fast-forward through its golf programming, then the network would be best served to shift more of its content to more popular sports. This should be done within hours, not weeks.

Big data is applicable across all market segments:

Research demonstrates that big data isn't relevant in just one industry, affecting that one sector alone. It affects multiple industries.

Research by the McKinsey Global Institute (MGI) and McKinsey's Business Technology Office examined the state of digital data and the significance of its value in various sectors. In retail, for example, utilizing big data can allow a retailer to "improve its operating margin by more than 60 percent."[20] In the health care sector, it has been predicted that better analysis of health care data in the United States could result in $300 billion in savings.[21] In economics and politics, there could be savings in operational efficiencies, which could reduce fraud and increase tax revenue collections.[22]

While there is a lot of buzz about big data in the market, it isn't hype. Plenty of customers are seeing tangible ROI when they have the right tools and structure in place:

- Researching call data and networking positively reduced processing time by 92 percent for some telecommunications companies.
- Analyzing petabytes of data allows utility companies to improve their accuracy in placing power generation resources by a whopping 99 percent.
- In the health care sector, patient data provided insights that resulted in a decrease of 20 percent in patient mortality.[23]

Another example is political elections—can big data help predict the future of elections? International Data Corporation (IDC) analyst Mike Fauscette thinks that social analytics applied to politics potentially has an edge over traditional polling. "The law of big numbers says the greater the sample size, the greater the chance of statistical significance," states Fauscette.[24]

Making these business predictions and profiling customers through social analytics can also be conducted through social customer relationship management (CRM). Social CRM assists marketers in tying social data to purchase information in order to model further business effectiveness. Items that can help in order to model said effectiveness include:

- Tie social data to sales, tracking down to the individual sale (e.g., coupon or click).
- Integrate social analytics with web analytics such as what drives people to the website and what makes them actually purchase the product from the brand.
- Monitor social CRM developments in order to stay on top of the latest technology in analytics.

Social CRM is a part of the listening, interacting, reacting, and predicting cycle, and it will play a large role in the future of business. Marketing analysts should be aware of how social analytics helps connect customer wants and needs to business objectives for tomorrow.[25] It's also important to realize that truly strategic companies don't use social media analytics as a stand-alone tool; rather, they "use a blend of transactional, demographic, life stage, and other customer data to develop a clearer picture of the real value that a customer is generating for them . . . and what their potential value is expected to be."[26]

As part of the business objectives of a company, executives must determine how to make social media actionable. In short, organizations need to move beyond simply capturing the buzz around their brand.

While listening is extremely valuable, it is simply the first step to getting to more actionable items (interacting, reacting, predicting). Going beyond basic listening will help drive real business results and assist in the future strategy of the organization.

The CMO needs to realize that social media is not a silo, but an integrated part of the revenue chain and business decision pyramid. Facebook, mobile apps, YouTube, blogs, message boards, LinkedIn, Twitter, Pinterest, and many others offer invaluable information if mined properly. In fact, 75 percent of executives believe that *customer* and client *data* generated by digital marketing can dramatically improve their commercial success.[27] The time is now to utilize social analytics and monitor the brand constantly in order to stay ahead of the competition.

Keys to Social Metrics

Marketing analysts have many rules for how to go after social analytics, but the overriding keys to remember are:

1. Start with the problem, not the data.
2. Listen before interaction, reaction, and prediction.
3. Share data to get data from consumers.
4. Assess your current data management and social analytic capabilities as an organization to determine if and where you need to upgrade.
5. Base the equation of your business on customer-centric metrics.
6. Let computers analyze and scientists analyze, respectively.
7. Stay up to date with the latest in social analytics and CRM technology.[28]

CHAPTER EIGHTEEN

Social Organizational Structure

Atop question from many executives is: How should social media be structured within an organization? This is a tricky question, as it depends on many factors having to do with how your organization or business is set up as well as how regulated your industry is. As I went from organization to organization, I did start to see some distinct patterns begin to shape and form on how companies structured around social media. These structures or models were dependent often on how advanced a company was in its social media practices. The more ingrained social media was within a company, the closer it came to an ideal structure — one in which virtually the entire company was involved; yet it was organized communication.

I wasn't alone in seeing these patterns or models. Jeremiah Owyang of the Altimeter Group had done extensive research on this specific question with many of his clients. When I saw his models I was blown away and realized that his models were better than mine. So in the following pages I use Owyang's models as a base and take the liberty of making an addition or a subtraction on some items. To see Jeremiah's incredible work, go to http://www.web-strategist.com/blog/2010/11/09/research-most -companies-organize-in-hub-and-spoke-formation/ or http://bit.ly/ socialnomics-owyang-models. See Figures 18.1 through 18.5 to see each model along with a table giving pertinent information about the pros and cons to each approach.

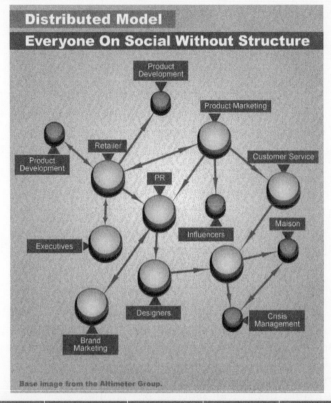

Model	Description	Pros	Cons	Good to Know
Distributed	Social efforts come from all areas of the company. As the name implies, there isn't much organized effort. Encourages a blogging culture for all employees. **Examples: Sun Microsystems, LPGA Golfers**	Conversations appear authentic since they are being "shot from the hip" from local or product level within the organization. This authenticity can increase trust from the consumer.	One side of the organization has no idea what the other side is doing. This can cause inconsistent and frustrating experiences for the customer. Impossible to manage from an IT and data perspective.	Most companies may start here, especially big companies where control is a little more difficult, but they quickly attempt to transition out of this model.

Figure 18.1   Distributed Model
10.8 percent of organizations use a distributed model.
Source: Jeremiah Owyang.

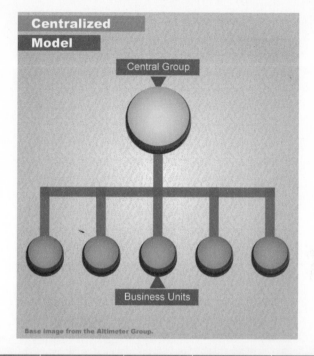

Model	Description	Pros	Cons	Good to Know
Centralized	All social communication is controlled by one department. **Example: Ford**	Consistent customer experience, coordinated resources.	Can result in slow response if the centralized team needs to reach out to the subject matter experts or is overwhelmed with volume. Often have to staff up and down for busy seasons.	Choice of many companies in highly regulated industries (government, pharmaceutical). Make sure to bring forward the employee voices (e.g., Ford's Scott Monty).

Figure 18.2   Centralized Model
28.8 percent of organizations use a centralized model.
Source: Jeremiah Owyang.

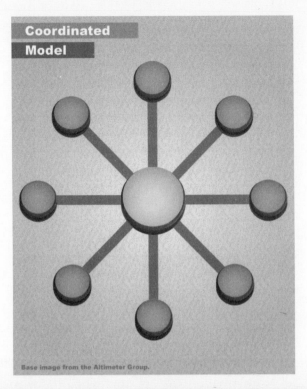

Model	Description	Pros	Cons	Good to Know
Coordinated	Cross-functional team sits in centralized position and helps various nodes such as business units, product teams, or geographies be successful via training, education, communication, support. **Example: Red Cross**	Central group is aware of what each node is doing and provides a holistic experience to customer with centralized resources.	Executive support usually is required. Costly Needs constant cross-departmental buy-in, or for multinational or holding companies cross-company buy-in.	Companies often land on this model as they make the progression to Dandelion or Holistic. Model will not work if the centralized team acts like social police instead of a valuable resource or shepherd.

Figure 18.3   Coordinated Model (Hub & Spoke)
41 percent of organizations use a coordinated model.
Source: Jeremiah Owyang.

Model	Description	Pros	Cons	Good to Know
Dandelion	Often in large multi national organizations. Companies within companies work autonomously from each other under a common brand. **Examples: Coca-Cola, IBM, P&G, HP**	Business units and some individuals are given freedom to run social media as they desire while there is a common thread among all units under the holding company or mother brand.	Requires consideration of cultural and executive buy-in. Constant internal communication can be difficult to keep up and sometimes breeds internal competition.	Allows big companies to act more local and responsive. If communication isn't solid, shared learning can be easily lost and there can be missed opportunities on efficiencies and group buying/ learning of tools. Key is to provide a way for spokes to connect to each others, not just to the hub.

Figure 18.4 Dandelion Model
18 percent of organizations use a dandelion model.
Source: Jeremiah Owyang.

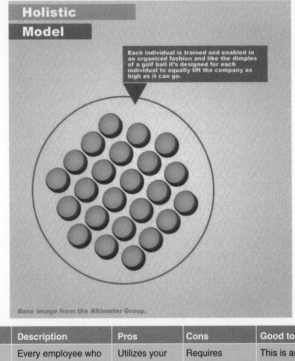

Model	Description	Pros	Cons	Good to Know
Holistic	Every employee who wants to be social is enabled. Different from Distributed in that this has ongoing coordination and training involoved. **Examples: Dell, Zappos**	Utilizes your entire workforce's knowledge **(Best Buy's Twelpforce is an example).** Entire company is focused on the customer.	Requires extreme trust and buy-in from executives. Culture needs to be ready for this. Employees need to live by the brand values 24/7. Constant training.	This is arguably the best model and very difficult to achieve. A formula for success is to have initiation training for every employee, ongoing shared learning sessions, and robust employee help resources.

Figure 18.5   Holistic Model

1.4 percent of organizations use a holistic model.

Source: Jeremiah Owyang.

This was only a quick overview of different models that are employed within organizations to properly address social media needs, but my hope is that you found it helpful. Also, remember that for most organizations as you progress from model to model you want to strive to reach the Holistic model where everyone within the company is engaged with social media to help improve the organization both internally and externally.

CHAPTER NINETEEN

FAQs

The following questions are a selection submitted from reporters, readers, and fans over the years, along with my answers:

Social media trends — which is the next big thing in your opinion?

LinkedIn isn't talked about enough. More people will move this out of human resources (HR) and put it into the hands of the digital team.

Putting structure to big data so we can make predictions is another important step.

Will mobile use change social media?

Advances in mobile technology will increase the usage of social media.

What are your recommendations of methods and tools to use? (Examples: QR codes, mobile geo-fencing, augmented reality, live streaming)

I love being able to augment the user experience in real time. Augmented reality is underutilized. If I have a menu in French and someone's smartphone can convert it to English, Spanish, and so on, that is value added.

What do you mean by "humanizing" your business? (Isn't this what we are getting away from with new social media?)

If done properly, social media allows us to listen, interact, and react to customers' input and feelings much better than ever before. We are making them feel as if their voice is being heard and they are helping to shape a brand/company.

Is social media going to consume our future marketing/ advertising? Why?

Yes, it will be the largest portion. Since the dawn of time, word of mouth has been the most important item for success. Social media is word of mouth on digital steroids.

Given modern technology, is easy accessibility a pro or a con? Why?

We have to live our lives as if our mother is watching us. The pros are these: less crime, less adultery, less lying, and the like. The cons: we have less privacy and fewer channels to release stress without ramifications.

Will social media be the end of PR? Is this experience tarnished (degrees in public relations, other education required)?

The only thing constant is change. One needs to adapt or die. PR specialists need to understand these new tools and techniques. So it's more of a change versus and elimination.

Do you think the future of social media is going to be more marketing orientated?

Actually, most people today just view it as another marketing channel. What they will discover in time — and great companies like Burberry, Cartier, Zappos, and Dell already have — is that it touches every facet of the business. This makes sense because social media is living, breathing. It is your customer. So in time companies will realize how to leverage it for customer service, PR, sales, outreach, recruiting, philanthropy, training, and so forth.

Some fashion retailers have recently developed shopping opportunities direct from social network sites like Facebook (enabling customers to shop directly from their social network). What do you think are the benefits of this?

Fish where the fish are. The easier you make it for your potential customers, the better off everyone is. It's win-win.

How has social media changed our romantic relationships? For better or for worse?

One out of five couples meet online. Three out of five gay couples meet online. One out of five divorces are blamed on Facebook. It has changed our relationships dramatically. The net is positive, but like anything there are some negative consequences. The fact that it is much more difficult to cheat is a positive development, as is the fact that we have so much more compatibility information at our disposal prior to deep relationships (although it's unromantic that there really is no such thing as a blind date anymore!).

How likely is it that we will become famous because of what we post on Twitter or Facebook?

Social media and digital tools allow anyone with enough talent and determination to become anything one wants to be. Barack Obama would not have beaten Hillary Clinton in the primaries without social media. The successes of Justin Bieber, Melissa Black, and Lady Gaga all started with social media. Success in this day and age is a choice.

What are your thoughts on the idea of ambient awareness — the idea that constant online status updates can give us a sense of the ongoing happenings in our social spheres? Is this something that can be harnessed for personal benefit?

Yes, if done properly it harnesses the old saying of it's not what you know, it's who you know. You can take this to an incredible level if you network properly.

Do you ever see social media fully overtaking traditional forms of communication (i.e., phone calls, e-mails, postal mail, etc.) as the go-to way to connect and form relationships?

Yes, it will become more and more dominant. However, there is something beyond social media that we don't even know about yet that will rise in the coming years.

Do you believe there is a quality in face-to-face interactions that cannot be duplicated through online mediums?

Yes, you can't replace face-to-face interaction. You can augment it, but you can't replace it. I can give my keynote presentations via Skype; but it's not the same. That's why companies still pay to fly me in.

What are your thoughts on the criticism that social media has led to a wave of oversharing where people flood the Internet with mostly meaningless information?

We are still in a learning curve. With any new technology it takes some longer than others to adjust. Remember the annoying friend that used to send 10 jokes a day via e-mail?

What makes social media, as you once said, the biggest technological shift since the industrial revolution?

Word of mouth is the most important item for *any* company, nonprofit, organization, or small business. Social media puts word of mouth on digital steroids.

How has the speed and efficiency of communications — both socially and professionally — been affected by social media?

We need to look no further than the revolution in Egypt to see just how powerful social media is. Many kids in Egypt have been named Facebook.

In comparison to past generations, how much do modern business owners rely on technology like social media? Is effective use of social media essential to running a successful business?

We don't have a choice on *whether* to do social media. The choice is in how *well* we do it. The ROI of social media is that your business will still exist in five years.

What reforms — corporate, legal, etc. — have been prompted by the revolution of social media?

There are many reforms in the works and still many more to come concerning privacy. In Germany it's illegal for companies to look at social networks like Facebook to determine whether or not to hire a job applicant. Fifty-four percent of companies block social media usage to their employees.

Social media is all the rage, and there are so many outlets. What are your recommendations to achieve the best possible results? Should one use all the different avenues or pick and choose?

Don't try to boil the ocean with social media. Select one or two areas where you believe you can achieve initial success and then when comfortable grow from there. For example, if you have a dance studio, then maybe you start with Yelp and YouTube and then grow into Living Social, Facebook, and Twitter initiatives. As a telecom provider you may start with Twitter and Facebook and then grow accordingly.

How should a company devise a long-range, comprehensive strategy for using social media?

The company needs to make it a part of its business ethos rather than having it as a separate campaign or silo.

What are the best ways to achieve buy-in from management and IT departments, which often are the major roadblocks in establishing social media for their organizations?

A great way to get buy-in from upper management is to take a few weeks and create a listen report for your products and services as well as your top competitor. This will give you good insight into the fact that your brand is no longer owned by you, so if you want to have influence you will need to learn to (1) listen, (2) interact, and (3) react to what is happening on social media.

What's the difference between "bleeding edge" and "cutting edge"?

Bleeding edge is when you are too far ahead of the market, whereas cutting edge is where you are ahead of your competition, but not too far ahead of the market and consumers. When Google Wave launched, it was too bleeding edge; the general market couldn't grasp it. When the iPhone originally launched, it was cutting edge; it was ahead of the competition, but still easy for consumers to understand and use.

Do most companies seem to have clear strategies and direction with social media?

Some of the good companies have a clear strategy, while others aren't properly integrating it with all of their other initiatives and their overall strategy. The key with social media is to fail fast, fail forward, and fail better. You probably aren't going to get it right the first time, but you aren't going to learn anything if you don't take that first step. It is the world's largest focus group on steroids. It's imperative that companies incorporate their social media strategy into their overall business strategy. A big mistake is making it a one-off strategy or simply running social media campaigns.

Do you know an agency or a brand that is doing it right in social media?

Zappos, Comcast, Ford, JetBlue, Skittles, Starbucks, Oreo, Nike, Lady Gaga, Ben & Jerry's, Bazaarvoice, Burberry, Dell, HubSpot, and Virgin are leaders in the space. Crispin Porter & Bogusky, Likeable Media, Brickfish, Wildfire, Buddy Media, Wieden + Kennedy, and Razorfish have been progressive agencies in this area as well.

Debate between Content Curators and Creators

Today, everyone is a potential media outlet. A curator (someone who summarizes other original content) understands the audience and is able to package created content in a digestible manner for that audience. Creators need to view curators as distribution points for their content rather than as pirates. Content creators and curators who will thrive in this new world understand the importance of this symbiotic relationship. But

(continued)

(*continued*)

is it symbiotic? In the end, almost every person is a little of both (creator and curator). After all, there is no such thing as a new idea, and imitation is the sincerest form of flattery. These clichés symbolize the irony of the topic being discussed.

What do you say to small business owners who want immediate results? What are realistic results?

It depends on what you define as success and also what you are selling. Immediate results are possible—Naked Pizza in New Orleans had record pizza sales for a day by effectively utilizing Twitter. However, this is the exception; for the most part you need to think strategically and long term with social media. It's not a magic pill, and if your client thinks it is going in, that's going to make it difficult to succeed.

What is the disadvantage for companies using social media?

Great companies embrace social media because they have nothing to hide and they welcome everyone to discuss their products, services, and so on. Social media is a big disadvantage for companies that have mediocre products/service/offerings and are attempting to hide behind big marketing budgets, distribution advantages, and the like. There is nowhere to hide.

Do you think most companies should go in-house with their social media?

Since social media touches every facet of the business, it inherently lends itself to the majority being taken in-house. Also, the conversations need to be genuine, and it's easier to establish that trust if it's coming from you, not a surrogate. Social media is not an *or*, but rather an *and* in your business. Dell originally had 40 people focused on social media, but soon realized it's not just the 40 people who need to own social media; it's the entire company. Hence, Dell has trained tens of thousands of its employees. Every person, whether it's someone on the phone answering customer service or any other employee, might have a Facebook, LinkedIn, or Twitter account, and they are representing Dell, whether it is during working hours or not.

While a majority of social media activity should reside in-house, it still makes sense to bring in help from an external agency or a consultant for certain aspects of the strategy and execution. If you look at the successful Old Spice Guy campaign, this was produced externally by Weiden & Kennedy.

How should marketers be measuring the success of their social media efforts?

Some items can be measured directly, similar to pay-per-click (PPC) search or direct response. For example, if you run Facebook ads with a direct action, you can measure the return on investment (ROI) similarly to how you do for PPC search — it has its own nuances, but it's pretty close.

A majority of other social media activity affects your entire business, so it's really measured by the overall health of your business. In fact, the Altimeter Group did a study that showed that companies actively engaged in social media increased revenues by 18 percent while those least engaged saw a decrease in revenues by 6 percent.

Do you feel that it is imperative for companies, organizations, and nonprofits to have a blog?

If you have something of relevance to say and you enjoy saying it, then yes, you should have a blog. Blogs are one of the best ways to create inbound traffic. However, they are a lot of work to maintain. Make sure you are willing to put in the time and commitment before launching a blog. They are free from a tangible hard cost standpoint, but they are far from free in other respects. Blogs are free like puppies, not free like beer.

My students tend to get sloppy with their grammar online. What do you think about the importance of using good grammar on digital posts?

Language is a living and breathing item and will constantly evolve. Hence, this is why we see *Twitter* as the most used word in 2009, beating out Michael Jackson, Barack Obama, H1N1, and so on. Some social media tools have character limitations that require people to use shorthand like "u" instead of "you." I wouldn't view this as sloppy. That being said, some people are sloppy with the written word and online posts live online forever, so it's always prudent to put your best foot forward as you are representing the brand that is you.

Does social media mean more content, less advertising, and better results? Why or why not?

Historically, word of mouth has been the most beneficial marketing effort for businesses. Social media takes word of mouth and puts it on digital steroids and essentially turns it into World of Mouth.

I am in the process of expanding e-learning (online) classes here at my college. Which of the many social media products would you say is the best to select for online projects, communication, chats, and so forth?

Fish where the fish are. If you are teaching college students, most likely they are on Facebook, Twitter, and YouTube. It would be tough to go wrong here. But it depends on your goals and what you are teaching. Take advantage of free online content from TED (Technology, Entertainment, Design), Stanford, Yale, MIT, and Khan Academy.

What actions should BP have taken digitally within the first 24 hours of the Gulf Coast oil spill?

BP should have immediately posted the high-definition video images and indicated how they were deriving their flow estimates. We live in a fully transparent world, and it's always better to point the finger at yourself rather than wait a few days to have someone else point the finger at you (e.g., Bill Clinton, Tiger Woods, Enron, Lehman Brothers, Eliot Spitzer). This is counterintuitive to how we've done business in the past with the legal mind-set of trying to keep the bodies buried. However, with social media you have to assume the bodies will be exhumed quickly.

What should BP have done in the days after the oil spill?

First and foremost, it should attempt to humanize BP. The company should have put cameras with their employees down on the Gulf showing what they were doing to help the region. People who work for BP are human; try to humanize BP rather than continuing to be simply a logo hated by so many. Not everyone who works for BP is evil. The company should have showcased, via video, real people accessing claims to give a sense of the process. Also, it should ask for feedback, listen, and react accordingly.

Rate BP's online strategy on a scale of 1 (worst) to 10 (best).

I'd give BP a score of 4. One good thing BP did was to not overreact and go after parody accounts like BPGlobalPR on Twitter that posted tweets like "50 percent off blackened shrimp today" and "Hey, if you see any oil in the Gulf it's ours, please return it." Going after parody accounts right away would have been adding fuel to the fire as people would have been upset that BP wasn't focusing on the important task of capping the well.

Another positive is that BP has many resources posted on www.bp.com, and you can also drill down (no pun intended) to specific regions (e.g., Alabama, Florida).

BP needed to do a better job of listening to how big politically this was becoming and adjusted its PR and spokespersons accordingly. It also wasn't easy to find BP's social presence (Facebook, YouTube, etc.) on www.bp.com.

How has social media changed the attitude and usage of media, consumer behavior, and enterprises?

We no longer search for the news; the news finds us. A good example of this was seen in the United States during the 2008 elections. Tina Fey of *Saturday Night Live* did some wildly popular Sarah Palin skits. More people watched the five-minute clip online than via regular television. This is a good example of the massive shift in how we consume media. We don't sit in front of the television to watch 90 minutes of *SNL*, nor do we walk down to the sidewalk to grab the morning paper. News, information, products, and services are pushed to us.

What does social media mean for publishers? How could they integrate it into new business models?

The beautiful thing about digital publishing is that it eliminates so many costs (shipping, printing, paper, etc.). In fact, many of you are probably reading this digitally right now. There are also possibilities to make money off pass-alongs. Books are social by nature. Historically when a paperback gets passed along, there is no additional revenue derived. With digital distribution you can charge $1 for this pass-along. Also, product placement is now possible with items in a digital format. We can also track what is being read the most so that we produce more of that and less of the items being ignored. We can track how many people read a particular book, or even page. The education front is even more exciting.

Many business travelers love the convenience of their favorite e-reader (Nook, Kindle, tablet, iPad, etc.). This is very similar to when we turned in our bulky music CD cases (sorry, Case Logic) for lighter and more elegant iPods. As we peer into the future, the thing that excites me the most about e-readers, iPads, and the like is the social component. Here is one quick example:

When I went to college and purchased a used book, I'd spend a few minutes sifting through the various copies in the student bookstore before placing one into my shopping basket.

After selection, I hoped and prayed that the person who took the notes in the margins and highlighted certain passages was smart. Sure, I had my own system — a tattered book was better than a fresher-looking one, as I assumed it was read more. I also saw neat handwriting and color-coded highlighting as a sign of aptitude. This was not a perfect system by any means, but it got me through college.

With the sharing capability of e-readers, though, buying used books will quickly become a thing of the past. How great will it be to have one tiny e-reader or iPad to tote around campus rather than straining the straps of a backpack loaded with books? Also, students will be able to perform quick digital searches and sorts for all the notes from the A+ students. Imagine the improved knowledge transfer from student to student. This is what excites many about the future world of education being enabled by social components of e-readers and iPads.

How will media consumption change for Generations Y and Z?
There will be more mobile consumption as technologies like smartphones, netbooks, and tablets improve. Wireless broadband penetration will make for an always-on world.

How long will it take for online marketing budgets to match traditional marketing budgets?
Not long. In 2009 Ford moved its digital spend from 10 percent to 25 percent. Keep in mind that most television as we know it today may be fed through an IP or Internet protocol (i.e., via the web) in the future. Budgets should also shrink when social search improves, as we'll be able to see the products and services that others like; paid search will become less effective and relevant.

You wrote about how Generations Y and Z are more creative and collaborative, and young adults are more willing to promote brands online. Should marketers be focusing on this group in their social media campaigns?
Companies should focus on this group only if they provide a product or service that is of value to these generations, or if they are influencers. If you are selling denture cleaner, targeting this group isn't going to do you much good.

How do you think the marketer's role in the nonprofit sector differs in comparison to the for-profit world?
The same constructs apply. Sometimes nonprofits have fewer resources, but that is the beauty of digital media; it helps mitigate these disadvantages. It rewards those willing to work

hard to develop relationships, not necessarily those with the most money.

What, in your view, are the most common ways that corporations embrace social media? Is it making a Facebook page, sending official tweets, or maybe a mix of things?

The good companies know a solid social media strategy is much more than a Facebook page or setting up a Twitter account. The good companies know that social media has to be integrated into everything that they do — it's a part of their overall strategy since it touches every facet of the business. They also understand that you get out what you put in; it's hard work. Just like offline relationships, it takes time and commitment. For some companies YouTube and LinkedIn may achieve the best results, whereas for other companies it might be Twitter and their own blogs.

What do you see about using podcasts?

There is still a strong market for podcasts, especially in commuting cities and cities heavily dependent on public transportation. Podcasts take commitment, which many aren't able to maintain. Hence, you can stand out if you produce a timely and consistent podcast.

What is the worst thing about social media?

Some people start to hide behind social media, and their interpersonal communication skills diminish.

What objectives are realistic for a small business owner who is only now just starting to practice social media?

Take the proper steps: (1) listen, (2) interact, (3) react, (4) soft sell. Even if you only do step 1, you will at a minimum have a much better understanding about your business and also your customers and their needs — this is invaluable. Take the next progressive steps from there. Define what success looks like before you start.

Can social media increase your vulnerability to viruses and identity theft?

If you leave your house, you are more vulnerable to catching the flu or getting hit by a bus. Yet living your life confined to your house can cause other problems. The same holds true here. Yes, you are more susceptible, yet common sense goes a long way! The nefarious tactics in social media are very similar to those used on e-mail and other parts of the web.

Can traditional online news in some way take advantage of social media?

CNN and ESPN are great examples of this.

Do you believe social media could become a threat to democracy because the news doesn't reach the broad layers of the population?

I would say the opposite is true. Social media allows for democracy to flourish since there is more transparency and it allows for more ownership and input from the people. In the United States, Barack Obama would not have been able to win the presidential race without the Internet — and social media played an enormous part.

Some classified information is easy to leak, which isn't necessarily good. Wikileaks posted some confidential intelligence around the war in Afghanistan, which may have put coalition troops and Afghan citizens in harm's way. This type of activity is not good.

Who is going to lead this new marketing? Big agencies? Specialized agencies? Media agencies? Brands themselves?

It's a people-driven economy — people will lead the charge. People who shepherd brands (e.g., Tony Hsieh, Morgan Johnston, Scott Monty) will also play leading roles. Technology development (application development, etc.) will continue to be outsourced to specialists.

How will we avoid ad saturation on social media?

Only advertising that delivers value to users will be tolerated. The days of shouting are over. Many of these sites have thumbs-up and thumbs-down ratings for advertisements. What people care about is what their friends are buying and using and what they like or don't like.

People often ask: What's the cost of social media? What's the ROI?

An important question to pose is: What is the cost of doing nothing? The ROI of social media is that your business will still exist in five years.

Which one do you think is the best business model for social networks? Is advertising the only way?

That is already proving to be one effective revenue stream for social networks, but there are many more. Think about people exchanging gifts in social media, small businesses setting up their businesses and using PayPal type functionality (many are already doing this), social search, social commerce, social gaming, Craigslist functionality, and so forth.

One of Google's vice presidents for engineering, Udi Manber, said his job is to do rocket science that will be taken for granted. How do you suppose social media fits into that rocket science?

A lot of success is dependent on execution rather than idea. Think of how much high school reunion activity Facebook has captured. Why didn't this all go to Classmates.com a decade ago? I agree with Manber in the sense that you want to be cutting edge rather than bleeding edge. The end users don't care how things work; they just want them to work. Pinterest was basically a new skin on things like Digg, Delicious, and Reddit, hyper-focused on images.

Marshall McLuhan once famously observed that "The future of the book is the blurb." Is social media eroding our collective attention span and ability to concentrate? It seems like our minds have been conditioned to absorb information the same way Twitter distributes it: in a rapidly flowing stream of bite-sized updates.

Often people believe that evolution is a negative thing. On the contrary, it's just a different thing. People today are used to contributing, collaborating, and multitasking; this is not necessarily a bad thing. It reminds me of an old saying that was attributed to Mark Twain: "I didn't have time to write you a short letter, so I wrote you a long one instead." The fact that we are becoming better as a society at getting to the essence of things quickly should be celebrated rather than frowned upon.

However, there has been some erosion in terms of interpersonal communication skills, and that's a trend I hope stops. About 80 to 90 percent of all communication is nonverbal; hence social media should be used as an "and" rather than an "or" when it comes to communication. I still fly around the world to give presentations. There is still nothing like face-to-face communication.

How does social media impact the process of job recruitment?

The traditional resume is dead. LinkedIn is the end game and may eventually be the most powerful social media player of them all.

How important to the future of political discourse is social networking?

Very important. It helps break down all types of social and cultural barriers created by distance. We all can't afford to travel internationally, but we can all hop on a social network to better understand our friends globally.

Impersonation on social networking sites has been described as both fraud and satire. How do you see them?

As long as you are up front that you aren't the real person, I have no issue with this. If there is an audience for it, then let Perez Hilton provide entertainment or @BPGlobalPR bring environmental concerns to life.

What about people sending friend requests to their kids, nieces, nephews, and others? When and why would that be a good or bad idea?

If minors are on social media, I highly recommend that parents be connected with their children on social media—this is just good parenting; in fact, over 70 percent are connected with their kids.

Should people use sites like Facebook or Twitter for dating, or is that best left to dating-specific sites (like Match.com)?

I believe it makes more sense to go on a date with someone a good friend of yours knows rather than a complete stranger, so by all means some of the social media players like Facebook can be used in this manner.

What was the original intent of social networks? Do you feel there are many negative aspects to them?

The original intent of social networks was to allow people to more readily stay connected with friends and family. Today, that is still the major goal of social media. Many other positive items have sprung up around it: being able to easily voice your political opinion (e.g., in opposition to the Stop Online Piracy Act [SOPA]), social search (being able to see what my friends and peers like and don't like), and entire country revolutions (kids in Egypt have been named Facebook since it played such a prominent role in the democratic revolution). At the same time, however, many negative items have also been associated with social networks, such as cyberbullying and loss of privacy.

This negative piece is nothing new when it comes to advances in technology. When credit cards were first being used for online transactions, many nefarious people and even companies were successful in stealing this information. Over time this becomes less, but never goes away completely. Whether it's the introduction of taking credit card transactions online or social networks, it's not the tools that are the problem; it's the people who are trying to take advantage of such tools. Over time the tools help mitigate the issues and problems (never completely eliminating them), and I'm certain that will be the case with social networks.

What role should the government have with regard to the Internet? Should it interfere and regulate as in ACTA/SOUP?

Until governments have a better grasp and understanding of technology, they should have limited involvement. How can you govern something you don't use or understand?

Do you believe that the power social media engagement has scares politicians?

It scares those who don't fully understand it. Those who do understand it embrace it to win elections and stay better connected with their voting base.

How is sociability changing now that we have access to all kinds of information about people before even meeting them?

It helps reduce small talk, as we have access to their information before we meet with them. It lets us get into the meat of a topic or conversation.

What do you think about the freedom of expression Internet users have — creating, modifying, and sharing?

Freedom of expression is always a good thing. People need to learn, though, that there isn't freedom of consequence on what you post, so be smart about it.

What are your personal strategies to connect with your consumers/audience in live settings (if any) and in general?

The key is to give them something of value. Spam is not value. Take their viewpoint — what would be the most useful and beneficial to them — not what is most beneficial to the company. The age-old adage is that it's more important to be interested than to be interesting.

How well can social media monitoring predict the future?

Putting structure to big data so companies can make predictions is just starting, but will be important for years to come. When Politico and Facebook shared data during the 2012 Republican primaries, they were able to predict fairly accurately the winner of each state primary based on the conversations happening online.

What are some of the pitfalls in using social media?

If you try to push a corporate agenda on social media, it's like throwing water balloons at a porcupine. You can waste a lot of resources and money doing this.

How did you become so interested in the social media, and what prompted your book?

Technology is always exciting, but what interests me most about social media is that it's less about technology and more about personal relationships. The inspiration for the original version of this book (2009) was that I really wanted everyone to understand the monumental shift that was coming in the way we all live as a result of social media.

Like everything in high tech today, social media evolves quickly. What tools do you see on the horizon that may eclipse the current tools we use today?

In time I really see the big play being that everything will be rated and we will have access to our friends' reviews and comments on products, services, people . . . everything!

Could you list the jobs in the United States today linked to social media and a give a brief description, such as social media analyst, community manager, and so forth?

There are many. I'd suggest you search LinkedIn for a full list, but included will be chief of social media, social media strategist, social media manager, social media director, director of social media, social media intern, community manager, and customer evangelist.

How do you understand the social media profession? Is it like a project manager (specialist in doing one thing) or it is like an IT professional (several specialties in different knowledge areas)?

Long term, everyone in the company needs to be trained on social media as it touches every piece of the business. This makes sense because social media is the customer. It's a living, breathing, always changing organism.

What are the different ways to get to an ROI?

Like search, some social media items are directly trackable to ROI. Often this is paid versus earned media. The earned media within social media is a little more difficult to track. It's analogous to asking what's the ROI of your telephone, or what's the ROI of a handwritten note? Or what's the ROI of your mother (via Gary Vaynerchuk). Much of social media is engaging with the customer to develop long-term relationships. You need to look at the other side of the coin as well.

What is the cost of not properly engaging within social media?

The cost of doing nothing will outweigh anything we can think of. That is why I say the ROI of social media is that your business will still exist in five years.

How will social media change doing business, and why?

We will no longer search for products and services; they will find us via our friends and peers. Only 14 percent of us trust advertisements, whereas 90 percent of us trust peer recommendations.

What are the advantages of using social media in recruitment?

The company knows *much* more about the candidate, and the candidate knows *much* more about the company and individuals at that company.

Does social media violate personal privacy, and how come?

This is a complex question, but at the end of the day most of social media is voluntary. If you don't want something out there, then don't do that activity.

Are people aware of all the information they share on the Internet?

At this point, no, but this is a learning curve, especially for the younger generations, who are starting to realize we all need to live as if our mother is watching.

Social media is certainly raising the transparency between brands and consumers. Do you think that social media will eventually kill the opportunistic marketing of bad products and services? Are we entering the era of 100 percent honest marketing?

Yes. Socialnomics is word of mouth on digital steroids, so it makes all of this possible and it's a beautiful thing. It's not a question of if, but a question of when. To get to 100 percent honest marketing may take a little longer than we expect, but we are making our way toward that.

Many businesses out there are using social media simply as another message delivery system. These same businesses tend to focus exclusively on ROI, and are constantly comparing social media with traditional media. Do you think that social media will regulate itself and purge this behavior, or are we moving toward a more "spammy" social media world?

Social media is user regulated, and the good companies already realize that this is a different animal from traditional channels. It's analogous to writing a handwritten thank-you note. The good companies do it, and in the long term they continue to have success. Social media is less about technology and immediate gratification and more about developing long-term relationships.

Why isn't there stronger security on our information that we post on social networks?

The more open the information, the more Facebook, Twitter, and other social networks can monetize to advertisers. Also, the purpose of a social network is to be social, which requires some level of openness. That being said, the tools are getting better at providing us easier security controls. Google+ and Path (company started by the former Facebook head of product, Dave Morin) have done a good job of increasing privacy measures, which in turn provides pressure to Facebook, Twitter, and others to improve their privacy controls. Nothing is ever 100 percent fail-safe, as evidenced by 8 million accounts on LinkedIn being hacked.

How can we monitor age limits on social networks like Facebook and Twitter?

This has always been an issue online; the only technology so far is the logins on sites like Budweiser.com asking for your age. As a result there is a thought to develop a social network specifically for children (e.g., Facebook). While this sounds revolting to many, if you think about it, a tool like Webkinz isn't too far away from this.

Where do you see the future of social media?

Much will be around big data aggregation and the sharing of this information with the social graph. What have my friends purchased? What services or restaurants have they rated highly? You will see search and social media begin to merge, with the end result being that we will no longer search for products and services via a search engine. Rather they will find us via social media. This is one of the true powers of social media! I care more what my friends and peers link to than about what an algorithm or opaque rating system spits out. A large part of Socialnomics is social commerce. Think word of mouth on steroids. Mobile and geolocation will be other major factors that will help both advertisers and consumers.

Consumers will also demand to have more control of their privacy. In a simplified example, there are some photos a consumer doesn't mind sending to the universe, but other photos that are to go to only five select people.

Some of the more exciting items revolve around education and politics.

Online voting and the ability for individuals not only to express their opinions, but to provide pressure and influence for change will cause all governments to become a little more open and truly powered by the people.

The education model we have known for centuries is being changed radically, and this is being driven by open technologies. The fact that soon, if you have access to the Internet, no matter where you live, your ethnicity, or the color of your skin, you will have access to the best educational content in the world is inspiring.

Oh, and 30 other things we haven't even dreamed up — that's what *is* exciting.

These questions are only scratching the surface; feel free to send me your questions by commenting at www.socialnomics.com, or send a tweet to @equalman.

CHAPTER TWENTY

Teacher and Company Resources and Exercises

Please often check www.socialnomics.com/education for up-dated lesson plans, new material, videos, and recommended exercises. If you are from a company, some of the class lesson plans are applicable for your team as well. I offer some specific corporate exercises here as well.

Class Lesson Plans

1. The book has been designed with the purpose of being able to parse individual chapters according to the goal or subject matter of your class. If your class is entirely on social media and you are going to meet more than 15 times as a class, then you may cover a chapter or two each time you meet. If you aren't going to meet this often or your class is more on general marketing or general management, then you can easily select the chapters most relevant for what you want to accomplish. Since the chapters are modular in fashion, this should make things easy for you.

2. There are Key Points listed at the end of each chapter. Select one or two of the bullet points from the summary list. Have your class focus on these as they read the chapter, and ask them to select an example that they've seen in the

prior week where this is being used. Have them present this example in class on-screen.

3. Have each student in class complete a social media case study with the following format: Situation > Action > Result > Learning. Suggest that the content of the case study be broken down to 10 percent for Situation, 20 percent for Action, 30 percent for Result, and 40 percent for Learning.

    Option: The two best case studies delivered by the students you will post to Socialnomics.com.

    Option: If you have corporate relationships, you can dive deeper on these case studies with these specific companies.

4. *Blog competition:* Have the students start a blog or, if they already have one, continue an existing blog. Break the class into teams. Hold a competition to see which blog can generate the most site traffic, retweets, Facebook likes, comments, or pick-ups from national or regional media outlets. If the blog already exists, then you will need to measure increases in the metrics. At the end of the project have each team write a summary of their initiatives. What actions did they take? What type of content performed the best? Where did they struggle? Did they reach out to get hyperlinks? What social media tool helped drive the most traffic? What did they learn?

    Suggestion: Use either Tumblr or WordPress as the blog platform. If the students are going to use existing blogs, I'd strongly suggest that everyone use the same blog software or platform, so pick either Tumblr or Word-Press.

5. Have the students go two days without using any digital tools. The next class, have an open discussion about the struggles and benefits.

6. Have each student fill out his or her profile on LinkedIn so that it's 100 percent complete (LinkedIn will show 100 percent completion in the upper right-hand corner). Have a teaching assistant check to see if this is complete by the assigned date.

7. Assign the students to determine which part of *Socialnomics* is now the most outdated. What do they believe is the next big thing? Why?

8. Hold a class Skype or Google+ Hangout FAQ session with me, the author. Simply send me a note at equalman@gmail.com.

   Option: This can also be used as an extra-credit project.

Corporate Ideas/Exercises

1. Have each member of your team complete a social media case study on one of your top competitors. Use the following format: Situation > Action > Result > Learning.
2. Videorecord a large sample of your employees (for larger companies I suggest 100 people). Ask them three questions:
   1. What is our mission as a company?
   2. What is our advantage over/difference from our competitors?
   3. If our company were to go away tomorrow, what would be the hole left to society?

   The reason you do this is that you are turning brand ownership over to your customers and clients. You need to shore up any gaps you have internally for those externally to have a chance of properly shepherding your brand.

   Option: Many companies and small businesses prefer the Socialnomics team to come in over two days to complete the interviews and provide unbiased strategic feedback on strengths, weaknesses, and opportunities around the company and its culture.
3. Take the top problem your company is facing and break into groups.
   a. Give the same problem to each group.
   b. Assign a well-known external company to each group (suggest: Nike, FedEx, Domino's, Amazon, Google, Apple, Caterpillar, Intel, Cartier).
   c. Have each group approach the problem according to the company they were assigned. For example, Domino's may approach the problem based on admitting fault, listening to the customer, allowing the customer to see the product being made, and delivering it quickly.
   d. Circle back as a large group and have one representative from each team present for five minutes on how their brand would attack the problem.
      Suggestion: This is a great two-hour exercise to conduct at an offsite.
4. Assign a team to act like a prospective job candidate investigating your company.

a. Are jobs easy to find on LinkedIn, CareerBuilder, and other sites?
b. What does your digital presence look like to an external candidate? Is it blah or exciting?
c. Are top executives easy to find digitally? Do their digital personalities say anything about the company?
d. Is the careers page on your website outdated? Are there any personalities or photos of current employees?
e. If you do a search on search.twitter.com around your company name, are their exciting dialogues? Are the jobs posted on Twitter?
f. Who are the most searched LinkedIn profiles for your company?
g. Is there anything very negative about the company online?
h. How is the company's Wikipedia page? Are there Wikipedia entries for your top executives?

15 Company Cultures to Learn From

1. Deckers Outdoor Wear
2. Zipcar
3. Salesforce
4. HubSpot
5. QuickenLoans
6. SAS
7. Zappos
8. Wegmans Food Markets
9. Chesapeake Energy
10. Intuit
11. SAS Institute
12. Likeable Media
13. Yard House Restaurants
14. Google
15. Montblanc

SOCIALNOMICS SUMMARY

I t's about the economy, stupid. No, it's about a *people-driven* economy, stupid. Whether you are a businessperson or a high school student, social media transforms the way you live and do business.

As an individual, you need to live your life as if your mother is watching, because she probably is via social media. Individuals behaving appropriately is a good thing for society. But is it beneficial for the individual? On one hand, if we can no longer have split personalities (Work William versus Weekend Warrior William) providing necessary stress relief, will more and more individuals experience nervous breakdowns? On the other hand, being able to constantly update their status and microblogs allows individuals to take real-time inventory of their collective lives. It also allows us to be connected with the ones we love like never before.

Because of this, there may be no looking back on a wasted youth. Social media is not a waste of time; it actually makes people more productive. We no longer look for the news or things of interest—they find us. If a person is updating his or her status or microblogs with "watching reruns of *Saved by the Bell*," that certainly isn't quite as cool as "learning how to kayak white-water rapids." Reality TV has been replaced by reality social media—it's all about my friends and my own reality.

And that is what social media does—it rewards first-class behavior and punishes improper behavior (what happens in Vegas stays on YouTube). Time will tell if our newly transparent world cuts down on crime, infidelity, and so on.

And it's not just criminals and unfaithful spouses who can't hide; inferior companies and products can't hide behind massive marketing budgets. The days of shouting and imposing your message on the masses are gone. Successful companies in social media function more like entertainment companies, publishers, or party planners than as traditional advertisers.

The 30-second commercial is being augmented and replaced by the 30-second review, tweet, post, status update, and so on. Not all great viral marketing ideas need to originate in the marketing department — businesses need to be comfortable with consumers taking ownership of their brands. The marketers' job has changed from creating and pushing messages to one that requires listening, engaging, and reacting to potential and current customer needs. And it's not just marketing that has changed; business models have shifted. Simply digitizing old business models doesn't work; businesses will need to fully transform, both strategically and culturally, to properly achieve success in the digital decades ahead.

But who is the winner in this new world? Customers and good companies win — which, as a society, we have been trying to achieve since the industrial revolution. Good companies view negative feedback as an opportunity to act on and adjust their products or services accordingly; bad companies view it as a nuisance or something they need to put an effort toward hiding.

Social media enables a truly global community. This results in tremendous time savings for individuals. It eliminates millions and millions of people performing the same tasks — multiple individual redundancies. Now only a few people need to research and test the best vacation spot or child car seat. Others in your network can leverage your experiences and learn, creating the world's largest referral program.

People care more about what their friends and peers believe is the best Italian restaurant in Manhattan than what Google thinks. That is why it is no surprise that Google continues its attempts to succeed in the social media world, from Google Wave to Google Buzz to Google+ to its successful purchase and running of YouTube. Google understands that its future competition isn't other search engines; it's the Twitters, Pinterests, and Facebooks of the world.

Making multiple mistakes within digital media is far better than sitting back and doing nothing at all. Businesses, organizations, and governments understand they don't have a choice on *whether* they do social media; the choice is in how *well* they do it. The ROI of social media is that our business will still exist in five years. The best way to increase our rate of learning in the digital decades ahead is to increase our rate of failure. We need to fail fast, fail forward, and fail better. This is the world of Socialnomics.

Socialnomics Winners and Losers

Winners

- Good companies that deliver products of great value.
- Team players (employees).
- Education.
- Society.
- Democracy.
- Referral programs.
- Good talent.
- Entrepreneurial talent (including musicians, comedians, etc.).
- Consumers: For consumers, good products will be easier to find and decisions will be easier to make because recommendations from people you trust and conversations with companies you develop a relationship with will replace the traditional one-way marketing messages.

Losers

- Companies solely reliant on great marketing: all sizzle and no steak is a recipe for failure.
- Undisciplined individuals: individuals exhibiting schizophrenic behavior.
- Companies that *deliberate* rather than *do* will quickly die in a Socialnomic world.
- Intermediaries.
- Search engines — if they fail to properly integrate social components.
- Established celebrities, singers, reporters, writers, and others who lack talent.
- Privacy.
- Traditional media.
- Businesses that don't listen or react.

NOTES

Introduction

1. James Carville, "It's the Economy, Stupid," Wikipedia, accessed April 23, 2009, http://en.wikipedia.org/wiki/It%27s_the_economy,_stupid.

Chapter One   Word of Mouth Goes World of Mouth

1. Josh James, "CEOs Afraid of Going Social Are Doing Shareholders a Massive Disservice," *Forbes*, July 12, 2012, www.forbes.com/sites/victoriabarret/2012/07/12/ceos-afraid-of-going-social-are-doing-shareholders-a-massive-disservice/.
2. Hitwise, June 2008.
3. Chris Anderson, *The Long Tail* (New York: Hyperion, 2006), Chapter 2.
4. Christoph Marcour, personal interview.
5. Business Analysis and Research, Newspaper Association of America, October 2008, www.naa.org/TrendsandNumbers/Advertising-Expenditures.aspx.
6. Daisy Whitney, "SNL Palin Skits: Seen More on Web than TV," *TVWeek*, October 1, 2008, www.tvweek.com/news/2008/10/snl_palin_skits_seen_more_on_w.php.
7. Julie Johnson, "Playboy Considers Radical Changes to Flagship Magazine," *Chicago Tribune*, May 11, 2009, www.chicagotrib.com/business/chi-biz-playboy-magazine pla,o,12113400.story.
8. Alan D. Mutter, "Print Drives Online Ad Sales at Newspapers," *Reflections of a Newsosaur*, February 3, 2009, http://newsosaur.blogspot.com.
9. Nielsen Global Online Consumer Survey, July 2009.
10. Larry Weber, *Marketing to the Social Web* (Hoboken, NJ: John Wiley & Sons, 2007).
11. Jim Giles, "Internet Encyclopaedias Go Head to Head," *Nature*, December 15, 2005.
12. Brian Morrissey, "Small Brands Teach Big Lessons," *AdWeek*, October 27, 2008, www.adweek.com/aw/content_display/news/digital/e3ia353f77f11f28ab 959172cf3f7595abb.

13. Jose Antonio Vargas, "Obama Raised Half a Billion Online," *Washington Post*, http://voices.washingtonpost.com/44/2008/11/20/obama_raised _half_a_billion_on.html.

14. Mary Schenk, "YouTube Co-Founder Tells Grads to Be Persistent, Take Risks," Department of Computer Science, University of Illinois at Urbana–Champaign, www.cs.uiuc.edu/news/articles.php?id=2007 May15-266/.

15. David Wilson, "American Airlines Crisis Management and Response," *Social Media Optimization*, April 2008, http://social-media -optimization.com/2008/04/american-airlines-crisis-management-and -flyers-response/.

16. Hitwise, 2008.

17. Ibid.

Chapter Two   Social Media = Preventive Behavior

1. C. C. Chapman, "Managing the Gray," May 23, 2008, http://www .podcastjunky.com/category/podcastjunky-podcast/.

2. "JetBlue Engages in Real Conversation on Twitter," *Socialized*, March 17, 2008, www.socializedpr.com/jetblue-engages-in-real-conversation -on-twitter/.

3. Jeff Jarvis, "Dell Hell," *BuzzMachine*, June 21, 2005, www.buzzmachine .com/archives/cat_dell.html.

4. Michael Michelson Jr., "Turning Complaints into Cash," the *American Salesman Journal*, 2003 (December), 22.

5. American Express® Global Customer Service Barometer, http://about .americanexpress.com/news/pr/2012/gcsb.aspx.

6. Ibid.

Chapter Three   Social Media = Braggadocian Behavior

1. "CMOs Not Ready to Embrace Social Networking Sites, Survey Shows," survey conducted by Epsilon, November 24, 2008, www.corporatelogo .com/hotnews/cmo-marketing-social-networking-sites.html.

2. Bill Tily, personal interview.

3. Heather Endreas, personal interview.

4. Melissa Dahl, "Youth Vote May Have Been Key in Obama's Win," MSNBC.com, November 5, 2008, www.msnbc.msn.com/id/27525497.

5. Facebook Application Statistics.

6. Jerry Seinfeld, www.wittcom.com/fear_of_public_speaking.htm.

7. Anick Jesdanun, "OMG! :(It Ain't Write," AP–*New York Post*, National Commission on Writing at the College Board, April 27, 2008, www .nypost.com/seven/04252008/news/nationalnews/omg_it_aint_write_ 108037.htm?CMP=EMC-email_edition&DATE=04252008.

8. "Young Adults Eager to Engage with Brands Online, Global Research from Microsoft and Synovate Reveals," November 11, 2008, www

.synovate.com/news/article/2008/11/young-adults-eager-to-engage
-with-brands-online-global-research-from-microsoft-and-synovate
-reveals.html.

9. Ibid.

10. Ibid.

11. "Advertising Nielsen Online: Kids Encounter Ads Less than Adults,"
E&P Staff and the Associated Press, October 13, 2008, https://listserv
.temple.edu/cgi-bin/wa?A3=ind0810&L=TEMPLE-GOLD&E=0&P=
2558622&B=--&T=TEXT%2FPLAIN;%20charset=US-ASCII&header=1.

Chapter Four   What We Can Learn from Politics

1. David Carr and Brian Stelter, "Campaign in a Web 2.0 World," *New
York Times* — Media and Advertising, November 2, 2008, www.nytimes
.com/2008/11/03/business/media/03media.html?_r=1&ei=5070&em
c=eta1.

2. Facebook Fan Data, October 2008.

3. YouTube View Data, October 2008.

4. Ibid.

5. Carr and Stelter, "Campaign in a Web 2.0 World."

6. Lance Muller, personal interview, June 2008.

7. Barack Obama, *Barack Obama: Connecting and Empowering All Americans Through Technology and Innovation*, November 2007, http://
lessig.org/blog/Fact%20Sheet%20Innovation%20and%20Technology%
20Plan%20FINAL.pdf.

8. David Needle, "Huffington: 'Obama Not Elected without Internet,'"
Internetnews.com, November 7, 2008, www.internetnews.com/
webcontent/article.php/3783741/Huffington+Obama+Not+Elected+
Without+Internet.htm.

9. "Web 2.0 and the Internet Delivered the Vote for Obama," *Huliq
News*, November 10, 2008, www.huliq.com/2623/72572/web-20-and
-internet-delivered-vote.

10. Ibid.

11. Brian Solis, "Is Obama Ready to Be a Two-Way President?," *Tech
Crunch*, November 15, 2008, www.techcrunch.com/2008/11/15/is
-obama-ready-to-be-a-two-way-president/.

12. Ibid.

13. Brian Reich, personal interview, November 2008.

14. YouTube, October 2008.

15. Burt Helm, "Who's Behind the 'Wassup 2008' Obama Ad? Not Budweiser," *BusinessWeek* — Innovation, October 27, 2008, www.business
week.com/the_thread/brandnewday/archives/2008/10/whos_behind
_the.html.

16. YouTube, October 2008.

17. John McWhorter, *All About the Beat: Why Hip-Hop Can't Save Black
America* (New York: Gotham Books, 2008).

18. Ismael AbduSalaam, "Ludacris Explains Controversial Obama Song," *All Hip Hop*, November 6, 2008, www.allhiphop.com/stories/news/archive/2008/11/06/20666656.aspx.

19. Miguel Helft, "Google Uses Searches to Track Flu's Spread," *New York Times*—Technology, November 11, 2008, www.nytimes.com/2008/11/12/technology/internet/12flu.html?8au&emc=au.

20. Ibid.

21. Google Trends, April 2008.

22. Ibid.

23. Ibid.

24. Kate Kay, "Web Ads Mattered More than Ever in 2008 Election," *ClickZ*, November 4, 2008, www.clickz.com/showPage.html?page=clickz_print&id=3631395/.

25. Needle, "Huffington: 'Obama Not Elected without Internet.'"

26. "America Goes to the Polls," A Report on Voter Turnout in the 2008 Election, Nonprofit Voter Engagement Network, November 2008, www.nonprofitvote.org/Download-document/America-Goes-to-the-Polls-A-Report-on-Voter-Turnout-in-the-2008-Election.html.

27. Kim Estes, personal interview, November 2008.

28. "Free Pancakes Anyone?," December 1, 2008, http://socialnomics.net/page/2/.

29. Ibid.

30. Facebook Fan Data.

31. "America Goes to the Polls."

32. "2008 Election Polls: How Long Would You Wait in Line to Vote?" *Soda-Head*, November 4, 2008, www.sodahead.com/question/184094/2008-election-polls-how-long-would-you-wait-in-line-to-vote/.

33. "Population Division," U.S. Census Bureau, July 1, 2007, www.census.gov/popest/states/asrh/SC-EST200701.html.

34. Stuart Elliott, "Army to Use Webcasts from Iraq for Recruiting," *New York Times*, November 11, 2008, www.nytimes.com/2008/11/11/business/media/11adco.html?pagewanted=print.

35. Ibid.

36. "Army Exceeds Recruiting Goal for Fiscal Year 2008," Army.mil/news release, October 10, 2008, http://www.army.mil/article/7221/army-meeting-2008-recruiting-goals/.

Chapter Five   I Care More about What My Neighbor Thinks Than What Google Thinks

1. "Nielsen Online Global Consumer Survey," Nielsen, April 2007.

2. Stewart Quealy, "*Interview:* John Gerzema," *SES Magazine*, March 2009, 57.

3. Facebook Statistics, retrieved April 2010, www.facebook.com/press/info.php?statistics.

4. Ken Robbins, personal interview, December 1, 2008.

5. Quealy, "Interview: John Gerzema."

6. iCrossing, "How America Searches: Health and Wellness," January 14, 2008, http://news.icrossing.com/press_releases.php?press_release=icrossing-study-finds-internet-top-resource-for-health-information.

7. Ibid.

8. Ibid.

9. YouTube View Data, 2008.

10. Acme Travels, in-house data.

11. "Jumping the Shark," Wikipedia, April 2009, http://en.wikipedia.org/wiki/Jumping_the_shark.

12. Facebook Application Active User Data, April 2008.

13. Razorfish, "The Razorfish Consumer Experience Report 2008," http://feed.razorfish.com/publication/?m=2587&l=1.

14. Ibid.

15. "Credit Union Members Vote on Logo Makeover," FinancialBrand.com, November 21, 2008, http://thefinancialbrand.com/2008/11/21/companion-logo-contest/.

16. Ibid.

17. Sri H. Kurniawan and Panyiotis Zahiris, "Reading Online or on Paper: Which Is Faster?," University of California at Santa Cruz, Institute of Gerontology and Department of Industrial and Manufacturing Engineering, http://users.soe.ucsc.edu/~srikur/files/HCII_reading.pdf.

18. Quealy, "Interview: John Gerzema."

Chapter Six Death of Social Schizophrenia

1. Schizophrenia is a very serious illness, and our intent by the use of this term is not to make light of its serious conditions or those who suffer from this illness.

2. "Texas Lineman Facebook Status Gets Him Booted Off Team," World of Isac.com, November 6, 2008, www.theworldofisaac.com/2008/11/texas-linemans-facebook-status-gets-him.html.

3. Ibid.

4. B. G. Brooks, "Coaches Deal with Athlete's Social Network," *Rocky Mountain News*, October 12, 2008, www.rockymountainnews.com/news/2008/oct/12/coaches-deal-athletes-social-networking/.

5. "Patriots Cheerleader Fired after Facebook Swastika Photo," Fox news.com, November 6, 2008, www.foxnews.com/story/0,2933,448044,00.html.

6. Facebook.com, 2008.

7. Tony Blair, "Challenge of Change," speech, 2008 World Business Forum, New York, September 2008.

Chapter Seven Winners and Losers in a 140-Character World

1. *Fantasy Football Today* Podcast, ESPN, November 2008.

2. Twitter postings, October 15, 2008.

3. Twitter posting, October 21, 2008.

4. "News from the Olympics," Nascar Licensedathletics.com, September 3, 2008, http://nascar.licensedathletics.com/news.php.

5. "Not Ye Old Banners," *The Economist*, November 27, 2008, www .economist.com/business/PrinterFriendly.cfm?story_id=12684861.

6. "Online Ad Spending Grows 10%; Video Ads Strong (Just Not at Google)," *Marketing Pilgrim*, March 31, 2009, www.marketingpilgrim .com/2009/03/online-ad-spending-grows-20-video-ads-strong-just-not -at-google.html.

7. "March Video Streaming Soars Nearly 40% Compared to Last Year," *Nielsen Wire*, April 13, 2009, http://blog.nielsen.com/nielsenwire/tag/ youtube/.

8. Brian Stelter, "Website's Formula for Success: TV Content with Fewer Ads," *New York Times*, October 29, 2008, www.nytimes.com/ 2008/10/29/business/media/29adco.html.

9. Ibid.

10. Ibid.

11. Mary Alison Wilshire, personal interview, December 5, 2008.

12. Stelter, "Website's Formula for Success."

13. Out of Home Advertising Bureau PDF, www.ovab.org/OVAB_ANA_ Guide_2008-09.pdf.

14. "Hulu Celebrates First Anniversary, Gains Popularity by Serving Fewer Ads," blog.wired.com, October 29, 2008, http://blog.wired.com/ business/2008/10/hulu-turns-one.html.

15. Stelter, "Website's Formula for Success."

16. "OMMA Panel: David vs. Goliath," *Online Video Watch*, www.online videowatch.com/omma-panel-david-vs-goliath/.

17. Facebook Active User Data, 2008.

18. "War of the Words: Scrabulous Is Off Facebook, but Did Hasbro Win the Game?" Knowledge@Wharton, August 6, 2008, http:// knowledge.wharton.upenn.edu/article.cfm?articleid=2029.

19. Ibid.

20. Facebook, 2008.

21. www.businessweek.com/debateroom/archives/2008/08/scrabulous_ face.html.

22. "War of the Words."

23. Ibid.

24. Razorfish, "The Razorfish Consumer Experience Report," http://feed .razorfish.com/downloads/Razorfish_FEED08.pdf.

25. Frank Rose, "How Madison Avenue Is Wasting Millions on a Deserted Life," *Wired*, July 24, 2007, www.wired.com/techbiz/media/magazine/ 15-08/ff_sheep/.

26. Newt Barrett, "Millions for a Virtual Coke on Second Life," *Succeeding Today*, June 25, 2007, http://succeedingtoday.com/2007/07/25/ millions-for-a-virtual-coke-on-second-life/.

27. Rose, "How Madison Avenue Is Wasting Millions."

Chapter Eight   Next Steps for Companies and the Glass House Generation

1. World Business Forum, Radio City Music Hall, New York, October 2008.
2. "Student 'Twitters' His Way Out of Egyptian Jail," CNN.com, April 25, 2008, http://edition.cnn.com/2008/TECH/04/25/twitter.buck/.
3. Ibid.
4. Jessica Guynn, "MTV Networks in Deal to Monetize Uploaded Videos," *Los Angeles Times*, November 3, 2008, www.latimes.com/business/la-fi-myspace3-2008nov03,0,6256914.story.
5. Steve O'Hear, "MTV and MySpace Partner to Monetize Pirated Content," ZDNet, November 3, 2008, http://blogs.zdnet.com/social/?p=602.
6. Organizing for America, www.barackobama.com/issues/technology/.
7. Author's estimate.
8. Erik Schonfeld, "Google Makes Up 88 Percent of Mozilla's Revenues, Threatens Its Non-Profit Status," *TechCrunch*, www.techcrunch.com/2008/11/19/google-makes-up-88-percent-of-mozillas-revenues-threatens-its-non-profit-status/.
9. 2008 Interactive Advertising Bureau Online Marketing Report.
10. PubMatic AdPrice Index Q4 2008, www.pubmatic.com/adpriceindex/AdPriceIndex_Quarterly_Q4_08.pdf.
11. Patrick Smith, "Digital Media: Facebook, Yahoo!, Microsoft Profit from Open Networks in Europe," March 9, 2009, www.paidcontent.co.uk/entry/419-ft-digital-media-facebook-yahoo-microsoft-profit-from-open-networks-in-/.
12. "College Student and Teen Web Tastes," *eMarketer*, November 19, 2008, www.emarketer.com/Article.aspx?id=1006736/.
13. "Is the Mobile Web Replacing the Wired Web in Southeast Asia?," *Fierce Wireless*, November 20, 2008, www.fiercewireless.com/press-releases/mobile-web-replacing-wired-web-southeast-asia.
14. Jason Ankeny, "NPD: 75% of Android Users Access Facebook from Their Phone," *Fierce Mobile Content*, March, 2012, www.fiercemobilecontent.com/story/npd-75-android-users-access-facebook-their-phone/2012-05-17#ixzz1vMz0q8dM.
15. Ibid.
16. https://generationfly.com/lounge.
17. Bob Garfield, "Widgets Are Made for Marketing, So Why Aren't More Advertisers Using Them?," December 2008, http://adage.com/article/news/garfield-advertisers-widgets/132778/.
18. Wikipedia, s.v. "walled garden (technology)," http://en.wikipedia.org/wiki/Walled_garden_(technology) (accessed December 21, 2008).
19. "Microsoft's New Windows Live Aims to Be Hub for Web," InfoTech .TMCnet.com, November 13, 2008, http://it.tmcnet.com/news/2008/11/13/3783709.htm.

20. "Facebook Aims to Extend Its Reach Across the Web," SM2, www.sm2.com.au/content/view/777/76/.

21. NPR Radio, *Weekend Edition*, November 22, 2006. www.npr.org/temp lates/story/story.php?storyId=6522523.

22. Wikipedia, s.v. "chava," http://en.wikipedia.org/wiki/Chav (accessed November 25, 2008).

23. Cem Sertoglu and Anne Berkowitch, "Cultivating Ex-Employees," *Harvard Business Review*, June 2002, http://hbr.org/2002/06/cultivating -ex-employees/ar/1.

24. www.videoactivereport.com/southwest_airlines_ding_widget_racks_ up_150_million_in_ticket_sales.

Chapter Ten   Social ROI

1. Gentry Estes, "Alabama Gets Back to Work in Preparation for BCS Championship Game," December 20, 2009, http://blog.al.com/press -register-sports/2009/12/alabama_gets_back_to_work_in_p.html.

2. John Maher, "Title Game Rarely Meets Month-Long 1 vs. 2 Hype," *Austin American Statesman*, January 2, 2010, www.statesman.com/ sports/longhorns/title-game-rarely-meets-monthlong-1-vs-2-159734 .html.

3. Nathan Golia, "Marketers Pull Products into Online Perks," *DMNews*, June 7, 2010.

4. Jon Swartz, "More Marketers Use Social Networking to Reach Customers," *USA Today*, August 28, 2009.

5. Lee Odden, "Book Review: *Crush It*, by Gary Vaynerchuk," Online Marketing Blog.

6. Jan M. Rosen, "Be It Twittering or Blogging, It's All about Marketing," the *New York Times*, March 11, 2009.

7. Wetpaint/Altimeter Group Engagement db study, 2009, http://www .marketingcharts.com/interactive/social-media-engagement-directly- linked-to-financial-success-9858/ and www.altimetergroup.com/2009/ 07/engagementdb.html.

8. Swartz, "More Marketers Use Social Networking."

9. www.advertolog.com/burger-king/print-outdoor/whopper-sacrifice -316211/. Estimate based on taking 32 million impressions at an average CPM of $13 based on *eMarketer* estimate found here: www .emarketer.com/Article.aspx?R=1007053. Less than $50,000 is a very conservative estimate (it probably cost much less) to actually build the application plus the cost to Burger King to give out fewer than 20,000 coupons/Whoppers. Please note these are estimates, but they fall on the conservative side.

10. Based on state populations of Arkansas, Kansas, Utah, Nevada, West Virginia, Nebraska, Idaho, Mississippi, Maine, New Hampshire, New Mexico, Hawaii, Rhode Island, Montana, Delaware, South Dakota, Alaska, North Dakota, and Vermont, http://en.wikipedia.org/wiki/ List_of_U.S._states_and_territories_by_population.

11. Kristen Nicole, "Will It Blend Videos Boost Sales 5x," Mashable, September 27, 2007.

12. Claire Baldwin, "Twitter Helps Dell Rake in Sales," Reuters, June 12, 2009.

13. Larry Weber, *Marketing to the Social Web* (Hoboken, NJ: John Wiley & Sons, 2007).

14. David Kiley, "Ford Spending 25% of Marketing on Digital and Social Media," *BusinessWeek*, October 16, 2009, www.businessweek .com/autos/autobeat/archives/2009/10/ford_spending_2.html.

15. Jacob Morgan, "Two Examples of Companies Measuring Social Media ROI," *Social Media Globetrotter*, October 12, 2009, www.jmorgan marketing.com/two-examples-of-companies-measuring-social-media -roi/.

16. Karl Greenber, "VW Goes All Mobile for Launch of GTI," *MarketingDaily*, October 22, 2009, www.mediapost.com/publications/?fa= Articles.showArticle&art_aid=115919.

17. ResponseMine Interactive Agency, Atlanta, Georgia.

18. Intuit Inc., Mountain View, California.

19. "Increase B2B Lead Generation Using Social Media," *Social Media B2B*, July 14, 2009, http://socialmediab2b.com/2009/07/b2b-lead -generation-social-media/.

20. Jose Antonio Vargas, "Obama Raised Half a Billion Online," *Washington Post*, http://voices.washingtonpost.com/44/2008/11/20/obama_raised_ half_a_billion_on.html.

21. Ed Bennett, "Hospitals and Social Media," SlideShare, www.slide share.net/edbennett/hospitals-social-media.

22. Daniel Adler, "Twenty-One Top Twitter Tips," *Forbes*, July 31, 2009, www.forbes.com/2009/07/31/top-twitter-tips-entrepreneurs -technology-twitter.html.

23. Marshall Kirkpatrick, "Social Media ROI: Dell's $3m on Twitter and Four Better Examples," *ReadWriteWeb*, June 12, 2009, www.read writeweb.com/archives/social_media_roi_dells_3m_on_twitter_and_ four_bett.php.

24. Adler, "Twenty-One Top Twitter Tips."

25. *Social Media in the Enterprise*, White Paper, Vignette Software, February 2009, www.vignette.com/dafiles/docs/Downloads/Social-Media -in-the-Enterprise.pdf.

26. Samuel Axon, "Old Spice Sales Double with YouTube Campaign," Mashable, July 26, 2010.

Chapter Eleven   Social Success Secrets
(Give Them to Me Now!)

1. Ethan Bloch, "The Value of an Existing Customer," *Flowtown*, October 17, 2010, www.flowtown.com/blog/the-value-of-an-existing -customer?display=wide with credit in infographic to Frederick Reicheld of Bain & Company.

2. Ibid.
3. Ibid.
4. "Social Media Raises the Stakes for Customer Service," AmericanEx-press.com, May 2, 2012, http://about.americanexpress.com/news/pr/2012/gcsb.aspx.
5. 2009 Giving Customer Voice More Volume, CMO Council and Sat-metrix; online survey of 480 executives, www.clearaction.biz/customer-engagement.
6. AP, "What's the Secret to Volkswagen's Success?" Three questions with VW marketing chief Tim Mahoney, *MLive.com*, January 11, 2012, www.mlive.com/naias/index.ssf/2012/01/whats_the_secret_to_volks wagen.html.
7. Austin Carr, "How to Sell Social inside Your Company," *Fast Company*, June 2012, 91, www.fastcompany.com/most-creative-people /2012/leslie-berland.
8. Ibid.
9. Bloch, "The Value of an Existing Customer."

Chapter Twelve   Blogging: What Works

1. NielsenWire, "Buzz in the Blogosphere: Millions More Bloggers and Blog Readers," blog.nielsen.com, March 8, 2012, http://blog.nielsen .com/nielsenwire/online_mobile/buzz-in-the-blogosphere-millions -more-bloggers-and-blog-readers/.
2. Ibid.

Chapter Fifteen   Social Media for B2B

1. Alexander Hotz and Lisa Waananen, Mashable.com infographic, www.socialnomics.net/2011/01/27/social-media-on-the-rise-for-b2b -marketing/. Source: March 2010 White Horse marketing survey.
2. Jeffrey Cohen, "12 Revealing Stats about B2B Social Media Market-ing," socialmediab2b.com, January 26, 2012. Read more: http:// socialmediab2b.com/2012/01/b2b-social-media-marketing-statistics -revealing/#ixzz1xK6pbQmS http://socialmediab2b.com/2012/01/b2 b-social-media-marketing-statistics-revealing/ (original source: Penton Marketing Services).
3. Phil Merson, "How B2B Marketers Use Social Media: New Research," *SocialMediaExaminer*, April 24, 2012, www.socialmediaexaminer.com/ b2b-social-media-marketing-research/.
4. Not sure of the originator of the term *flawsome*. I first became aware of it when being interviewed by Ann Hadley; by showing our *flaws* as an individual or a company and owning up to them, this shows our *awesomeness*.
5. Rajesh Kadam, "B2B Social Media Best Practices for the Integrated Age," *Business2Community*, June 8, 2012, www.business2community.com/ b2b-perspective/b2b-social-media-best-practices-for-the-integrated-age -0189092.

Chapter Sixteen   Case Studies

1. http://cloudcomputing.sys-con.com/node/1292141/blog.
2. www.facebook.com/GRLipDub?sk=info.
3. http://cloudcomputing.sys-con.com/node/1292141/blog.

Chapter Seventeen   Social Analytics: Big Data and Beyond

1. "Brands Ignore Negative Social Buzz at Their Peril," *eMarketer*, July 16, 2012.   www.emarketer.com/Article.aspx?R=1009189#ZgZdVK0mkrH MBF6z.99.
2. "Marketing in the Digital Age," DataXu, 2012, 2.
3. "IBM Social Analytics: The Science Behind Social Media Marketing," IBM, 2011, 2.
4. Susan Etlinger, "A Framework for Social Analytics," Altimeter, August 10, 2011, 26.
5. "Best Time to Tweet or Post to Facebook for Click-Throughs (Infographic)," *Silicon Republic*, June 18, 2012, www.siliconrepublic .com/new-media/item/27801-best-time-to-tweet-or-post/.
6. Chuck Hemann, "The Five Ws of Social Media Listening," Social Media Explorer, August 18, 2009.
7. "Cashing In on Customer Insight: Customer Analytics Can Help Companies Increase Loyalty, Profitably Grow Revenue, and Outmaneuver the Competition," Peppers & Rogers Group, 2012, 2.
8. Etlinger, "Framework for Social Analytics," 28.
9. "Social Media Analytics — Making Customer Insights Actionable," IBM, 2011, 3.
10. Wes Simonds, "Big Data: Transforming Raw Info into Successful Strategies," IBM, September 6, 2011.
11. James Manyika, "Big Data: The Next Frontier for Innovation, Competition, and Productivity," McKinsey Global Institute, May 2011, 2.
12. Farhad Manjoo, "Google's Creative Destruction," *Fast Company*, May 2012, 107.
13. "What Is Big Data?," IBM, 2.
14. Manyika, "Big Data," 2.
15. "Integrating Social Media and Advanced Analytics for Richer Customer Insight," IBM, 2011, 1.
16. "Measuring the Impact of Social Media," IBM, 2011, 1.
17. Rahul Dubey, "Facebook Fans Are Brand Advocates: Forrester," exchange4media.com, July 3, 2012, www.exchange4media.com/47065 _facebook-fans-are-brand-advocates-forrester.html.
18. Barry Hurd, "Social Media Analytics and Big Data," Barry Hurd: Thoughts on the Digital Divide, 1.
19. Marc Teerlink and Michael Haydock, "Customer Analytics Pay Off: Driving Top-Line Growth by Bringing Science to the Art of Marketing," IBM, 2011, 9.
20. Manyika, "Big Data," 1.

21. L. Siegele, "Welcome to the Yotta World: Big Data Will Flood the Planet," *The Economist*, November 17, 2011, 2.

22. Manyika, "Big Data," 1–2.

23. "Big Data in Action," IBM, www-01.ibm.com/software/data/bigdata/industry.html.

24. Scott Martin and Jon Swartz, "Can Social Media Predict Election Outcomes?" *USA Today*, March 6, 2012, http://bre.ad/11sl2w.

25. Mike Lewis, "Evolving Social Media Analytics: Insights from Marshall Sponder," Socialnomics, May 1, 2012, 1.

26. "Cashing In on Customer Insight," 8.

27. "Marketing in the Digital Age," 3.

28. Andreas Weigend, "Eight Rules for Big Data," People & Data, April 2012, 1.

ABOUT THE AUTHOR

Erik Qualman is the author of *Digital Leader*, *Crisis*, and *Alex Azure & the Forbidden Door*. The first edition of *Socialnomics: How Social Media Transforms the Way We Live and Do Business* made Amazon's #1 Best Selling List in the United States and United Kingdom within three weeks of publication and later went on to be #1 in South Korea, Germany, Japan, and Canada. The book was also a finalist for the American Marketing Association's "Book of the Year" award. These books and his personality helped Qualman earn the selection as the second "Most Likeable Author" in the world behind Harry Potter author J. K. Rowling. Qualman is a frequently requested international speaker of the Fortune 500 and has been highlighted in numerous media outlets, including *BusinessWeek*, *60 Minutes*, the *New York Times*, CNET, the *San Francisco Chronicle*, Mashable, *USA Today*, ABC, *Forbes*, the *CBS Nightly News*, and the Huffington Post.

He has been fortunate to share the stage with Alan Mulally (Ford CEO), Lee Scott (Walmart CEO/chairman), Olli-Pekka Kallasvuo (Nokia CEO), José Socrates (prime minister of Portugal), Al Gore (former U.S. vice president), Julie Andrews, Tony Hawk, and Sarah Palin.

Qualman has recently advised/given keynotes with Coach, IBM, Sony, Facebook, ADP, Starbucks, M&M/Mars, Cartier, Raytheon, Montblanc, TEDx, Polo, UGG, Nokia, Google, and many more companies. He gave the commencement address to the graduating class of McCombs Business School of the University of Texas.

Under his Equalman Productions company, Qualman has written and produced the most watched social media video series in the world (http://bit.ly/RTzPe).

Qualman is an MBA Professor of Digital Marketing at the Hult International Business School and has been ranked one of the Top 50 Professors in the world.

For the past 18 years Qualman has helped grow the online marketing and e-business capabilities of many companies, including Education First, Cadillac, EarthLink, Yahoo!, Travelzoo®, and AT&T. He is the founder and owner of the social media blog Socialnomics.com.

Qualman holds a BA from Michigan State University and an MBA from the University of Texas. He was Academic All–Big 10 in basketball at Michigan State University and has previously been awarded "MSU Alum of the Year."

twitter@equalman
equalman@gmail.com
www.socialnomics.com

Qualman is no stranger to the executive suite, having served as the head of marketing at Travelzoo®; today he sits on several company boards. In his spare time he enjoys scuba diving, golfing, tennis, and MSU hoops; he has been fortunate to speak in more than 42 countries. He lives in Cambridge, Massachusetts, with his wife and two daughters.

INDEX